Pilots and Rebels

The Use of Aircraft
in Unconventional Warfare
1918–1988

Titles of related interest from Brassey's

CHANT
Air Defence Systems and Weapons

JAMES
Imperial Rearguard: Wars of Empire 1919–85

LAFFIN
The World in Conflict 1989: War Annual 3

MASON
Air Power

MASON
War in the Third Dimension

SABIN
The Future of UK Air Power

TAYLOR
The Terrorist

WALKER
Air Superiority Operations

WALKER
Air-to-Ground Operations

Pilots and Rebels

The Use of Aircraft in Unconventional Warfare 1918–1988

PHILIP ANTHONY TOWLE

BRASSEY'S, UK

(A member of the Maxwell Pergamon Publishing Corporation plc)

LONDON · OXFORD · WASHINGTON · NEW YORK · BEIJING
FRANKFURT · SÃO PAULO · SYDNEY · TOKYO · TORONTO

UK (Editorial) (Orders)	Brassey's (UK) Ltd., 24 Gray's Inn Road, London WC1X 8HR, England Brassey's (UK) Ltd., Headington Hill Hall, Oxford OX3 0BW, England
USA (Editorial) (Orders)	Brassey's (US) Inc., 8000 Westpark Drive, Fourth Floor, McLean, Virginia 22102, USA Pergamon Press, Inc., Maxwell House, Fairview Park, Elmsford, New York 10523, USA
PEOPLE'S REPUBLIC OF CHINA	Pergamon Press, Room 4037, Qianmen Hotel, Beijing, People's Republic of China
FEDERAL REPUBLIC OF GERMANY	Pergamon Press GmbH, Hammerweg, 6, D-6242 Kronberg, Federal Republic of Germany
BRAZIL	Pergamon Editora Ltda, Rua Eça de Queiros, 346, CEP 04011, Paraiso, São Paulo, Brazil
AUSTRALIA	Brassey's Australia Pty. Ltd., PO Box 544, Potts Point, NSW 2011, Australia
JAPAN	Pergamon Press, 5th Floor, Matsuoka Central Building, 1-7-1 Nishishinjuku, Shinjuku-ku, Tokyo 160, Japan
CANADA	Pergamon Press Canada Ltd., Suite No. 271, 253 College Street, Toronto, Ontario, Canada M5T 1R5

First edition 1989

Library of Congress Cataloging in Publication Data
Towle, Philip, 1945–
Pilots and rebels: the use of aircraft in unconventional warfare/Philip Anthony Towle.—1st ed.

p. cm.
Bibliography: p.
Includes index.
1. Air warfare—History. 2. Guerrilla warfare—History.
3. Special operations (Military science)—History. I. Title.
UG632.T65 1989 358.4′425′09—dc19   89-635

British Library Cataloguing in Publication Data
Towle, Philip
Pilots and rebels: the use of aircraft in
unconventional warfare
1. Unconventional warfare. Air operations, 1918–1988
I. Title
355′.02184

ISBN 0-08-036712-7

Printed in Great Britain by BPCC Wheatons Ltd, Exeter

To My Parents

Acknowledgements

I would particularly like to thank Air Commodore Henry Probert of the Air Historical Branch who encouraged me to write this book. I am also most grateful to all those who have read and commented on the various chapters, who have supplied invaluable information and who have saved me from many errors. In particular, I would like to thank General Sir Hugh Beach, Colonel Peter Blaker, Dr Robin Bidwell, Dr Anthony Clayton, Colonel Cecil B. Currey, Air Commodore Timothy Garden, Air Commodore Mike Gibson, Group Captain Gordon Gilbert, Colonel F. Graham-Bell, Dr John Grantham, Mr Eric Grove, Mr Harry Hilton, Colonel Bruce Jackman, General Garry Johnson, Dr John Lonsdale, Professor Robert O'Neill, Mr Peter Rogers, Mr Radek Sikorski, Mr Charles Smith, Group Captain Andrew Vallance, Group Captain Marten van der Veen, Colonel Don Walbrecht, Air Commodore Ted Williams and Colonel Adrian Wray. All the errors and opinions which the book contains are nevertheless my own. I am also immensely indebted to Mr Chris Hobson, the Librarian of the Royal Air Force Staff College at Bracknell, Mr Lake the Librarian at Adastral House and to the Archivists at Churchill College, Cambridge who were consistently helpful. Josephine O'Connor Howe and the staff of Brassey's provided invaluable assistance during the editorial process.

I am extremely grateful to the Master, Scholars and Fellows of Churchill College in the University of Cambridge for permission to quote from their archives and in particular to Mr D. C. Grigg for permission to quote from the papers of Sir Percy Grigg, to the Honourable Francis Noel-Baker for permission to quote from the papers of Lord Noel-Baker and Mrs S. Corbett for permission to quote from the papers of her late husband, Lieutenant General Thomas Corbett. I would also like to thank Sir Fitzroy Maclean for permission to quote from *Eastern Approaches*, Mr William Deakin for permission to quote from *The Embattled Mountain*, General Sir John Akehurst for permission to quote from *We Won a War*, Lady Glubb for permission to quote from *War in the Desert* and Dr Peter Slugett for permission to quote from *Britain in Iraq*. I am also most grateful to Routledge Publishers for authority to quote from *Afghanistan, the Soviet War* by Edward Girardet, to Stackpole Books and Games for authority to quote from *Street Without Joy* by Bernard Fall, to Jonathan Cape for authority to quote from *Journal of a Vietcong* by Truong Nhu Tang, to Faber and Faber for authority to quote from *Last Post Aden 1964–1967* by Julian Paget, to Longman Publishers for authority to quote from *Guerrilla Warfare and Eoka's Struggle* by George Grivas, to Century Hutchinson for authority to quote from *Rebellion in Palestine* by John Marlowe and to Collins Publishers for authority to quote from *Last Sunset* by Stephen Harper. I am most grateful to Peters Fraser and Dunlop for permission to quote from Christopher Robbins' book entitled *Air America*, the Corgi paperback edition. Crown copyright material in the Public Record Office is reproduced by permission of the Controller of Her Majesty's Stationery Office.

Queens' College, Cambridge   PHILIP ANTHONY TOWLE
March 1989

Contents

Contents

Introduction

UNCONVENTIONAL WARFARE is by far the most common form of warfare in the modern world. Every part of the Third World from Latin America to the Middle East and from South-East Asia to Afghanistan has experienced this sort of violence since 1945. Sometimes, as in the Confrontation between Indonesia and Malaysia in the 1960s, unconventional warfare took the simple form of a guerrilla struggle, with small numbers of men—civilians or occasionally soldiers—operating in a 'hit and run' fashion against the government's regular forces. In other areas, such as China and Vietnam, it amounted to a 'people's revolutionary war' in which the insurgents tried to involve the whole nation and promised the economic and social transformation of society.[1] Often the wars since 1945 have been a mixture of both types, as in Algeria and Aden. Together guerrilla and revolutionary wars have far outnumbered inter-state conflicts in recent years.

If unconventional warfare is thus a central part of the history and a symptom of the problems of the developing countries, the use of air power epitomizes the technology and economics of the developed nations. The Great Powers use aircraft in unconventional wars because they have them, their armed forces are trained around them and they can bring enormous firepower to bear on their enemies. Aircraft have thus been employed against guerrillas or insurgents on many occasions from Iraq, Aden and Afghanistan in the 1920s to Vietnam and Afghanistan in the 1960s and 1980s. Third World governments have also acquired aircraft and are using them increasingly to counter guerrillas in Sri Lanka, Nicaragua, El Salvador and East Timor.[2] On their side, some of the guerrillas have begun to use anti-aircraft missiles which, for the first time, give them power to shoot down many of the aircraft which attack them and turn the struggle into one between rival technologies.

1

Imperial Policing

This book looks at how the conflicts between aircraft and guerrillas have developed over the last seven decades. Despite the scepticism expressed by some recent commentators, the Royal Air Force employed aircraft and armoured cars very effectively to maintain order in large parts of the Middle East between the two World Wars.[3] Aircraft were useful at that time because of the nature of the terrain and the lack of sophistication of the people they controlled. The tribesmen who troubled the British in Iraq, Aden and Afghanistan in the 1920s were simple nomads. Although they enjoyed fighting in guerrilla style and regarded it as a noble pastime, they felt no humiliation at surrendering when attacked by almost invincible aircraft.[4] Thus 'air control' often does seem to have involved relatively little death and destruction when used carefully. But even then, as the British found out in India and Palestine, these methods did not work in urban or more developed areas where nationalism was spreading. The uprising in Palestine from 1936 to 1939 took on some of the characteristics of a national war and was only contained by political concessions and the massive use of ground as well as air forces. Air power had been most effective in the desert and against relatively unsophisticated enemies. Most post-1945 insurgencies were to take place either in cities or in the jungle and neither location was ideal for the use of air power.

Insurgency

Many of the important postwar conflicts were on an even wider scale than the Palestinian revolt; they involved huge numbers of people and held out the prospect of changing the very nature of society as Mao Tse-tung did in China. In the early 1930s the Chinese Communists were able to survive repeated attacks by the Kuomintang's ground and air forces on their base areas in the south of China. When they were finally forced to abandon their base in October 1934, it was very largely because the Communist leaders had ignored Mao's advice and given up guerrilla for positional warfare.[5] During the epic year-long march from Kiangsi to Yenan in the north, the Communists were again repeatedly attacked by aircraft. These caused massive casualties, severely wounding Mao's wife and on another occasion, killing the aide standing next to him.[6] Air reconnaissance also meant that the Kuomintang could follow the progress of the marchers even when they were passing over the most difficult mountains or through grasslands.[7] Yet, at the end of the day, the side with the air power lost. European air forces might despise the Kuomintang pilots for their incompetence but, although the struggle would have been bloodier and more ferocious, it is doubtful whether the outcome would have been any different if a more efficient air force had been involved. Mao and the other survivors of the Long March established themselves in the caves of Yenan as a protection against air attacks. They thrived despite the hostility of the nationalists and, after 1938, of the Japanese as well. Ten years later the Communist forces had ceased to be merely guerrillas and were defeating the Kuomintang's troops. The power of insurgency had been demonstrated once and for all.

Such struggles were political as well as military and could not be defeated by military technology or tactics alone, however subtly, determinedly and effectively they were employed. After 1945 they were also usually supported by some friendly neighbouring state which offered sanctuary to the insurgents and gave them weapons and others supplies. Air power, as the American war in Vietnam showed in the 1960s and 1970s, is rarely an answer to the problems presented by such sanctuaries.

The new leaders were far more sophisticated than their predecessors. Ho Chi Minh, the Viet Minh leader, lived and worked for many years in London and Paris. He thus began the Vietnam war in 1946 with a keen insight into the strengths and weaknesses of those who fought against him. Ho Chi Minh and other guerrillas, such as Chin Peng in Malaya, had fought alongside the Western powers against the Japanese. They had long experience of guerrilla techniques and knew, when they took up their struggle against their erstwhile allies, how to oppose them most effectively. Above all they realized that the patience of the peoples of the developed world was limited and thus that they would probably prefer to make terms rather than to face the prospect of fighting an apparently interminable guerrilla war. As Ho Chi Minh told the French, 'you will kill ten of our men and we will kill one of yours and in the end it will be you who will tire of it'.[8]

Public Opinion and Air Power

Any attempt to force the new guerrilla movements to surrender by the use of air and fire power alone was likely to lead to a bloodbath and Western opinion was becoming ever more sensitive to the danger of causing civilian casualties. Even in the 1920s the RAF had to strive continually to convince the government and public to allow it to maintain order in the Middle East in its own way. There were many bitter critics of its policies, in the British Labour Party, amongst the delegates to the League of Nations and in the Indian National Congress Party. These pressures were amongst the factors which forced the RAF to limit civilian casualties to the maximum extent possible. In the Second World War the situation was completely different and the Germans and Japanese could, without fear of criticism, use whatever aircraft were available to destroy the insurgents who fought against them. However, such concerns restricted the use the British made of bombers in Kenya and Cyprus. They surfaced again during British operations in Aden in the 1960s and far more extensively in the American campaign in Vietnam in the 1960s. That war was seen by many as a symbol of the exaggerated and brutal use of air power to crush a brave enemy. Air power was immensely effective at halting large-scale attacks by North Vietnamese troops on South Vietnamese forces but it also played a decisive part in causing disaffection amongst the American people and opening what the insurgents called the fourth front, alongside politics, war and diplomacy.[9]

Some commentators have felt that air power is particularly brutalizing because the pilot can dissociate himself from people on the ground who become mere 'targets'. As critics of the US war in Vietnam put it,

> participants remain emotionally detached, not only because flying the plane and operating its complicated gadgets demand all their attention, but also because of the magnitude of the forces they control; the extent of the destruction they unleash, would otherwise overload their emotional reserves. These men operate in an atmosphere where professionalism is essential not only for technical reasons, but for psychological ones as well.

In some cases pilots have gone beyond dissociation and revelled in the brutality. Bruno Mussolini wrote of his experiences in the Abyssinian war:

> We had to set fire to the wooded hills, to the fields and little villages . . . It was all most diverting . . . After the bomb-racks were emptied I began throwing bombs by hand . . . It was most amusing: a big Zariba surrounded by tall trees was not easy to hit. I had to aim carefully at the straw roof and only succeeded at the third shot. The wretches who were inside, seeing the roof burning, jumped out and ran like mad.[10]

On the other hand, there have been plenty of cases where the airmen have sympathized with those on the ground and used their power with discretion. One of the most remarkable examples occurred during the Vietnam war when troops of the American Division ran amuck, killing women and children at My Lai. Warrant Officer Thompson landed his observation helicopter and loaded it with women and children whom he flew to safety. He also ordered the accompanying helicopters to fire on American ground troops if they interfered with his actions. As General Peers, who carried out the official enquiry, commented later: 'Occasionally we encountered a witness who, like Warrant Officer Thompson, had maintained his basic integrity . . . They kept alive our faith in the American soldier.'[11] They also showed that the distance between ground and air forces could sometimes work to limit rather than to increase brutality towards civilians.

Technology

Yet another reason why aircraft became less effective at fighting guerrillas after the Second World War was that the technology was changing. The aircraft used by the RAF in Mesopotamia and elsewhere in the 1920s were left over from the fighting in Europe. By chance they were quite suitable for the operations they had to undertake. The de Havilland 9a and the Bristol Fighter—to take two classic examples—could land in the desert and were slow enough to use their weapons accurately. They were sufficiently strong to withstand rifle shots in less vital parts and they were cheap and easy to maintain. As technology developed in the 1930s, aircraft became steadily less suitable for such operations. The Spitfire and Hurricane were much less robust than their predecessors and their stalling speed was far higher. In the Second World War it was often obsolete army co-operation aircraft, such as the Lysander and Storch, which proved most effective either at helping or at hunting down the guerrillas. The jet aircraft which came into service at the end of the Second World War were even less useful for anti-guerrilla operations than the fighter aircraft of the late 1930s. Thus the colonial powers made growing use of training aircraft in the strike role in Greece, Malaya, Algeria, Indochina and Kenya. As far as unconventional warfare was concerned, the Harvard or T 6 was by far the most important fixed-wing aircraft of the decade after 1945 and its successor, the T 28, played an important role in South-East Asia in the early 1960s.

It is remarkable that so little of the military technology of the Great

Powers was devoted to producing weapons for use specifically in unconventional warfare even though this was the dominant form of conflict. There were a number of reasons for this not least the looming shadow of another world war, the preference of armed forces for fighting and training for conventional wars and of the arms industries of the developed world for producing the appropriate weapons. Consequently, with notable exceptions such as the Helio-Courier, aircraft had to be adapted at short notice from their original purposes when the need arose for anti-guerrilla operations.

The types of aircraft required for fighting conventional and guerrilla wars thus became more and more distinct from 1934 onwards until this process was reversed by the advent of the helicopter. These were first used to move troops and evacuate casualties on a very small scale by the Americans in Burma in the Second World War, by the British in Malaya and by the French in Indochina. They were employed far more widely and more innovatively in Algeria by the French, who developed the helicopter gunship. The Americans utilized the same weapons on an even more extensive scale in Vietnam in the 1960s, as did the Russians in Afghanistan in the 1980s. The British followed a more conservative path, continuing to use helicopters mainly to transport and supply troops in unconventional wars. Helicopters are of course vastly more expensive than the 'string-bags' of the 1920s but they can land and take off from more inaccessible areas, their maximum speed is roughly the same (100 to 125 miles per hour) and they can hover in the air. Thus from about 1952 onwards the development of helicopters reversed the tendency for aircraft to become less suitable for countering guerrillas. One history of helicopters, written in 1983, referred to them as 'the supreme counter-insurgency weapons'.[12]

Technology started to change once again from the 1970s onwards, when hand-held anti-aircraft missiles, such as the Soviet SAM-7, British Blowpipe and American Stinger began to spread around the world. Already in the 1950s General Grivas had concluded from his experience fighting against the British in Cyprus that only the vulnerability of helicopters would limit their role in counter-insurgency.[13] Thus SAM-7s were used against American and South Vietnamese forces in Vietnam and against the British in Dhofar. Ironically they were also used against the Russians in Afghanistan in the 1980s. But it was the American decision to send Stinger missiles to the Mujahadeen which really changed the face of that war. It is still unclear whether, in the long run, these missiles will alter the balance of power between governments and irregular forces or whether parallel advances in the aircraft and bombs will not help to preserve the *status quo*. Either way the struggle will revolve round technology to a greater extent than in the past.

The Individual Struggle

Apart from conflicts between technologies, there have been the struggles between individuals, between the pilot and the guerrilla. The one was often a product of university and military college, educated and trained at massive cost (several million pounds in the case of a fast jet pilot); a professional in control of machinery which has become increasingly complex and expensive over the years, motivated by pride in his task and loyalty to his service and fellow officers. On the other side there was the dirty and unkempt guerrilla, sometimes also a product of university, more rarely of a military college and most frequently of a village school. The guerrilla was usually moved by nationalism and loyalty to his fellow guerrillas, sometimes by Communism or religion. Both pilot and guerrilla often needed great courage and dedication if they were to survive and emerge on the winning side. Thus governments and commentators alike must beware of assuming that weaponry alone is the key to victory.

The Future

Some felt that the Vietnam war proved the opposite and that courage and determination would always be more important than weaponry in unconventional wars. If the Americans could not win with all their technology, then insurgents had established their supremacy over the science of the West. In fact technology, tactics, courage and the support of the people all play a vital part in guerrilla warfare and insurgency. The use of helicopters for reconnaissance and transport has become ever more important, even in urban guerrilla wars such as Northern Ireland. Elsewhere, Third World nations and nations which feel they are fighting for their lives and have nothing to lose in terms of world public opinion—notably Israel and South Africa—still also use offensive air power on a very wide scale in rural areas against insurgents. The struggle between aircraft and guerrillas is therefore by no means over. Thus this book is not only an historical examination but also an analysis of a continuing struggle. It is not a history of contemporary guerrilla warfare as such and includes only enough political background to make each war intelligible. It cannot be remotely comprehensive since guerrilla warfare has been so widespread; it therefore concentrates on those wars which have been particularly significant in the struggle between air power and insurgents and for which information is available to me. It is strictly limited by the sources, firstly because government papers have not been released for more recent campaigns and secondly because in contrast to conventional warfare, very few guerrilla campaigns have been well documented from both sides. The Iraqis, Adenis and Afghans who were 'policed' by the RAF in the 1920s were often illiterate and consequently left little record of their reactions. Similarly there are far more accounts from the government side of the guerrilla wars after 1945 in Malaya, Kenya, Aden and Indochina than from amongst the guerrillas.[14] Conversely, it is the government side which is least well documented in the guerrilla campaigns of the Second World War, In Greece, Yugoslavia and Malaya, whilst two of the best accounts of the war written in English—Fitzroy Maclean's *Eastern Approaches* and F. Spencer Chapman's *The Jungle is Neutral*—were written by British officers who accompanied the guerrillas. The guerrilla side is also better documented than the government's in the current struggle in Afghanistan but only now is much useful information becoming available from the insurgents who fought against the Americans in Vietnam.[15] These limitations have to be kept firmly in mind when attempting to write about the effect of aircraft on irregular wars.

1

Biplanes and Nomads 1918–39

Iraq and Jordan

Introduction

When the First World War began, aircraft were little more than string and canvas toys. During the course of the fighting tens of thousands of aircraft were built and they evolved into effective (though mechanically unreliable) fighting machines.[1] It is not, therefore, surprising that they were used very extensively by the colonial powers in the interwar period to expand or maintain control over their empires. The French used them in Indochina and Morocco, the Italians used them in North Africa and in Ethiopia, the Spanish used them in their part of Morocco and the Americans in Nicaragua. Aircraft increased the strength of Europeans relative to non-Europeans by at least as much as the machine-gun had done in the nineteenth century. Moreover, while machine guns had still to be carried into battle by the troops, the aeroplane, backed up by the armoured car, conquered distance. Deserts were no longer a protection against government control; quite the contrary, they were the most suitable areas for the use of aircraft and armoured cars. Consequently regions which had never been dominated by central governments in recent history, such as Cyrenaica or the Aden hinterland, were brought under European control. In many areas the Ottomans and other rulers had run the towns but had left the desert tribes to manage their own affairs.[2] Ironically, therefore, the European grasp on the rest of the world was in some ways most effective and extensive in the decades when it was already being challenged by the Congress Party in India and by the stirrings of nationalism elsewhere.

Of course the use of aircraft was not a sure recipe for success in colonial wars, though it sometimes helped to moderate defeat or to speed up victory. The Spanish had aircraft in Morocco when the Krim brothers led the Rif rebellion against them there in July 1921. Never-

9

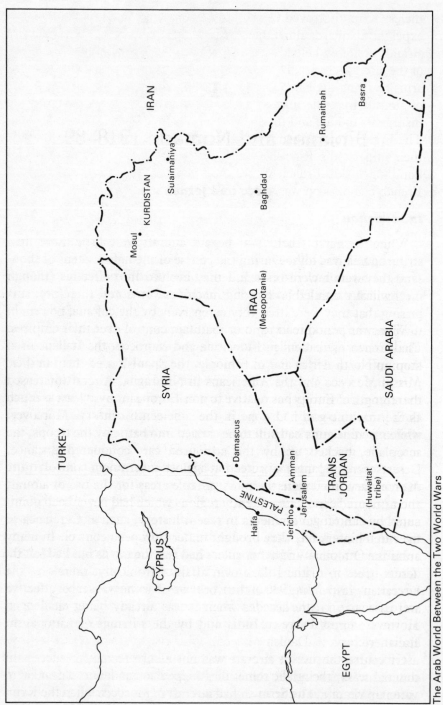

The Arab World Between the Two World Wars

theless Krim destroyed General Silvestre's army and seemed about to expel the Spaniards altogether.[3] However the colonial forces rallied and aircraft certainly helped to steady them. The Spanish even made use of the aircraft-carrier, *Dedala* to blockade the rebel area and to prevent arms reaching the Rifs. The two main handicaps to the successful use of aircraft were the uneven nature of the country which allowed the insurgents to hide and the sheer incompetence of the Spanish airmen. The French complained not so much that the Spaniards were missing their targets, the Rif rebels, but that they were actually sometimes bombing inside French rather than Spanish Moroccan territory. A French commission was sent to investigate and

> along with several Spanish officers, who scornfully denied the inefficiency of their aviators, the commission made sorties into the hills and although they stayed within [French] zonal borders, they were lucky to escape being blown to bits by Spanish planes, which unloaded bombs within yards of them.[4]

When the war spread to French Morocco in 1925, the French also used aircraft against villages suspected of harbouring guerrillas and to stop outposts such as Rihana and Beni-Derkoul from being overrun. Missions to supply garrisons with ammunition, ice and food were extremely dangerous because the aircraft had to fly very low to drop their loads accurately. One machine returned from a sortie of this type with forty bullet holes from the besiegers. Aircraft also made the first maps of Morocco which greatly helped the French ground forces.[5]

Just as the Spanish were for a while hard-pressed to hold on to Morocco, so the Italians were struggling in the early 1920s to maintain their grip on Tripolitania and Cyrenaica. In 1922 they were reduced to supplying the town of Azizia by air. Subsequently, when they went over to the offensive, they used aircraft to cow some of the tribes into submission. John Wright, in his account of the war, argues that the Zintan gave in to the Italians after gas bomb attacks from Caproni aircraft in 1925.[6] In 1930, when Graziani became Governor, aircraft were used to drive the last surviving rebels over the frontier into Egypt. However, aircraft were certainly only one of the factors leading to the Italian victory. A Danish Moslem, who visited the area at the time, ascribed Italian success in part to their policy of sealing wells in the desert and so forcing the rebels to decide between surrender and starvation.[7] Aircraft and chemical weapons simply made the Italian victory easier.

But it was the British, with the largest empire, who made the greatest use of aircraft to control their territories. They also developed the most articulate doctrine of 'air control'. The reasons are straightforward. They had expanded the area under their control during the First World War at the expense of the Ottoman Empire. Yet their capacity to maintain their empire was reduced by four years of total war and their forces were stretched by unrest in India and elsewhere. Finally the RAF had been established on 1 April 1918 and it was determined to preserve its independence even after the end of the 'war to end wars'. The Royal Navy was to struggle bitterly throughout the 1920s until it finally regained control of the aircraft of the Fleet Air Arm from the RAF. The Air Staff was afraid that this would be the signal for the abolition of a separate air force, not least because many army officers also regarded the new Service with dislike and distaste. It vitally needed an imperial role to survive.

Unrest within the Empire provided it with just such a role. In 1919 RAF aircraft helped to put down rebellion in Egypt. The following year they were used in the Sudan but it was in Somalia in 1920 that they were first used most extensively. The British had had trouble there from the forces belonging to the man whom they disparagingly referred to as the 'Mad Mullah' at several periods between 1903 and 1914. However their campaigns against the Mullah had always been half-hearted and his power remained unbroken. In 1918 the Governor of Somalia suggested that this situation should be changed and the War Office sent General Hoskins to plan the campaign. However the government decided that such an effort would be too expensive and Hoskins was recalled in January 1919. Then in May 1919 the Colonial Secretary, Lord Milner asked Trenchard, the Chief of the Air Staff (CAS) for advice. Trenchard argued that the RAF could defeat the Mullah single-handed. The Chief of the Imperial General Staff (CIGS), Henry Wilson, was totally opposed to the idea but the government allowed the RAF to try.[8] In the event the Mullah's forces were destroyed not by six DH9as alone but by a combination of air and camel power.[9] Nevertheless the RAF argued later that aircraft had been decisive and the Governor of Somaliland himself suggested that 'the interests of the Protectorate will best be served by the retention of a small air force and a reduction in the Camel Corps. I consider that threats from the air offer the surest guarantee of peace and order in Somaliland.'[10]

Iraq

Aircraft were only involved for three weeks in the Somaliland campaign and thus their employment over two decades to maintain control in Mesopotamia (Iraq as it later became) was much more significant. The country had been captured from the Ottomans during the First World War after bitter fighting but the cost of garrisoning it was high. On 19 February 1920 an official in the Air Ministry in London minuted to the Chief of the Air Staff:

> Secretary of State [Winston Churchill] tells me today that the General Staff profess themselves unable to garrison Mesopotamia. As you will remember the original estimates provided for £21.5 million for this purpose which is considered to be more than the country is worth. Secretary of State has had to cut this down very considerably with the result . . . that the General Staff now proposes complete evacuation of the country. He wishes to know whether you are prepared to take on Mesopotamia. If you can give him an answer in the affirmative he will announce the scheme in his speech on Monday next in the Army Estimates.[11]

Obviously this was not the first time that the subject had been discussed by Winston Churchill, who was the Secretary of State for both Air and War, and the CAS. They would already have discussed the possibility of using the newly-founded RAF to police the Empire and thus Churchill was simply seizing this opportunity to put their ideas into operation. Nevertheless, Churchill was perhaps the only minister who would have taken the gamble of turning so vast an area as Mesopotamia over to a new and essentially untried method of control. For his part, Trenchard was only too willing to grasp the opportunity offered, despite the risks involved.

Ten days after the CAS had been informed of Churchill's original query, the Secretary of State wrote to him: 'I shall be glad if you will, without delay, submit a scheme and state whether you consider the internal security of the country [Iraq] could be maintained by it,'[12] Churchill said that the RAF would not be expected to protect the country against external enemies such as the Russians or Turks. He had obviously been giving its duties within Iraq some thought and called for the establishment of 'a series of defended areas in which air bases could be securely established'. These would be ringed by blockhouses and also protected by a few tanks. The RAF would need to be able to move two or three companies of troops quickly around the country and it should examine the possibility of developing what would now be called incapacitating or irritating chemical agents to help it maintain order. Furthermore some 4,000 European and 10,000 native troops might be maintained in the country to back up the air force.[13] This scheme, with some exceptions such as the development of chemical weapons, bears a good deal of resemblance to what eventually happened and Churchill must be given credit both for his prescience and for his courage in taking responsibility for the idea.

The Air Staff followed up Churchill's initiative by asking for a meeting with the India Office, since Iraq was administered from India. They could make little progress until the Peace Conference decided at the end of April 1920 that Syria and Mesopotamia should be independent but 'subject to the assistance of a mandatory until such time as they are able to stand alone.' Plans were then thrown into even greater confusion by the outbreak of a full-scale rebellion in Iraq in the middle of 1920 caused by growing Arab nationalism and resentment against British methods of administration and taxation.[14] Four of the five roads leading to Baghdad were cut, troops had to be rushed to the country from India and elsewhere and many garrisons had to be supplied by air. Rumaithah held out for sixteen days whilst aircraft dropped ammunition to the troops and drove the Iraqis away so that the besieged forces could leave the fort and raid the bazaar for provisions. Kufah held out for eighty-nine days with aircraft dropping medical supplies, ammunition and other necessities. It was some months before the situation could be brought under control as a result of extensive ground and air operations.

The rebellion hardened opinions within Britain. Those who had never been in favour of accepting the mandate believed that the rebellion proved the enormity of the task involved. Those who believed that the RAF should be given charge of the country asserted that rebellion had only shown the inability of the army to carry out the task, except at excessive cost. According to Trenchard's biographer, the issue suddenly came to the forefront again in November 1920. Churchill sent a motorcycle despatch-rider to the CAS who was staying in Cambridge. The Secretary of State wanted Trenchard to rehearse the arguments for using the Air Force to control Iraq so that his views could be presented to the next Cabinet meeting. In the event they had to defend their views against the bitter hostility of Henry Wilson but they succeeded in winning Cabinet support.[15] In February 1921 the pivotal figure, Winston Churchill, moved from the War Ministry to the Colonial Office. Iraq had now come under that Ministry rather than under the India Office so that he was in a position to decide its fate. On the other hand, he had lost control of the army and it was to become a redoubtable opponent of his efforts to hand Iraq over to the new Service.

In March 1921 Churchill summoned a conference in Cairo of senior British officials and serving officers in the Middle East to discuss the future of Palestine, Trans-Jordan and Mesopotamia. Many of the officials were doubtful about the RAF scheme. Sir Percy Cox, the very experienced High Commissioner in Baghdad, appears to have led the opposition. He argued that unless air action 'is intensive or followed by the movement of troops, its effect is transitory and gradually decreases',[16] Cox expected the impact of aircraft to decline as the Arab tribes became more used to them. All in all he concluded: 'I can't regard the "air force scheme" in the light of a practical solution to the problem.' General Sir Aylmer Haldane, the commander of the military forces in Iraq, was also sceptical at this stage. However he suggested that the outlying garrisons should be withdrawn to Baghdad so that the RAF could test its ability to maintain order.[17] Trenchard emphasized the cheapness of the RAF's scheme which relied on aircraft still in service from the war. Their bases would be defended by ground troops raised by the RAF whilst an Iraqi army would gradually be built up.

Despite Cox's opposition and Haldane's scepticism, by the third meeting of the Military Committee in Cairo the delegates were talking about the time 'when the Chief of the Air Staff's scheme comes into operation'. However, when the political and military committees met together, Sir Percy Cox continued to argue that a large British garrison was needed until an indigenous Iraqi army could take over. The decisive counterargument was financial. Churchill told the combined political and military committee on 13 March 1921 that a British garrison would cost £25 million a year and that this was more than Britain or Iraq could afford.[18] There was thus only a choice between abandoning the mandate or following the RAF's proposals to maintain control with eight squadrons of aircraft and limited numbers of troops with armoured cars. They would also have to placate Arab nationalism by supporting the Emir Feisal as ruler of Iraq under the mandate. Feisal was the third son of Sherif Husein who had co-operated with the British against the Turks during the war. Subsequently he had tried to establish an Arab kingdom in Syria but had been driven out by the French. He seemed popular in Iraq and the only possible Arab ruler. However, with or without Feisal it was astonishingly risky to put so much faith in the RAF's untried scheme and many Middle East experts must undoubtedly have returned to their posts predicting disaster. The Air Staff itself noted

> these and other questions have not yet been fully explored but Mesopotamia offers a good field for their exploration. Weather conditions are more favourable for aerial operations than was the case on the Western Front . . . and much of the country is flat and offers suitable landing grounds.[19]

Trenchard had said that it would take the RAF a year to make its preparations to take over Iraq. He raised RAF armoured car units to defend the air bases there, though the army made as much difficulty as possible about supplying weapons or helping with the training of these units.[20] The Adjutant General objected to leaving any army personnel in Iraq after the RAF took over and the officer commanding armoured car units in Iraq announced flatly that none of his men would want to transfer to the RAF's new armoured car squadrons.[21] Nevertheless by the middle of 1921 the Air Staff had received one influential recruit. Sir Aylmer Haldane reported that the RAF had demonstrated the feasibility of maintaining control from the air:

> The test was one that covered operations in the desert, over marshy country and the hilly borders of Kurdistan so that it must be regarded as a representative one. Wholesale reductions on the strength of the results would of course be unwise but I think that it shows that disturbances can be checked or prevented from arising by the speedy arrival of aircraft . . . Indeed I now feel that had I had sufficient aircraft last year I might have prevented the insurrection spreading beyond the first incident at Rumaithah.[22]

However, the army as a whole continued to oppose the RAF scheme up to 1 October 1922 when the RAF officially took over. Afterwards it went on criticizing RAF methods on humanitarian grounds.

The RAF air and armoured car squadrons in Iraq were certainly kept active. The armoured car squadrons operated amongst the nomads on the ill-defined frontier with Saudi Arabia. The squadrons of aircraft distributed propaganda leaflets amongst the tribes, transported political officers who worked amongst the rural population as well as 'punishing' malcontents by air action. The High Commissioner reported on 9 December 1922 that they had been used nine times on punitive missions since April. On three occasions demonstrations by aircraft brought tribal feuds to an end. On another occasion planes destroyed a dam illegally built by a sheik to deprive his neighbours of water, and dropped bombs on a sheik and his followers who refused to pay taxes, held up travellers and attacked a police station. One person was killed and thirteen wounded.[23]

The RAF was not only concerned with internal disturbances. In 1922 war seemed likely with Turkey over the Chanak crisis and it was possible that it would spread into Iraq. Consequently the War Office maintained that the Mosul area in the north of Iraq should be abandoned, but the Air Ministry and the High Commissioner in Iraq argued that this would turn all Iraq against Britain. Moreover there were no air bases between Mosul and Baghdad and so the RAF could not easily oppose a further Turkish advance from Mosul. Trenchard himself believed that an invasion would be limited to two Turkish divisions and he agreed with Sir John Salmond, the Air Officer Commanding (AOC) in Iraq, that 'the RAF would give a good account of themselves against two Turkish divisions'.[24] Negotiations with Turkey dragged on over the next three years; the situation never quite exploded into war though no one was sure that it would not do so. On several occasions the RAF bombed small groups of Turks who had crossed the frontier, driving them back into their own territory.[25]

The Kurds also caused constant problems because of their desire to establish a separate state. Their leader, Sheik Mahmund, was determined if ultimately ineffective and, because of the efficacy of his guerrillas, he was jokingly referred to by the RAF as their Director of Training.[26] In retaliation for his attacks on government officials the RAF bombed villages and towns where he was hiding, including his 'capital city', Sulaimaniya. Most future RAF leaders were involved in these operations, including Sir John Salmond, the future CAS who was AOC in Iraq in 1922, 'Bomber' Harris, Sir Gerald Gibbs who was to be the last AOC in India, Sir Basil Embry and many others. Embry recalled that he flew seventy-four missions against the Sheik's men in the four and a half years he was in Iraq.[27] In 1926 the British tried to persuade Mahmund to settle in Persia but he was still at large in 1930 when the RAF reluctantly supported the Iraqi army's attacks on his guerrillas.[28]

Apart from unrest amongst the Iraqi tribes and threats from Turks and Kurds, the RAF also had to deal with tribal raids across the ill-defined frontier with what is now Saudi Arabia. The situation there has been brilliantly described by Sir John Glubb who came to know it better than any other foreigner. Raids by one tribe on another had been endemic since time immemorial, though the situation worsened in the chaotic years after the war. Protecting the Iraqi tribes by armoured cars and aircraft was very difficult. Armoured cars often arrived too late to help and pilots, on being informed that an attack was in the offing, had to identify both the attackers and the defenders. How difficult this could be was demonstrated by an incident during the early 1920s. Aircraft were pursuing Sheik Balaibel who had raided a village. They saw two lines of horsemen in white cantering towards each other and, to maintain order, they dropped a 20 lb bomb in the area. It was only later that they discovered that they had disrupted the wedding celebrations of the daughter of a friendly Sheik.[29] At one time Glubb persuaded pilots to fly routine patrols over the frontier during the raiding season to deter attackers. Such patrols had a dramatic effect but they were much disliked by the pilots who generally saw nothing but empty sand. The RAF also made the situation worse by trying to force Iraqi tribes to keep away from the frontier region, even though they desperately needed to graze their flocks there. In the end the problem was solved by the combined efforts of the RAF, Glubb's ability to persuade the Iraqi tribes to defend themselves and King Ibn Saud's decision in 1929 to crush the Wahhabis, the fierce, puritanical sect which had helped him to power but had subsequently become increasingly rebellious.[30]

Flying the machines available in the 1920s—DH9as, Sopwith Snipes, Bristol Fighters, Vickers Vernons—was by no means easy. They had been developed very rapidly during the First World War, primarily to meet conditions in France; flying across arid deserts was very different. Sir John Glubb wrote subsequently:

> It is difficult to imagine how precarious was flying in the desert in the 1920s. Forced landings were the rule rather than the exception . . . The worst was that, if a machine force-landed, it was not certain that it could be found again and a slow death from thirst 150 miles out in the desert was not a pleasant prospect.[31]

In the first years engines overheated, propellers warped, tyres were punctured by thorns and shock absorbers perished. Bristol Fighters had to be refuelled from the top with the hot desert winds blowing petrol on to the bare skins of the pilots and mechanics. Nor were the design and unreliability of the machines the only problems; 'sandstorms are prevalent during the summer months; they reach a height of anything from 1,000 to 8,000 feet and it is utterly impossible to see anything if caught in one, either in the air or on the ground'. The only solution was to land ahead of the storm, tie the plane to the ground and to wait for the storm to pass. Fortunately the aircraft were usually strong enough to survive unscathed, yet their very lightness could also be a help. One pilot, whose DH9a was shot down, kept off enemy tribesmen by lifting up the tail of his aircraft and moving it round so that his gunner could fire at them until help arrived.[32]

Problems with the aircraft were gradually sorted out and by the 1930s they were well suited to their task. They were not as fast as later machines and the pilot had a good view of the ground and the target; 'no threat from the Continent was in sight . . . under the circumstances, increased reliability and extra load-carrying were considered as the main requirements for aircraft employed in the various overseas commands on policing work with no air opposition'.[33] Even in 1924 the AOC in Iraq felt sufficiently confident of his men and machines to stage a bombing demonstration in front of Iraqi officials and civilians: 'The very first bombs dropped from 2,000 feet, a salvo of four fell bang in the middle of the target. There was hardly a bomb that was not within 20 or 25 yards of the spot aimed at . . . from what I heard the effect on the populace was very marked.'[34]

It is perhaps somewhat surprising that such accuracy was achieved so early, considering that the RAF in the first years of the Second World War was sometimes incapable of finding the city it was supposed to be attacking. Conditions were, however, different. In Iraq, bombs were dropped from tens or hundreds of feet, not thousands. The aircraft involved flew slowly and in the daytime. There was no opposition from the air though there was some from the ground. One RAF officer concluded that the average Iraqi tribesman was a good shot since 'he wasted very little ammunition on the fabric parts' of the aircraft. Aircraft were shot down by such marksmen but by 1932 the RAF had only had fourteen pilots killed and eighty-four wounded in air policing operations.[35] If they were shot down there was a considerable possibility that pilot and gunner would be killed but it was also possible that they would be captured. To try to ensure their safety the RAF offered a reward for their release, at the same time threatening dire penalties if they were molested.[36] The Air Staff was very insistent that, even if an officer were captured, this should not prevent operations continuing against the captors.[37]

Bombing recalcitrant tribes to force them to pay taxes and conform in other ways to British wishes was certainly not without its critics. Many in Britain remembered the German raids in the First World

War and the civilians that had been killed. Some felt that there was something 'unsporting' about using aircraft against tribes which did not possess them. The army grumbled that 'the only means at the disposal of the air force and the means now used are the bombing of the women and the children in the villages'.[38] The Labour government which came to power in 1924 was, of course, particularly sensitive to the charge that it was behaving in an inhumane manner. George Lansbury referred to 'this Hunnish and barbarous method of warfare against unarmed people'.[39] The Colonial Secretary, James Thomas, wrote to the High Commissioner in Iraq in January 1924 pointing out that critical press stories were appearing about bombing attacks on the rebellious Beni Huchaim tribes. He explained that he did not want to make the High Commissioner's task more difficult but that heavy casualties 'will not be easily explained or defended in Parliament by me'.[40] The High Commissioner replied that British ground forces in Iraq had been run down—by 1924 there were only two battalions there—while the Iraqi army was still too weak to take the field. Thus the only alternative to present policy of air control was to resort to the 'Turkish' policy of stirring up one tribe against another. An (unspoken) alternative was to abandon Iraq altogether but such a policy had been rejected after prolonged discussions and disagreements by the previous government on 6 February 1923.[41] In the circumstances, the Colonial Secretary and his successor could do little but complain when they thought that tribes were being bombed too frequently.[42]

Concern about the effects of the RAF's policy encouraged the Air Staff to write *Notes on the method of employment of the air arm in Iraq*, which Thomas presented to Parliament in August 1924. The first drafts of this paper tended to stress the military effectiveness of air power. Rebellious Kurds and others knew that 'within 45 minutes a full-sized village . . . can be practically wiped out and a third of its inhabitants killed or injured by four or five planes which offer them no real target and no opportunity for glory or avarice'.[43] Later drafts put much less emphasis on efficiency and more on the relative humanity of control from the air. The Air Staff stressed that destruction was neither the aim nor the normal result of its actions. Rebellious villages were warned that they would be bombed if they did not give in to government demands within a certain time. Then, when the people had been given the opportunity to evacuate the area, their houses would be attacked with small, and later with larger, bombs. The aim was not so much to destroy the houses but to interrupt daily life; 'the real weight of air action lies in the daily interruption of life which it can inflict, if necessary for an indefinite period while offering negligible chances of loot or of hitting back'.[44]

This was the theory but how humane was the practice? We know that in the early years Churchill was horrified by a report that aircraft had attacked women and children and insisted that Trenchard investigate. Conversely, we also know that the RAF refused to bomb tribesmen who fled from Ibn Saud in 1930 partly because women and children were present.[45] Furthermore, if the theory of air policing was that villages rather than people were to be attacked, we know that officers sometimes protested in the early days against the wastefulness of this policy.[46] The difficulty is to be sure how typical any of these incidents were and how great an impact the Air Staff's refinements had in the field. Historians of other colonial empires have been very critical of the use of air power against civilians. According to David Woolman, in the Moroccan campaigns, 'bombers were used by both the French and the Spanish who seemed to have no qualms about bombing villages from which all the men were absent.'[47] Some reporters even suggested that they bombed at sundown to catch people in mosques and kill them more easily. The British Air Staff maintained that the Italians did not apply the correct 'air policing' methods.[48]

The problem for the historian of the RAF's activities is that the people who were controlled by the RAF did not usually leave written records of their reactions or sufferings. The RAF tried to answer the critics by arguing that their aircraft landed in rebel areas as soon as the tribes had come to terms and found no evidence of resentment or widespread destruction.[49] They also maintained that, if the army were sent to 'punish' a tribe, the campaign would be more destructive because the tribes would fight harder. This seems to be plausible for the period and peoples in question. Many of them regarded war as a sport 'which produced the colour and excitement to counteract the monotony of the pastoral life'[50] but they also felt that they could honourably avoid war against aircraft and armoured cars. Very often they were prepared to come to terms when such equipment appeared and thus the bloodbaths which later characterized the wars in Indochina do not appear—on the evidence currently available—to have typified British methods between the two World Wars.

Historians have, however, supported allegations by some contemporary administrators that air control increased the gap between rulers and ruled. According to Peter Slugett, the historian of Iraq, perhaps the most serious long-term consequence of the ready availability of air control was that it developed into a substitute for administration. Several incidents during the mandate period indicate that the speed and simplicity of air attack was preferred to the more time-consuming and painstaking investigation of grievances and disputes.[51]

The Air Staff denied this and argued that political and intelligence officers were far more free, in the areas under their control, to wander around and assess the conditions of the people than they were under less efficient administrations.[52]

Sir John Glubb, who as an ex-officer could hardly be accused of hostility to the Service, believed that air power sometimes gave government control over the tribes which it lacked the knowledge to use wisely. In 1923 Glubb was involved in the operations against the Beni Hucheim tribe which so worried John Thomas. Glubb found that the tribe's attacks on travellers and their unwillingness to pay taxes were the product of their appalling poverty and that the government's request that they forfeit their rifles was equivalent to asking them to commit suicide, given the traditions of the area.[53] Nevertheless the Beni Hucheim were forced by bombing attacks to make their peace with the government and this was cited as a great success by the Air Staff. Of course, this occurred in the early days of the British mandate and it may well be that greater wisdom was shown later on. Certainly the Air Staff was constantly cautioning officers in Iraq that bombing should only be used as a very last resort.

Before the end of the 1920s the RAF's role in Iraq was decreasing as the Iraqi army became stronger—a process regarded with mixed feelings by Britain's armed forces. Trenchard opposed the Labour government's idea of creating an Iraqi air force in 1924, partly because of the costs involved. The British also wanted the Iraqis to develop their ground forces more slowly than the Iraqi government would have liked.[54] The CAS expected the RAF to remain in Iraq after it became independent. When the issue was discussed in 1927 the question was, who would protect RAF bases in an independent Iraq? Up to that time they had been defended by the RAF's own armoured car squadrons, by Indian infantry and by levies raised by the RAF in Iraq from amongst the Christian Assyrians. The CAS hoped that the Iraqis would absorb the Assyrians into their own armed forces once the country became independent, but the Iraqis decided to kill them instead.[55] Gradually, however, British strength in Iraq was reduced. In

November 1928 the last imperial infantry battalion was withdrawn and in April 1929 the RAF abandoned two of its bases in Iraq. In 1930 Britain signed a treaty with Feisal's government and the country became fully independent two years later.[56] However the RAF retained some bases in the country until 1958 and intervened decisively during the Second World War to crush a pro-Nazi government.[57] The RAF and Iraq were thus bound together for more than three decades. Without Iraq, the RAF would have found it very difficult to retain even the residual strength which it maintained in the 1920s; without the RAF, the British would have abandoned Iraq much earlier and Feisal's government would not have survived.

Jordan

The RAF found itself in very similar situations in Jordan and Iraq. Towards the end of the First World War, as the Turks were driven back, Britain's ally Feisal set up an Arab government in Damascus which for sixteen months ruled the area east of the Jordan river as well as Syria. However, his system fell to bits in 1920 under French pressure and the League of Nations gave the British 'Trans-Jordan' as part of their mandate for Palestine.[58] The following year Sherif (now King) Husain of Hejaz sent his second son, Abdullah, to avenge Feisal's humiliation by the French. The Amir Abdullah appeared with his army in Jordan shortly before Churchill presided over the meeting with British officials in Cairo. The British decided to dissuade Abdullah from attacking the French and in return to recognize him as ruler of Jordan under the British mandate.[59] Thus, after the Cairo conference, Churchill met Abdullah in Jerusalem and agreed to back him as ruler of Trans-Jordan for a trial period. Abdullah hoped that the whole of Palestine would come under his control but Churchill explained that this would not be possible because of British plans for the region. Thus, while the RAF retained aircraft and armoured cars in Trans-Jordan, the new state gradually established itself until, in 1928, London signed a treaty with the Amir recognizing the country's independence but retaining some military and financial control.[60]

The Turks had made little effort to occupy the area around Amman until the 1880s when the Hejaz railway was extended to the region. Four-fifths of the country was made up of desert occupied by Bedouins who were never effectively ruled by the Turks but after the dislocation of the war years there was more confusion then usual in the whole region. Indeed one writer has commented 'all combined to stir the

Arabian deserts to a frenzy such as they had seldom, if ever, known before . . . Every Bedouin tribe was a law to itself and a terror to others.'[61] In April 1920, for example, tribesmen attacked a goods train at Semakh in Palestine. They also set upon a patrol of Indian cavalry which went to investigate. Thus British aircraft had to be sent to disperse the tribesmen, 200 of whom were killed.[62] In January 1922 two of the tribes began fighting each other. The British tried to mediate but made no progress until they deployed aircraft. Five Bristol Fighters from Ramleh airfield near Amman demonstrated above the unruly tribesmen; 'two machines photographed the town; others flew low and performed aerobatics, zoomed over the crowd and fired Very lights'.[63] The tribes then agreed to compromise. But Trans-Jordan remained very fragile for a number of years whilst its armed force, the Arab Legion, was built up; one officer wrote to Trenchard, in December 1928: 'The situation . . . is not good. If the armoured cars and aeroplanes are taken away my opinion is that the Amir's government will not last a fortnight.'[64]

The British and the Arab Legion had to deal with a constant series of rebellions and threats to the new government.[65] In September 1923 one Sultan who was giving particular problems was warned that unless he co-operated he would be attacked. When he failed to do so and instead assaulted an Arab Legion post, two RAF armoured cars were sent to disperse his forces. The tribesmen were unimpressed by these marvels of advanced technology. The two cars were assailed by over 4,000 Arabs:

> Number One was halted in order to watch over Number Four as a number of men were rapidly approaching her from the hilltops . . . at this period the near front wheel and near rear wheel of Number Four car were punctured; in addition Sergeant Kenny had got a stoppage with the Vickers gun.

At this stage the car's second gun also failed and its occupants had to defend themelves with revolvers. The car stalled and one of the men had to jump out and restart it. Both cars had their radiators hit and their tyres shot away, reducing their speed to ten miles an hour. In the end the vehicles had to reverse towards Amman, defending themselves all the time. Nevertheless St John Philby, the British representative in Amman, felt that they had fulfilled their role and that the offending tribe had learnt its lesson.[66]

The greatest threat to the new state came in the early years from

Wahhabis or Ikhwan who raided Jordan from what is now Saudi
Arabia. They were a fanatical sect, utterly determined to stamp out
such practices as smoking and drinking and to restore Islamic purity.[67]
The Wahhabis formed the main power behind Ibn Saud in the early
years and enabled him in 1925 to expel King Husain, the father of
Abdullah and Feisal, from the Hejaz, and to unite Saudi Arabia under
his control. They also wanted to overrun Jordan and other 'corrupt'
states in the area. In 1922 they invaded Jordan and began killing members of the Beni Sakhr tribe. Fortunately however an RAF aircraft
chanced to fly over the area. The aircraft had no idea what was going
on but the raiders thought that they were going to be bombed and fled.
The RAF explained that 'as the aeroplane had only a mechanic without
goggles or cap in the back seat and the pilot was watching land marks
it is understandable how the fighting was altogether missed'.[68] Abdullah was not very pleased that the opportunity to inflict casualities on
the invaders had not been taken but the RAF was gratified by this
example of the effect of air power.

A far more serious incident occurred two years later when several
thousand Wahhabis invaded and approached Amman itself. If they had
taken the town, as they might well have done had the RAF not been
there, Abdullah would have been overthrown and the townsfolk
killed.[69] Trans-Jordan might even have become a province of Saudi
Arabia. According to the RAF's version of events, at five o'clock in the
morning of 16 August 1924 a lorry driver carrying petrol from Amman
to Ziza was informed that Wahhabi tribesmen were attacking villages
in the area. The driver returned to Amman and by 6.55 a.m. one DH9a
had been sent out to confirm the report. By 9.15 a.m. three DH9as
had attacked the Wahhabis with bombs and Lewis guns. According to
Glubb, the aircraft caused few casualties but they forced the Ikhwan
to stop plundering the villages and to concentrate their forces.[70] The
aircraft also dropped messages to the armoured cars warning them of
the whereabouts of the Wahhabis and returned to Amman to refuel.
Repeated attacks on the tribesmen turned them into a rabble and the
RAF believed that they had inflicted 500 casualties whilst the raiders
in turn had killed forty friendly Arabs. Again, according to Glubb's
reconstruction of events, it was the armoured cars rather than the aircraft which inflicted most of the casualties.[71] All the aeroplanes had
been hit by rifle fire and two of those on board had been wounded.[72]
Arab versions of the battle put far less emphasis on the importance of
the armoured cars or aircraft. Some maintain that the RAF's bombs
hit the friendly Beni Sakhr tribe and yet that it was these tribesmen

who really won the battle and drove the Wahhabis away. Glubb's version seems more convincing; according to this, one Sheik, Dirdah Ibn Bakhit, had indeed defended his village for some hours before the armoured cars dispersed the raiders. Subsequently the Beni Sakhr pursued the Ikhwan and cut off the stragglers.[73]

Their raids nevertheless continued for a number of years. In March 1928 the British believed that a general rising by the Wahhabi had taken place in the Nejd and that the tribesmen might descend upon Jordan or Iraq in armies up to 20,000 strong.[74] In fact the Ikhwan were frustrated by Ibn Saud's unwillingness to attack Iraq and Jordan even if the Wahhabis believed that the people there had lapsed from the true faith. Thus in 1927 three of the most powerful tribes had begun to carry out raids without the King's permission. 'Recent raids have been undertaken by camels and horses, the camelmen being mounted two to a camel. Raiders ride in open formation which is a difficult target for air attacks.' To protect Amman, aircraft were to attack the invaders as far as possible from the capital; 'should aircraft have no effect on the attack, the armoured car battle would be fought at about thirty miles distance'. Finally, if the armoured cars failed, the Arab legion would organize a defence amongst the town's inhabitants.[75]

In the end, the massed attack did not take place but it was not until the Wahhabis were defeated by Ibn Saud himself in 1929 and 1930 that the menace really disappeared. In 1932 Sir Henry Cox, the British Resident in Amman, led a delegation to Jedda to negotiate a frontier agreement with Ibn Saud. Later that year, Trans-Jordan and Saudi Arabia signed a treaty in Jerusalem establishing inspectors on the frontier to clear up any future disputes.[76] The two first inspectors, John Glubb and Amir Abdul Aziz ibn Zeid met on a number of occasions. But the meetings became more and more a social event as raiding had ceased.[77] From then on, the main problems in the area concerned smuggling.

French activities in Syria caused the British and Jordanians intermittent problems. In 1923 the French wanted British help in hunting down Sultan Arrash whom they believed had attacked one of their generals. The British were not particularly enthusiastic but felt that they had to give the minimum of co-operation.[78] In later years Druse tribesmen attacked by the French fled across the frontier into Jordan where Abdullah wanted to give them support. The British had some sympathy with the Druse, whom they believed had been goaded into rebellion by French behaviour. Nevertheless, they vetoed the Amir's plans for political reasons. However, when they allowed the Druse women and children to stay in Jordan, they found that the area became a base for guerrilla operations in Syria. In the end British orders against this had to be enforced by the threat of air power.[79]

Gradually the Arab Legion was strengthened until it became, in British eyes, the most efficient Arab army in the Middle East. Correspondingly, the RAF's role in defending Jordan declined. Nevertheless for a number of years a handful of armoured cars and aircraft, working with the Arab Legion, had protected Amman from the Ikhwan and imposed a greater degree of order on the area than it had previously experienced. Undoubtedly the British and their Arab allies made mistakes. They had also begun to destroy a way of life which included raiding other tribes and yet which, in the eyes of Sir John Glubb and others, had had its own beauty.

Aden

If Iraq and Jordan were the first areas where the RAF fully tested its 'air control' methods, the Aden Protectorate was the next. Aden was far more mountainous than Iraq but the people were similar. The main problems for the British rulers in the Aden Protectorate, as in Iraq and Jordan in the 1920s, were fighting between the tribes and encroachment by neighbouring states. The RAF was nevertheless able to support the political officers in Aden who brought a semblance of order which lasted until the forces of nationalism reached the area in the 1950s.

The port of Aden was seized by Britain in 1839.[1] The British found it easy to control Aden itself but the hinterland, the 9,000 square miles of the Aden 'Protectorate', was a different story.[2] Aden town was administered until the 1930s from India and the Indian authorities did not want to spend money on the tribes which they nominally protected—a determination which was perhaps increased by the knowledge that the Imam of Yemen to the north laid claim to the whole area.[3] Thus until well into the twentieth century the British did little more than sign treaties with the various tribes in the interior to keep out other colonial powers and prevent the tribes encroaching on Aden itself. In any case British expansion would have been hindered by the scorched, roadless mountains of the Protectorate and the warlike characteristics of the people who lived there and whose pastime from time immemorial had been attacking their neighbours.

Until 1928 the army was responsible for maintaining order in Aden town but, obedient to the dictates of the authorities in India, it did not often venture into the interior. Meanwhile the Imam of Yemen to the north was steadily extending his control over the hinterland and the army said that it would cost £1 million and require a division of infantry to throw his forces back to the line which the British considered the frontier between Yemen and the Protectorate.[4] In 1927, when a political officer wished to travel seventy miles across the interior he had to bribe the various tribes with 15,000 rupees to let him pass. Eight years earlier, Colonel Jacobs, the Assistant Resident in Aden had been made a virtual prisoner when he was sent to Bajil to carry out negotiations on behalf of the Indian government. The General Officer Commanding (GOC) in Aden had said that he would need a considerable force to effect his release but the Air Ministry claimed that they had achieved this by sending two obsolete Snipe aircraft to overfly the town. The inhabitants were so astonished that, according to the RAF, they released Jacobs forthwith.[5] Generally, however, as the Air Staff noted later, 'bounds were set at five miles outside the settlement . . . Beyond lay a virtually unknown land. Even the intelligence officers in the garrison knew little of either the country itself or of the tribes over which we professed to exercise control and to whom we gave what was little more than nominal protection.'[6]

Even before No. 8 Squadron of the RAF took over responsibility for the area in 1928, aircraft had already been used in the Protectorate not only to gain Colonel Jacobs's release but to try to bring some sort of order. In January 1922 aircraft had bombed and killed some thirty-five of the Imam's tribesmen who were raiding the Haushabi tribe at Dareja within the Protectorate; in May 1923 two Bristol Fighters had attacked the Mahkdumi and Mansuri tribes which had been raiding the trade routes through the area. The Bristols dropped two 20 lb bombs and the tribes surrendered. In 1925 they had been used against the Hukhais and Zeidis who had stolen thirty-three boxes of Martini ammunition.[7] Aircraft had also begun the process of mapping the area. The process was crude and apparently ineffective:

> We dropped a 20lb bomb on open ground about half a mile from the town or village required to be named, and there would be a few days for a report to come in that the Air Force had made an unprovoked attack on such-and-such a place, razed it to the ground and slaughtered all the inhabitants; we then added the name to our rapidly growing map.

Once the RAF took over, its control became more systematic. One of its first actions was to repel the Imam's forces. These had captured two friendly Sheiks and the Imam was warned that, unless his forces withdrew and the Sheiks were released, the Yemen would be bombed. When this warning was ignored, Mawia and Yerim were attacked. Twenty-one planes were also sent against Dhamar and, although only eight found their target, the Imam's forces felt compelled to withdraw.[8] On 5 April 1928 raiders from Yemen attacked a friendly village in the Aden area; within one and a half hours aircraft had reached the village and forced the raiders to flee. One aircraft was also ordered to fly to Sanaa, the capital of Yemen. The American Vice Consul in the town reported that this had had a considerable impact. Trade had come to a standstill and two-thirds of the population had fled. Even allowing for his exaggeration, it was a remarkable result and the Imam decided to sue for peace.[9] As the Permanent Under Secretary of the Air Ministry expressed it subsequently, 'in two months, by air action undertaken by a single squadron (which flew 900 hours under arduous and exacting conditions) the Imam had been forced to evacuate territory of which he had been in wrongful but virtually uncontested occupation'.[10] Finally in 1934 the British were able to negotiate the treaty of Sanaa with the Imam which temporarily improved relations. Unfortunately, however, the Imam continued to believe that the Protectorate belonged to the Yemen and so the issue could never be completely resolved.

Within the Protectorate itself, the results of air action were even more remarkable. Sir Stewart Symes, the Resident in Aden, reported in 1929 that the previous year the Subeihi tribe had stolen two camels and murdered a girl. The tribe was warned that air action would be taken against it and, when this threat produced no result, air attacks began on 30 January 1929 and continued until 30 March, preventing the tribe going about its normal business. The Subeini then submitted. Similarly in 1934, when part of the Quteibi tribe attacked a caravan from Yemen, its territories were blockaded until it agreed to pay fines and hand over hostages.

On other occasions the RAF was able to fly political officers rapidly to the area where a dispute had occurred and to negotiate a truce. This happened, for example, when the Amir of Dhala fell out with the Shai'iri tribe in 1930. The Resident was delighted with the RAF's achievements: 'The advent of the RAF has produced a considerable change in the relations of Aden to the Protectorate tribes. The shadowy protection whose obligations could often not be fulfilled has been converted into reality.'[11] Over thirty landing grounds were laid out by Wing Commander Rickards throughout the Protectorate and No. 8 Squadron was re-equipped in 1934 with the Vickers Vincent, an aircraft specially modified for Middle Eastern conditions.[12] Intelligence officers were able to cross the whole area and the Resident complained that he had too few political officers to take advantage of the new situation. The tribes benefited not only from the establishment of some degree of order but also from the ability of aircraft to carry the sick to hospital in Aden. The disadvantage was that, as air travel was so easy, there was a tendency to withhold funds for roads or railways.[13]

The Air Ministry papers in the Public Record Office emphasize the contribution which aircraft made to extending British control over the hinterland. Subsequent historians and political officers, in their memoirs, have also emphasized the efforts of the political officers to bring order to the region and the transfer of administrative control over the area from India to the Colonial Office.[14] However, the two processes were complementary. The Resident, Sir Bernard Reilly, wrote to the Secretary of State for the Colonies in April 1935:

> I have felt for some time that increased contact between Aden and the interior of the Hadhramaut that has been brought about by the RAF and by the visits of political officers to that country makes it desirable that our policy to that part of the Protectorate should be reconsidered.[15]

Reilly was Acting Resident from 1925 to 1926, Resident from 1931 to 1937, and Governor from 1937 to 1940. A former army officer and civil servant, he was a great exponent of extending British control over the Protectorate. One part of it, the Hadhramaut, had hardly been visited by white men before the Resident sent W. H. Ingrams on a tour of the region. Subsequently Ingrams was able to negotiate a whole series of treaties with the tribes there, to maintain what was rightly called 'Ingrams' peace'—a peace backed up by the British-officered Hadhrami Bedouin Legion and ultimately by the RAF. There the system worked and order was generally maintained from the 1930s onwards. However Basil Seager's attempt to extend the treaties to the rest of the Protectorate was less successful and only five of the eleven principal chiefs had signed by 1946.[16]

Nevertheless the improvements which took place in the general state of order were dramatic. Some advances also occurred in the economy of the area. More crops could be planted as conflicts were resolved. Perhaps 100,000 people from the Hadhramaut worked abroad, where some of them became wealthy and eventually brought their money back to the area. Funds from taxes rose in consequence and schools were opened. The British also encouraged chiefs to send their sons to school in the Sudan and elsewhere. Indeed, J. H. Hall, the Governor during the Second World War, believed that the changes might have been too drastic;

> Recently the pace has been too hot and the methods rather too robust, and I am content to adopt a slower pace and a less direct approach, and the more so because there are insufficient aircraft available to maintain proper intercommunication within the Protectorate and to provide the necessary reminder of that ultimate sanction upon which our authority rests.[17]

Aircraft had been withdrawn from the Eastern part of the Protectorate as the Italian menace had grown in Africa and disturbances in the Hadhramaut had not been punished until 'much valuable ground had been lost'. Ingrams concluded in July 1941 that the Protectorate could be 'kept quiet if we had plenty of aircraft, plenty of political staff and much better, and more, security forces'. But the inhabitants would probably resent this in the long run and already 'our political officers are becoming too like civil servants'.

As the Second World War came to an end, sufficient aircraft became available but they were not suitable for the tiny airstrips laid out in the 1930s. Air Marshal H. T. Lydford pointed out in March 1946 that the Albacores being used for carrying political officers would be worn out within months.[18] Four years later the problem had still not been solved and another officer complained,

> When we were equipped with biplanes there were some dozens of small cleared spaces where aircraft could drop political officers to preach the gospel of peace and keep in touch with what was going on. Our aircraft have, however, outgrown these airfields and there is now only one in the Eastern Protectorate and six in the Western Protectorate which can be used. Consequently the political staff are out of touch with the tribes.[19]

The author thought that the Auster might be suitable temporarily though he preferred a two-engined aircraft as there were so few landing grounds available if an engine failed. In the meantime, he argued that many of the bombing operations which the RAF was carrying out could have been avoided if political officers had kept in contact with the tribes. Casualties could also have been evacuated had helicopters been available but, according to the same officer, there were none at all in Middle East Command at that time.

Most of the transport within the Protectorate was now carried out by twin-engined Avro Ansons. These had started life as coastal reconnaissance aircraft in 1936 but some 10,000 had been produced in the war years for training purposes. They needed more landing room than the old biplanes and some landing grounds were extended from 600 to 1,500 yards to accommodate them. The Anson's other main disadvantage was its limited ground clearance and, for this reason, there was some relief in the mid-1950s when the Pembroke high-winged monoplane replaced it. At the same period the Aden Protectorate Support Flight, which was responsible for transporting political officers, became a separate unit in recognition of the importance of its duties.[20]

Certainly the RAF was kept busy in the Protectorate in the postwar years. For example, at the beginning of 1946 large-scale ground and air operations were mounted against the Ahl Billeil and Algami tribes which had been causing disturbances.

> The tribesmen were so overcome with the strength of the force sent against them that they felt resistance was useless. Precise formation flying by flights of Mosquito aircraft and the fire-power of the 37 mm guns of the armoured cars were the factors in causing the surrender of hostages.[21]

In 1947 action was taken against the Quteibi tribe in the Radfan area. Forts in the area were smashed by Tempests and the tribe was forced to come to terms. 'There can be no doubt', Lydford concluded, 'that had a land force been employed then there would have been bitter fighting with resultant heavy casualties'. As it was there were no casualties on either side.[22] Lydford pointed out that in 1934 it had taken sixty-one days to force the same tribe to submit, in 1940 it had taken 127, and in 1947 only two-and-a-half. Lydford felt that this change reflected the greater power of modern aircraft though other factors may have been involved. The following year another tribe incurred the British wrath when it refused to accept the settlement to some dispute announced by a court of law.[23]

Operations against the Bal Harith tribe in 1948 were typical of the period. The tribe had been bombed the previous year for sixty hours and forced to submit. In 1948 the British offered to compensate them for the damage caused if they ceased their depredations and handed over hostages. However, 'they refused such gracious offers and proved conclusively that they continued to remain rebellious'. Thus in February 1948 they were ordered to give up fifty rifles, eleven hostages and 100 camel loads of salt, or to face reprisals. Their villages were only just within range of the Tempests so Lincolns with 1,000 lb bombs were flown in to Aden. After the expiry of the ultimatum on 23 February the Lincolns obliterated the Bal Harith's main village whilst the Tempests strafed smaller targets. Finally on 6 March they submitted; their villages had been destroyed and their crops damaged. Some of their camels were killed and their prized 'ilb trees burned or broken by the force of the explosions'.[24]

Problems with the Yemen also continued. In 1949 Yemenis built forts within the area the British considered to belong to the Protectorate on the Western slopes of Jebel Manawa. The British protested to the Yemeni government without results, and then dropped messages warning the people in the area that the forts would be attacked. On 2 September 1949 Tempests attacked the forts with rockets. As they were made of stone they were difficult to destroy but the thirty rockets eventually demolished them. One of the Ansons observing the operation was hit by a bullet but this was the only problem from the RAF's point of view; 'the operation followed the textbook pattern of air control of a semi-civilized people; it was decisive, the cost was insignificant, nobody was hurt'.[25]

Thus the situation continued into the 1950s. In 1953, when the British wanted to build a road joining the territory of the Audhali and Aulaqi tribes, the Imam of Yemen encouraged the tribes to rise.[26] In 1955 the Life Guards and Seaforth Highlanders were rushed from the Suez Canal Zone to deal with a rebellion amongst the Shamsi tribe. They had to make a 345-mile drive across the Protectorate to evacuate the garrison in Fort Robat, abandoning two of their Scout cars and seven of their lorries *en route* because of the difficult conditions. For much of the way they were escorted by aircraft and the most difficult 'Snake Pass' was bombed by Lincolns before they attempted it. In 1956 Saudi Arabian forces crossed the frontier and were forced to surrender by the RAF and local ground forces.[27] In 1958 Yemeni ground forces captured the town of Hadeya, ten miles within the Protectorate, and Durham Light Infantry as well as aircraft were used to expel them.[28] At the same time the British armed the Audhalis and Bayhanis and encouraged them to attack the Yemen in reprisal. 'Pitched battles developed and often British and Protectorate forces and political officers invited aggression so as to have an excuse to call for help from the RAF, a weapon that the Yemenis could not effectively counter.'[29]

Clearly, therefore, 'air policing' did not solve the Protectorate's problems once and for all but political officers, in their memoirs, have strongly defended it as by far the least destructive method of maintaining order. Indeed, they show that bombing became part of an elaborate and humorous game played between the government and the tribes to relieve the monotony of the nomadic life. P. S. Allfree, who was Assistant Adviser in part of the Hadhramaut, argued,

> tribal people could never allow themselves to confess that mere soldiers, even by the thousand, could overawe . . . stout-hearted fellows . . . But tanks and above all an aeroplane pushed up the stakes. They were like a nuclear threat.[30]

Similarly Dr R. Bidwell maintained that a tribe was prepared to accept collective punishment just as it would accept collective gains. The men feared the taunts of cowardice from the women and would thus only reluctantly submit to ground forces, whereas they would submit to air attacks which anyway did but little material damage.[31] 'People who knew little of Arabia constantly protested that bombing of villages was inhumane, but in fact it was for decades the best method of control.' Bidwell and others have pointed to the humour with which bombing operations were often received. He met one man who boasted that he had had four houses destroyed by the RAF, and subsequently rebuilt with the government's financial assistance. Such miscreants normally had to give a hostage for their good behaviour to the government; the hostage

> usually a small boy, had the time of his life drinking coffee with the soldiers all day instead of having to look after the family goats. Of course, if the tribe misbehaved again the possession by the government of a hostage was quite useless for one could hardly punish small boys.[32]

An RAF officer recalled seeing the villagers in the 1960s lining the hills to watch the RAF rocket their villages so that they could cheer the 'good shots' and boo the misses.[33] But by that time, as we shall see, 'air policing' had gone out of fashion and the political situation in the region had become far more complicated.

The RAF and the North-West Frontier of India

Iraq and Aden were not of great moment to the British army and it reluctantly accepted RAF control there. It was far more hostile to the Air Staff's suggestions that aircraft should play the predominant role in maintaining order amongst the tribes on the North-West Frontier of India and in defending India against the Afghans. In the inter-war period British governments savagely cut the budgets of the Services; the army's vote, which had already been greatly reduced, sank still further from £36.7 million in 1925 to £32 million in 1930. If it had lost its role on the Frontier this would have meant yet more reductions in its strength.

During the nineteenth century British India had co-existed uneasily with Afghanistan to the north. On several occasions the British had sent armies into Kabul's territory. Such expeditions often ended disastrously because of the ease with which the warlike Afghans could defend the Hindu Kush and other mountains rising to 16,000 ft above sea level.[1] The situations were complicated by the tribes along the frontier who often lived in areas which were claimed both by the Amir in Kabul and by the Indian authorities. The tribes were regarded by the British as a greater military threat than the Afghan army because of their fighting prowess and because they periodically descended into the settled areas of India to murder and loot. The British responded by sending large forces into the frontier provinces which burnt the villages of the offending tribes and then returned to the plains. They hoped that the frontier peoples would abandon their depredations and gradually accept peaceful incorporation into India but their ability to harass British forces actually increased towards the end of the nineteenth century, as they acquired more modern rifles.

In February 1919 the Amir of Afghanistan, Habibullah was murdered. He was succeeded by his son, Amanullah, who was extemely critical of his father's alleged subservience to the British and was evidently looking for a chance to show his enmity.[2] Two months after the accession of the new 'King'—as Amanullah wanted to be called—an uprising took place in northern India. General Dyer responded to widespread rioting and looting in the city of Amritsar by ordering his Gurkha troops to open fire, killing 379 Indians.[3] Amanullah snatched the opportunity to call for a *jehad* or 'Holy War' against the British and sent his army to the frontier where it seized disputed territory in the Khyber Pass. On 5 May 1919 the British declared war on Amanullah. British forces had been drastically run down and many of the officers

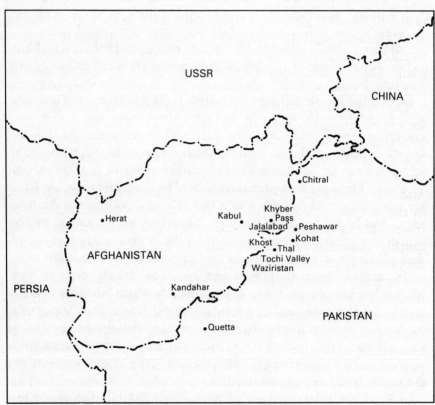

Afghanistan and the North-West Frontier of India in 1919

and men in the frontier region were hoping to return to England in the near future. Nevertheless General Crocker collected a force together and, supported by two elderly Be 2C aircraft, by 11 May, he had driven the Afghans back and recaptured the disputed territory. Two weeks later, as Crocker was advancing very slowly into Afghanistan, another Afghan force under the King's cousin, Nadir Shah, crossed the frontier and moved on Thal. The siege of the town began on 27 May and was raised by General Dyer four days later. Dyer quickly drove Nadis Shah's men across the frontier with the help of some 'exceedingly effective RAF bombing and machine gun fire' and the fighting ground to a halt. The second Afghan war in 1878–80 had involved 40,000 British and Indian troops; the third war in 1919 had involved 340,000.[4]

The frontier was unsettled by these events and the ferment continued for some years. There were 611 armed attacks on the settled areas in 1920 alone and these caused 1,100 casualties amongst British subjects. Waziristan with its population of Wazirs and Mahsuds was particularly unruly and in one battle 2,000 British and Indian troops and 4,000 Mahsuds were killed. To overcome the problem, the British built bases in the area which were capable of accommodating large numbers of troops. They also constructed roads so that the soldiers could be moved quickly. Nevertheless, the fighting went on and it was facilitated by supplies of arms and money from Amanullah.

Throughout the period, the RAF put forward its own solution for the frontier's problems. First of all the Air Staff believed that Afghan attacks could be deterred by the threat to bomb Kabul. It argued that the Afghan government came to terms in 1919 not just because of General Dyer's victories but also because of a demonstration of air power. 'On 24 May [1919] the bombing of Kabul by Captain Haley RAF in a Handley Page machine caused a panic in the capital and the evacuation of about half the inhabitants. The Amir himself was reported to be preparing to leave if the bombing was repeated.' However, although these assessments were contained in the War Office's history of Afghanistan, many army officers dismissed them as nonsense. They claimed that there was panic only in the royal harem and that it was the victories of Generals Crocker and Dyer which were decisive. Furthermore many opposed the idea of strategic bombing; as Amanullah himself put it in a letter to the Viceroy, 'it is a matter of great regret that the throwing of bombs by Zeppelins was denounced as a most savage act . . . while now we see with our own eyes that such operations were a habit which is prevalent among all civilized peoples of the West'.[5]

In the view of those sympathetic to air power it was not only Captain Haley's attack on Kabul which underlined the importance of air power in the 1919 campaign. As a result of attacks by 31 Squadron, 'large parts of the military quarters of [the Afghan town of) Jalalabad were burnt out and on one occasion a parade of 2,000 troops was attacked, with good results'. Similarly, when Dyer raised the siege of Thal, 'a flight of aeroplanes contributed largely to the retreat of the enemy'. Consequently Trenchard argued,

> the Air Staff are convinced that operations against Afghanistan can be carried out by air power as the primary arm—that it is the only method open to us of a quick final settlement by fire—and the affect will be to induce the Amir to sue for peace; such an operation would not cost a tithe of the money which a protracted military campaign would involve.[6]

The Air Staff noted that there were seven regiments of cavalry on the frontier, twenty-four batteries of artillery and forty-six battalions of infantry. These could be drastically reduced if the RAF took over, though bombing Kabul would not be easy. It was 145 miles from Peshawar airfield so that Bristol Fighters would need extra fuel tanks and this would severely cut their bomb load.

Trenchard's critics took a number of positions. Some argued that a strategic attack on Kabul might easily bring the King down and leave the country in anarchy, with nobody for the British to deal with.[7] Denys Bray, a senior official in the Foreign Department of the Indian government, stressed the international repercussions of such attacks; 'a few bombs on the Dilkusha palace [in Kabul] might crush the Amir by wiping out his harem but it would create a howl against us from Paris and New York'. He also suggested that the Amir would develop his own air force and that this would undermine the RAF's proposed strategy.[8] As early as 1921 the Afghans raised the possibility of buying aircraft from the British. Officials in London were unenthusiastic although they recognised that, if Britain did not supply the machines, some other state would do so.[9] At first it seemed that this might be the Soviet Union or Italy. But the Soviets failed to provide suitable machines and the Italians sold the Afghans aircraft which could not fly effectively at Kabul's altitude. Thus the Afghans imported DH9as and Bristol Fighters. Afghan pilots also trained in Karachi and Peshawar but it was doubtful whether they could have done much to protect Kabul from a British attack or that the King's acquisitions undermined the RAF's policy.[10] The British controlled the spares for their aircraft and the Afghan air force would thus quickly have become unworkable. The growth of Kabul's air power simply gave the Air Staff an excuse for asking for two more bomber squardons to be sent to India in 1927.[11]

As events turned out, after 1919 the Afghans were in any case much easier to deal with than the frontier tribes. However Trenchard believed that aircraft could 'police' the tribes effectively. Eight efficient squadrons were needed in India so that six could be used against the Afghans if they invaded, and two kept back for operations against the tribes.

> If, as has happened in the past, a rising of the tribes occurs without the intervention of Afghanistan, the whole eight squadrons will be available for immediate action, pending the mobilization of the army. Experience in the late risings suggests that intense air action, even if it is insufficient of itself to subdue a tribe once it has risen (and the Air Staff maintain that the possibilities in this direction have never been fully explored) will . . . often forestall a rising provided it is applied without delay.[12]

In fact the early years of RAF activity on the frontier had mixed results. Several of the villages in the Tochi valley of Waziristan were fined in 1919 because they had raided the settled areas. When they refused to pay or to hand in some of their rifles, 'the most recalcitrant villages were bombed by number 20, 97 and 99 squadrons and by four o'clock of that same date all the rifles and fines had been handed in'.[13] On the other hand, air action proved less effective against the Mahsuds who also refused to pay fines and extensive ground and air operations were needed to force them to do so.

The RAF believed that its case was strengthened by events near Wana fort. The fort had been built to dominate the surrounding countryside but it was overrun in 1919 and for years after it was recaptured the garrison had to appeal to the RAF for help. On 7 April 1922 the Viceroy reported to the Secretary of State for India that 'friendlies' near the fort were weakening and that aircraft were desperately needed to defend it. On 9 April he was happy to be able to inform London that 'aeroplanes flew over . . . and obtained good targets . . . and report signs of enemy contemplating withdrawal to hills'.[14] Curiously enough ten years later a lecturer at the Staff College in Quetta was still claiming that 'relieving beleagured garrisons by air [is] an attractive idea which is not however capable of being put into practice'. The Commander in

Chief, General Sir Henry Rawlinson, was at least prepared to agree that RAF intervention had been decisive but argued that this was because 'conditions were exceptionally favourable'.[15] This made the Air Staff particularly indigant because, out of the forty-six planes theoretically available in India, only seven Bristol Fighters, four DH9as and one DH10 could become airborne. One officer who arrived in India about this time found that tyres, inner tubes, shock absorbers and other essential spares were all in short supply. He also noted with indignation someone from another squadron trying to steal wheels from one of his aircraft. The situation improved somewhat after a campaign in *The Times* and by 1927 aircraft could communicate with ground forces by radio at least in a primitive fashion.[16] However India always lagged behind the air forces in Europe and eighty Wapitis dating from the beginning of the decade were still in service in India in 1939. Sir Philip Joubert de la Ferte, who took over as AOC in 1937, wrote later, 'aircraft were very few in number and very antique. The command was definitely in the bow and arrow stage of development.'[17]

In the 1920s Rawlinson remained unsympathetic to the RAF's pleas and particularly to its claim to be able to police the frontier. In August 1922 he wrote: 'After very considerable experience of the potential and limitations of aircraft, both during the Great War, in northern Russia and here upon the frontier, I am unable to accept the optimistic predictions set forth [by the RAF].' Rawlinson rightly pointed out that air action alone had not been decisive against the 'Mad Mullah' in Somalia or against the Mahsuds. He agreed that the air force in India should be increased by two squadrons but made clear that he was 'not willing to make any reductions in the covering troops or in the field army until the experiment [of air control] has incontestably proved a success' in Iraq.[18] In fact, however, some of Rawlinson's successors were equally sceptical, even though the RAF had long proved its value there. Rawlinson also contended that aircraft could not help maintain order inside India. They might frighten a crowd into dispersing but they could not attack it unless a full scale revolt took place, similar to the Indian Mutiny. With this, at least, Trenchard was in agreement. 'Even if a great degree of nicety of aiming from the air were granted, it is not normally possible to distinguish when in the air between the so-called "enemy", *ie* the rioters and the peaceful inhabitants.' Three aircraft had been sent to deal with the Amritsar riots in 1919. Two pilots had decided that it was impossible to distinguish the rioters from others, while the third, who believed that he had done so, actually injured innocent people. Nevertheless, there were circumstances even within

India where aircraft could help maintain order. In the Moplah and Akali rebellions in 1921 and 1923 aircraft dropped leaflets threatening further action, though their role was essentially peripheral to the army's.[19]

Many shared the Commander in Chief's doubts about air control. Lord Chelmsford, who was Viceroy from 1916 to 1921, thought that joint operations were acceptable but that it was 'rather inhuman and cold-blooded to send our airmen to bomb the villages while the rest of our forces keep the ring', Denys Bray, like many other members of the Indian Civil Service, was equally hostile. If one frontier tribe rebelled and was bombed, he believed this 'might precipitate a wholesale conflagration in sympathy'. Furthermore

> we have built up by generations of patient labour, a reputation amongst the tribesmen for . . . fair play—among other things for not warring on women and children. It is at least doubtful whether we should not stand to lose in the long run by continuous and intensive use of ruthlessness that cannot be other than promiscuous.[20]

Bray was chairman of a committee which supported the expansion of frontier forts and advocated permanent occupation of the area by the army rather than periodic control by the RAF. Many in the India Office in London felt the same way. In December 1923 Trenchard complained that the India Office had sent a telegram to India about the cruelty of bombing without informing the Air Ministry and thus giving it the chance to disagree.

Successive British Ministers in Kabul disputed the effectiveness and criticized the morality of air control. Sir Francis Humphrys argued that bombing would increase the hatred of the British amongst the tribes. If warnings were given so that they could remove their women and children from the villages, bombing would be ineffective. If warnings were not given, the women and children would be killed.[21] In 1933 Sir R. Maconachie, Humphrys's successor, maintained that the RAF either did not know or would not admit how many 'civilians' were killed by its methods and that it would not be able to distinguish from the air between friendly and unfriendly villages.[22] Certainly the RAF did not systematically compile statistics on bomb loads and casualties. Basil Embry was the intelligence officer responsible for the frontier when a Parliamentary Question asked for such information; 'An accurate reply would have been impossible even after weeks of research,' he wrote later. 'So I took a pencil and paper and wrote "number of bombs dropped = X approx . . . X was a figure I made up on the spot . . . number of persons killed = 1 . . . value of property destroyed = unknown . . . as there . . . were no house agents on the frontier".'

Such Parliamentary Questions were sparked off by continued discussions in the press about the morality of air policing. The policy of *The Times* varied. On 23 September 1932 it suggested that bombing caused bitterness and was ineffective against 'agile' tribesmen who could avoid the bombs.[23] On the other hand its aeronautical correspondent reported enthusiastically from the frontier in May and June 1933 about the RAF's 'entirely new technique of maintaining order in inaccessible country'.[24] One correspondent wrote to the *Manchester Guardian* on 25 May 1935 quoting a Lieutenant Colonel Osburn DSO as saying, 'when our troops enter a bombed village the pariah dogs are already at work eating the corpses of the babies and old women who have been killed. Many suffer from ghastly wounds, especially some of the younger children who . . . are all covered with flies and crying for water.' The Chairman of the Air League of the British Empire replied that all military actions caused casualties and that air action was the most humane method available.[25] Subsequently he discoverd that Osburn had not actually seen civilian casualties himself but the newspaper's correspondent was unconvinced by any of his arguments.

The Air Staff was fully aware of these criticisms, though naturally it did not find them justified. As we have seen, it refined its methods and argued that they were designed to make life difficult for dissident tribesmen rather than to kill them. Above all 'it is essential to attack the tribesman with constant propaganda. He must be reminded how easy it is to submit, how light the terms are, how air operations can be kept up indefinitely and how helpless he is to react.'[26]

The nationalists in the Indian Legislature were unimpressed by RAF claims about the humanity of their methods. They saw air control as an effective stick with which to beat the government. On 29 August 1933 Hossaim Imam asked in the Legislature if 'the bombing of inoffensive civil populations has been interdicted by the League of Nations?'[27] The Commander in Chief responded that there had been no such bombing on the North-West Frontier. The following day the Viceroy defended the bombing of the Upper Mohmands who had attacked the peaceful Halimzai tribe. The village of Kotkai in particular had been bombed because that was where the chief troublemakers lived. On the next day another member asked how many bombs had been dropped and how many casualties had resulted. The Commander in Chief replied that ninety bombs had been dropped and that one person had been slightly injured. Immediately the questioner asked how he knew that so few had been harmed. The President of the Assembly ruled that the question was frivolous and out of order but the questions went on during the following days. One speaker compared the bombing to the Amritsar massacre in 1919 and said that he had heard that there had been serious loss of life. However not all members of the House attacked the government, Mijor Nawab Ahmad Nawaz pointed out that it had a duty to protect peaceful tribes and argued that air control was the best method of doing so. But his was a rare voice.[28]

Where did the truth lie in these arguments? The Air Staff could argue that ground operations were far more destructive because they took so much longer and because the fighting was more extensive. It also seems likely that air control became less destructive as it was refined. Furthermore it is surprising that so few eyewitness accounts appeared of the butchery Osburn described, if it was as widespread as the RAF's critics implied. On the other hand, if ground operations took less time than air control, this may have enabled women and children to move from the area before the army actually arrived. Moreover the RAF's practice of using delayed action bombs to keep villagers away from their fields during the night and of bombing reservoirs to prevent irrigation were open to criticism on humanitarian grounds.

The critics argued that atrocities committed by frontier tribes in the 1920s were a reaction to air control. In 1920 Captain Foulkes and his wife were murdered in Kohat. Three years later Major Ellis and his wife were murdered in the same town and their daughter was kidnapped. The attacks on women were so unusual and so against Pathan custom that it seemed possible some new factor was at work. Moreover it is true that some of the tribesmen protested at the inhumanity of air attacks. One group complained: 'Men, women and children . . . fled. The women were disgraced on account of their coming out of Purdah . . . It has transpired that strength and tolerance are no longer qualities of government.' But the murderers themselves denied that there was any connection between RAF actions and their own, and British officials on the frontier took the same view.[29] The Chief Commissioner of the North-West Frontier Province, Sir John Maffey, argued that Indian 'extremists' were spreading rumours of the connection to discredit the British: 'they are afraid of the hold over the tribes that the aeroplane gives us . . . I regard the careful dissemination of this theory as a piece of cunning anti-British propaganda.'[30]

Much of the debate about the efficiency of air control turned on events which took place in 1930 in the Peshawar area. The RAF's critics argued that lashkars of tribesmen were able to reach the outskirts of the city because the defence of the frontier had been given to the new Service. RAF officers maintained that air power had been ineffective because it had been misused. On 13 May 1930 the Air Staff noted, 'telegrams seem to show that delays are ensuing in the taking of appropriate air action to prevent the spreading of unrest and that the action itself, when taken, is being fettered and that in this way a very serious situation is being allowed to develop'.[31] On 11 May the Resident in Waziristan had reported that the inhabitants of Bannu might rise against the government but, even when the rising materialized, the RAF was only given permission to bomb after what it considered unnecessary delay.

When the Afridi rose later in the year officers in the political department in India also became concerned at the dilatoriness of the response: 'If . . . steps are not taken . . . there is a genuine risk of the contagion spreading and leading to simultaneous risings along the frontier on a very much larger scale.'[32] The Air Staff agreed, observing 'for four days our forces were obliged to watch the Afridi lashkars advancing, obviously hostile and offering excellent targets, down the Basra valley to Peshawar. They were not however asked to attack them until late on the night before they reached Peshawar itself.'[33] Despite this setback, the Air Staff maintained that it was the RAF which prevented other tribes joining the Afridi. It pointed out that the military bases, built at such cost in Waziristan, had been completely ineffective at halting the Afridis without RAF help.

Army attitudes are well illustrated by lectures to the Staff College at Quetta. One lecturer claimed that the RAF were carried away by 'their success in other theatres such as Mesopotamia and by the part they played in smoothing minor disturbances on the frontier at their source [and] are apt to jump at conclusions, the foundations of which are still in the mud and water stage'.[34] The Acting Governor General of Baluchistan told the students that the RAF's plan 'leaves out of account . . . the fact that the aim and object of our policy is not the destruction of the tribes but should be a policy of civilization'.[35]

The arguments did not abate as the rearmament of the 1930s began. One very senior member of the Indian government wrote home in March 1935, 'the present CGS [in India]—and even more certainly the last one—hates the air and everything to do with it! Kitten Wigram's view always was that the Air Force were NBG in this country which is BS in my opinion'.[36] Despite such feelings, the two Services had to co-operate on the frontier and often did so very effectively. For example Basil Embry recalled later how army detachments laid out X signs to indicate their positions to passing aircraft and placed large 'Vs' with the apex pointing towards the enemy when they were under attack. Perhaps if the government had not squeezed them so hard in the 1920s the conflict would never have become so acute and the two Services would have co-operated more amicably together to deal with frontier problems. Joubert de la Ferte wrote subsequently: 'Probably a really intelligent co-operation between air and land forces would have produced the best results—the air being the striking force and the land the backers-up with limited objectives.'[37]

The Revolt in Palestine[1]

When the RAF replaced the army as the main military arm of the government in Iraq in October 1922 or in Aden in 1928 the Air Staff did not claim that 'air policing' methods were universally applicable. Indeed, although the RAF took over Palestine at the same time as Iraq, government and Air Staff were agreed that 'air action was not suitable to the particular problems of public security in a more-or-less civilized country like Palestine where the principal centres of trouble are the towns'.[2] Similarly, Trenchard reacted with horror when the Cabinet asked him whether Ireland, before its independence, could be controlled from the air.[3] The RAF was given control of Palestine, Trans-Jordan and Iraq for adminstrative convenience since the three states were so close together. But, as the years passed and as air policing seemed to work, the Air Staff became more confident. Trenchard suggested that aircraft could replace ground forces in rural areas including most of Africa and the North-East Frontier of India. It was not, therefore, perhaps surprising that, when widespread revolt broke out in Palestine and General Dill had to take command of operations from Air Vice Marshal Peirse on 19 September 1936, many should argue that air policing had failed.

The argument was unfair since the RAF had never claimed that Palestine could be controlled from the air but the experiences there from 1936 onwards did suggest that air policing would be decreasingly successful in much of the world. Indeed this was implicit in the Air Staff's admission that Palestine was 'too civilized' for air policing to be effective there. Operations in Iraq and Aden were aimed against people who very often simply wanted to avoid paying taxes and who lacked support from abroad. The Arab revolt in Palestine was both rural and urban. Many of the Arabs involved were motivated by nationalism and hatred of the Jews as well as other factors.[4] Their operations were directed by their religious leader, the Mufti of Jerusalem, who fled into exile in Lebanon in 1937 and they were encouraged by radio broadcasts from Italy and Germany. Thus the Palestinian revolt resembled the post-1945 guerrilla uprisings much more closely than any other insurgency with which the British had to deal between the World Wars and the revolt had to be controlled by combined operations rather than by the RAF alone.

The Palestinian revolt followed what we can now see to be a classic pattern. Fearful of the increasing flow of Jews into Palestine, the Arabs called a general strike in April 1936. The British authorities became fully engrossed in dealing with the strike and handling sectarian riots which killed many people. Meanwhile, armed bands of Arabs, including volunteers from Syria and Iraq, gradually assembled in the countryside and these grew in numbers until many bands had 20–70 members. They were able to set up base areas, particularly around Galilee, unmolested by British troops. According to a contemporary historian, some joined the guerrillas out of boredom during the strike but, whatever their motives,

> a greater organization and a greater purposefulness became apparent in their activities. They appeared to be more numerous, better drilled, better armed, better clothed. In fact a parallel, and what was to prove a more formidable rebellion, was taking shape in the hills alongside the passive rebellion in the form of the general strike in the towns.

The guerrillas were divided into two types; the Mujahideen attacked British soldiers and others whilst the Fedaji concentrated on sabotage.[5]

The British response was cautious for three main reasons. First, the liberal-minded High Commissioner, Sir Arthur Wauchope, hoped to settle Arab grievances by negotiation and to use the minimum of force. Thus the government stopped troops searching mosques for arms and insurgents and, when a road was driven through the rebel stronghold in the old city of Jaffa, pretended that this was for sanitary rather than security reasons.[6] Secondly, despite their problems with the general strike and incipient guerrilla warfare, many British officials sympa-

thized with the Palestinians' political aims. Thirdly for a long time
the government only had enough troops to act defensively—some two
battalions of infantry, an armoured car company, two RAF squadrons
and the British Palestinian Police. Such operations as they did carry
out in the countryside were frustrated by the terrain and by poor intelligence.

As the British found on so many later occasions, the NAFFI and
other military facilities were centres of Arab espionage and the only
way of keeping operations secret was to inform troops of them only at
the very last moment.[7] It was not until they showed their determination
by bringing the greater part of two divisions of troops and four
squadrons of aircraft (Nos. 6, 14 and 33 bomber squadrons and No. 208
army co-operation squadron) to bear on the situation and when the
Arabs became increasingly worried about how the general strike would
effect the citrus crop, that the Arab Higher Committee decided to call
off the strike and the first phase of the revolt ended on 12 October
1936.[8] According to the official figures some sixteen policemen, twenty-
one soldiers, eighty-nine Jews and 195 Arabs had already died and the
real figure for Arab deaths was probably far higher.[9]

The guerrillas in the rural areas did not disband, nor were they hunted
down by the British. Indeed most of the British troops left the country,
even though attacks against Jews and representatives of the government
continued. It was not until September 1937, when the District Commissioner of Galilee was murdered, that the British again took decisive
action.[10] The main Palestinian organization, the Arab Higher Committee, was declared illegal and many of its members were arrested. However, the Mufti escaped and the revolt continued.[11] The guerrillas were
able to expand their operations into the towns where they persuaded
or forced other Palestinians to give them money and to deny intelligence
to the British. Arab policemen and others who co-operated with the
government were killed or intimidated. By 1938 the insurgents probably had about 15,000 men under arms compared with 5,000 in 1936
and the British had lost control in many towns and rural areas. Insurgents' attacks on Jews were particularly vicious and bomb attacks on
Haifa market and elsewhere showed how difficult it was for the government to protect the people.[12] On their side the Palestinians accused
both the Jews and the British of persecuting innocent civilians. They
claimed, for example, that Jews shot three people in Kafr Mosr village
in July 1939 and charged British troops with torturing and starving
villages and raping a 12-year-old Palestinian girl the previous month.[13]
Whatever the truth of such claims, they obviously made good propa-

ganda and intensified the war. According to the official figures, in 1938 alone 486 Arab civilians, 292 Jews, 69 British and 1,138 rebels were killed.[14]

The British only very gradually felt their way towards the tactics which they were to adopt so often in guerrilla wars after 1945. Troops descended on villages to search for arms and guerrillas, though this proved time-consuming, irritating and frightening to the Arabs.[15] Eventually, when Wauchope's efforts at conciliation failed, the army took full control and links between the urban and rural areas were weakened by the introduction of identity cards and travel permits. When the Arabs protested against this by calling a transport strike to effect all but the crucial citrus harvest, the army refused to let them move the harvest until the strike was entirely abandoned.[16] The authorities also tried to prevent the guerrillas using Syria as a base by building a barbed wire 'wall' along the frontier, though this had only a limited effect as the insurgents could circumvent it to the south. The guerrillas' urban strongholds, such as the old city of Jerusalem, were stormed and the Royal Engineers drove roads through the countryside so that troops could attack the insurgents more easily.

Success came slowly for the British and there was the usual alternation between optimism and pessimism in government reports. In November 1937, for example, reports suggested that Arab villagers were now so hostile to the insurgents that many rebels were drifting back over the frontier into French territory.[17] Yet eight months later in July 1938, the new High Commissioner, Harold Macmichael, reported that the guerrillas' efficiency was increasing and that their domination of the villages was growing because of their use of 'murder, kidnapping and robbery with violence'.[18] Reports of successful actions against the insurgents followed but again in September there was 'a serious deterioration of public security throughout the country' whilst in October the High Commissioner concluded that it had been the worst month for 'terrorism' so far and that 'the rebellion has unquestionably become a national revolt involving all classes of the Arab community in Palestine'.[19] The war was to end in 1939 partly because of the increased efficiency of British military measures, partly because of the increasing poverty and war weariness of the ordinary Arabs and partly because the British government made political concessions to the Arabs, in particular severely limiting Jewish immigration and land purchases.[20]

On the British side the war emphasized the importance of good inter-Service relations. The War Office appointed a series of extremely able generals to take charge of operations, including Sir John Dill, the future CIGS, Archibald Wavell, the future Viceroy of India and Bernard Montgomery. Dill's relations with Air Vice Marshal Peirse, the commander of the RAF in the area, were particularly important during the period of transition from control by the RAF to control by the army. But they appear to have been more satisfactory than one might have expected. Dill wrote to one of his correspondents, Peirse had not only been perfectly charming but has also been a tower of strength.[21] Dill sympathized with the predicament in which political constraints had placed his RAF colleague for much of 1936 and apparently did not blame the RAF or 'air policing' for the rebellion; he wrote:

> I had no idea till I came out here how completely control had been lost. And yet if Peirse had been allowed by the civilian authorities out here to take a few strong measures, which he was perfectly prepared to do, there is little doubt that the whole conspiracy would have collapsed.[22]

Peirse found his new chain of command irksome[23] and some of his colleagues were worried that the army might 'misuse' aircraft. Sir Henry Brooke-Popham, the Commander of the RAF in the Middle East, wrote to Dill in September 1936: 'I hope the staff will remember that 208 squadron is trained and equipped for army co-operation and nor for air taxi work.'[24] Not surprisingly, however, the greatest strain on relations between the Services arose when the abrasive and arrogant Bernard Montgomery arrived on the scene declaring, according to Arthur Harris the commander of the RAF in Palestine at the time, that aircraft were of little use in such operations. Fortunately Montgomery soon realized how wrong he was.[25]

Whilst the struggle continued, the RAF could do little to help the army in the towns. Moreover the guerrilla struggle in the towns and countryside came to be closely linked, as it was to be in future struggles in Cyprus and elsewhere; 'every important rebel band has . . . assassins who operate in the towns as well as the band in the country'.[26] Defeated by troops in the open, the band would switch its operations to the town. Aircraft were useless against assassins and of only limited value against rioters. The RAF had found in the 1920s that urban mobs could sometimes be broken up by the threat presented by low flying aircraft. However it had also discovered that, if this method were ineffective—and it was likely to become increasingly so as 'mobs' became more sophisticated—pilots could not discriminate between rioters and peaceful citizens sufficiently to enable them to use their weapons to restore order.[27] Moreover the Palestinian government was determined in 1936 that civilians should be given the maximum protection. Thus the weapons which aircraft could use against the guerrillas themselves were carefully limited. Aircraft were at first only allowed to use 20 lb bombs and were not allowed to bomb buildings even when the guerrillas fired from them. In September 1936 they were permitted to use larger weapons after three aircraft had been shot down in one day, but they were still not able to employ them against buildings from which they had been fired at.[28] As the Services complained,

> the airmen had to find the enemy in precipitous country where cover from rock and olive groves abounded, had then to identify him . . . as a rebel . . . and finally had to engage him in strict accordance with a precise and complicated set of rules dictated by policy and varied with bewildering frequency.[29]

But in open country the RAF could be particularly effective for protecting convoys from ambush, as the French discovered later in Algeria. The Jerusalem–Jericho road, which was at first threatened by the insurgents, was kept open by a handful of troops and a single aircraft which 'pounced' whenever ambush threatened.[30] High-flying aircraft could in fact patrol several roads but low flying was more effective at deterring attack. In other operations the RAF needed to work closely with the army and it was only gradually that the two discovered the best ways of working together. Aircraft could sometimes locate rebel bands and summon ground help or *vice versa*. Troops moving along roads were accompanied by mobile 'wireless sets' for summoning aircraft. Those working away from the roads had to rely on visual signals.[31] In any case radio operations from aircraft were still primitive. Aircraft had to trail 250 feet of wire behind them and thus to break off any action in which they were engaged. If aircraft spotted the insurgents before ground troops did so, they had then to beware of dispersing them before the army could arrive. Their aim was, on the contrary, to pin the insurgents down until ground forces assembled. According to his biographer, it was Arthur Harris who invented the 'airpin' scheme for keeping people in a village by threatening them with air attacks until the army came up.[32]

Aircraft had to be ready to respond immediately to requests for help but to use their power in a discriminatory fashion. General Dill commented, 'the pace at which they respond to an "XX" call is quite extraordinary. At Ramle the other day when I was there the first plane was off the ground in about three minutes after an "XX" call came in.'[33] Thus the air force could respond with great rapidity, it was the ground forces which found movement very difficult. Moreover, flying through the air at more than 100 miles an hour, pilots only too often underestimated the time that it would take soldiers to struggle through the heat and dust to the scene of the action. The army's history of the operation emphasized the importance of close personal contact between pilots and soldiers to overcome such problems. It was perhaps largely because of the difficulty of moving on the ground that the army concluded 'most of the casualties were inflicted [on the enemy] by low flying air attacks'. But the army was not unhappy about the way inter-service relationships had developed by the end of the campaign;

> Once the armed band had made its appearance there were few engagements in which troops and aircraft did not work together in very close co-operation—so close in fact that combined operations is probably a better description.[34]

Apart from direct engagements, aircraft also transported officers, kept isolated troops supplied and dropped propaganda leaflets as they were to do in Malaya, Kenya and elsewhere after 1945.

RAF successes were not achieved without losses. In order to locate the enemy and to distinguish them from peaceful civilians, aircraft had to fly at a maximum height of 500 feet and this made them vulnerable even to small arms fire.[35] The RAF found the Hart biplane the most robust and suitable for these operations. In fact No. 6 Squadron had a variant of the Hart, named the Hardy, which was specially designed for operations in the Middle East. The Hart had been in service since 1930 and was supplemented in Palestine by Gladiators, Wellesleys and Lysanders. The Lysander was an army co-operation aircraft, which proved very useful for keeping officers in touch with what was going on on the ground, but the Wellesley's 2,000 lb bomb load could rarely be used effectively in Palestinian conditions.[36] The insurgents often moved by night and reports on engagements only too frequently noted that air attacks on insurgents had continued just until dark. Both aircraft and ground troops tried to operate at night but the use of flares was still in its infancy and night operations by aircraft had limited impact.[37] Thus the lesson of the campaign as a whole was clear; order could not be restored in the face of a national insurrection in a country such as Palestine without prolonged and carefully-thought-out operations involving both the army and RAF. The days when the appearance of aircraft alone was enough to disperse groups hostile to the government were ending.

Conclusion

The Palestinian uprising was a harbinger of the type of insurgency which was to spread across the world after 1945. In other parts of the Middle East aircraft were normally effective at maintaining imperial power in rural areas between the two World Wars. Indeed the British Empire would have contracted far more quickly had aircraft not been able to fulfil this role. But such a situation could not go on for ever because of the growth of urban communities, because rural peoples would find ways to combat aircraft, because the aircraft themselves would become less suitable and because public opinion was sensitive to the whole notion of using bombing to maintain order.

Thus, looking back, we can now see that the RAF was fortunate in the circumstances which it faced in the 1920s. It had plenty of cheap, fairly robust aircraft which could land in the desert. As the 1930s advanced and these were replaced by fast monoplanes, such as the Spitfire and Hurricane, aircraft became less able to use rough landing grounds and generally less suitable for maintaining colonial power. Secondly, the Iraqis, Jordanians and others who caused disturbances were conservative, rural people activated by nothing more profound than the natural desires to avoid paying taxes and to wage warfare periodically against their neighbours. The desert which had protected their ancestors against government interference was now only a minor hindrance to aircraft and armoured cars and they had little alternative but to give way. The tribesmen felt that they could do this without losing face because the odds were so uneven that their villages also had to accept collective punishment for their members' defiance of the government. When guerrilla warfare broke out in Palestine in 1936 or in the jungles of Asia after 1945, it became clear that aircraft would not be decisive against different enemies and in different terrain. Thus their monopoly of air power did not make it possible for the Japanese or the Kuomintang to destroy the Chinese Communists. Finally although colonialism was still accepted as normal and desirable in Europe in the 1920s, attitudes were, nevertheless, gradually changing and sensitivity to charges of inhumanity was increasing.

The British Air Staff emphasized that air control was unsuitable for 'civilized countries' and so, as civilization advanced, it was bound to become less effective. They saw that the main role of the RAF in the maintenance of order in developed areas would be to move troops rapidly to the scene of disorders. Already in 1931 the RAF flew 126 army personnel from Egypt to Cyprus within a day of riots breaking out there. The following year aircraft transported 560 troops from Egypt to Iraq within six days.[1] Moreover some commentators believed that even simple tribesmen were finding ways of avoiding the worst effects of bombing. When Wing Commander Peck gave a lecture on air power at the Royal United Services Institute in August 1928, he was taken to task by Captain C. T. Beckett, who argued that air control only worked because it was novel and this novelty would soon wear off. 'The Spanish conquered Mexico almost bloodlessly . . . by means of the [to the Mexicans] unknown gunpowder and armour. The effect, however, soon wore off and 200 years of trouble supervened.'[2] Similarly one correspondent wrote to the *Army and Navy Gazette* on 5 June 1933 suggesting that events on the Indian frontier in 1930 had shown that the tribes there already had the measure of air power. 'Once a serious outbreak takes place, the villages are evacuated whilst the fighting men carry on the war thus reducing air power's impact.'[3]

In fact, the RAF wanted the villagers to abandon their houses and expected their methods to work because they caused the tribesmen so much inconvenience rather than because of the casualties they inflicted. They were also aware that tribesmen could lose their fear of aircraft. Thus the Air Staff noted, 'the constant bombing of empty valleys by large concentrations of aircraft only undermines the moral effect of bombing by bringing it into ridicule'.[4] This was a phenomenon which occurred in many post-1945 guerrilla wars where insurgents took heart from the inaccuracy of bombing attacks.[5] Furthermore the Air Staff itself agreed that tribesmen were becoming less frightened of aircraft in the 1930s:

> Before the enemy became accustomed to aeroplanes, the mere sight of a machine in the distance was sufficient to send them scurrying for cover, but later they would move about in the open and would only disperse when bombed and machine-gunned.[6]

Thus the force necessary to defeat insurgents was going to grow at the same time as the Western public was becoming increasingly sensitive about bombing. The RAF's critics accused it of being callous and indifferent to the casualties it caused. As Major General J. F. C. Fuller put it, 'for unimaginative people it is easy to be brutal in the air for

they are out of touch with the burning homestead, the terror-stricken
women and the maimed children below. I do not believe our airmen
realize this for otherwise they would not suggest it.'[7] Fuller was
undoubtedly right about the possible effects of distance in blunting
sensibilities but we now know that many airmen did worry about the
effects of their weapons and the sufferings of their 'victims'. One officer
wrote later of his operations on the North-West Frontier, 'to me it
seemed a pity that we should be having to bomb these hardy people
who must have found life terribly difficult anyhow but, like naughty
children, I suppose they had to be taught a lesson'.[8] Sir Gerald Gibbs's
reaction to bombing the Wahhabis was similar; 'They were gallant if
misguided followers of the prophet and we were sad to see so many of
their wounded succumb.'[9] The RAF's use of air power to maintain
order must also be judged in the context of imperialism as a whole.
Those who felt that empires were beneficial to the people being ruled
usually believed that such use of force was justified to maintain them.
No European was ever closer and more sympathetic to the Arabs than
Sir John Glubb, yet he argued that the RAF's activities in general were
immensely beneficial, even if he criticized some of their actions.

    One manifestation of public hostility to bombing was the prolonged
attempt at the League of Nations' disarmament conference in Geneva
in 1932 to prohibit it altogether.[10] This put the British government in
a particularly difficult position. On the one hand they very much
wanted the conference to be a success because they feared that otherwise they would have to spend more on armaments and did not believe
the country could afford such expenditure. They also believed that the
public was very much in favour of disarmament.[11] Furthermore they
knew that Germany was covertly rearming and hoped that success in
Geneva would discourage this trend. They felt that, if ever war came
to Europe again, London would be more vulnerable than any other
centre because of its size and location and that bombing would cause
countless casualties. But there were insurmountable difficulties in the
way of banning bombing and of disarmament in general. For example,
many pointed out that civilian aircraft could easily be converted into
bombers. Thus some suggested that the League should take over the
running of civilian airlines, although it is difficult to see how this would
have worked in practice.

    The British had also to face the difficulty that any ban on bombing
would undermine the methods they used for maintaining order in much
of their empire. After the prohibition of bombing, they would have
either to give up large areas or to spend a great deal more on ground

forces. This in turn would undermine their desire to keep military expenditure to the minimum and to disarm rather than rearm. Sir Robert Vansittart, then Permanent Under Secretary at the Foreign Office, certainly wanted agreement at Geneva and greatly feared the results if Germany began to rearm but his correspondence with the Air Ministry in London shows how difficult the whole process was. The Chief of the Air Staff pointed out that

> the French made the agreement to the abolition of bombing dependent upon the effective international control of civil aviation; the Italians in their turn insist upon a concurrent abolition of 'offensive weapons' . . . [In any case] it is unthinkable that any country under invasion by land, or bombardment from sea would not use its military aircraft for self defence.[12]

The Admiralty was equally sceptical and Vansittart felt the need to remind their lordships that 'it is the duty of public servants to be helpful when their Ministers have recognized the necessity' for disarmament.[13]

To meet the need to maintain air policing the British government suggested at Geneva that bombing should be prohibited 'except for police purposes in outlying regions'. This, not surprisingly, produced a good deal of merriment and derision. As Vansittart put it, 'the police bombing reservation has come in for a lot of vehement criticism in this country and abroad and the government has declared more than once that they would not persist in it if it stood in the way of settlement'.[14] In fact it never did so. Germany's determination to rearm finally undermined the disarmament conference. The significance of the whole debate was that it demonstrated the prevalent fear of bombing in Europe and especially in Britain and also showed how much importance the British government ascribed to air policing. Its effectiveness might steadily decline but in the 1930s it was still playing a very important part in maintaining the British Empire.

2

Lysanders, Liberators and the Resistance 1939–45

Introduction

The most interesting aspect of the Second World War for the historian studying the use of aircraft in unconventional warfare is that aircraft were used by the Allies to support guerrillas on a scale undreamt of before or afterwards. After the British had been expelled from Dunkirk in June 1940 and from South-East Asia early in 1942, blockade, subversion and strategic bombing were almost the only ways they had of hitting back at their enemies.[1] Moreover some of the people in Yugoslavia, Greece, France, Poland, Malaya and elsewhere, who had been conquered by the Axis, rose spontaneously against the invaders. Allied support for these insurgencies depended very largely on whether aircraft could reach them to bring munitions, provisions and liaison officers. France was consequently the easiest area to supply from 1941 onwards and Yugoslavia from 1943; Poland and Malaya proved very much more difficult. Anti-German guerrilla movements could survive without such assistance, as the Partisans did in Yugoslavia from 1941 to 1943, but they became far stronger and more threatening to the invaders once Allied aircraft could support them.

The British Chiefs of Staff told Churchill in May 1940 that, together with strategic bombing, 'the only method of bringing about the downfall of Germany is by stimulating the seeds of revolt amongst the conquered territories'. As a result the government set up the Special Operations Executive (SOE) to encourage such revolts. Yet the other Services never gave SOE their full support. The RAF was unwilling to relinquish any but obsolete aircraft from the bomber offensive. As the Chief of the Air Staff explained, 'I cannot divert aircraft from a certainty to a gamble which may be a goldmine or may be completely worthless'. Thus the Special Duties (SD) squadrons based in Britain still had under thirty aircraft by the end of 1942 and never had more than sixty. Similarly in the Far East, where guerrilla operations were often beyond aircraft range, the Royal Navy would only allow its submarines to land agents in enemy territory whilst they were engaged in other missions. It was not, therefore, until the Americans began to mass-produce front-line aircraft that SOE acquired up-to-date machines such as the Liberator.[2]

For the most part supplies and liaison officers were dropped by parachute from bombers, such as the Halifax, which were being replaced by Lancasters in the front line of the strategic bomber offensive, or from transport aircraft such as the Dakota. Some idea of the scale of the operation can be gleaned from the fact that 7,000 agents were landed by the British SOE during the course of the war.[3] Medium bombers, like the Halifax, could deliver supplies and agents but other aircraft were needed to retrieve personnel. For short journeys of this type the British used Westland Lysanders. These had been introduced into Palestine and elsewhere in 1938 as army co-operation aircraft but, lacking manoeuvrability and with a cruising speed of 165 miles an hour, they proved very vulnerable during the battle for France and were superseded in this role in 1941. However the SD version was fitted with an 150-gallon fuel tank which enabled them to make a round trip of 1,150 miles. This aircraft proved ideal for sneaking agents into France (and later Burma) under the enemy's radars. The European squadron was based near Newmarket and later at Tempsford in Bedfordshire. Lysanders flew more than 260 sorties of this type between 1941 and 1944 of which 180 were successful.[4]

On longer journeys and where a larger airstrip was available, however crude, light bombers, such as the Hudson and the Baltimore, were also employed. The Hudson was built by Lockheed in the USA. The Tempsford SD squadron inherited a Hudson from the King's Flight and, after experiments, discovered that it could land away from runways. Subsequently SD Hudsons flew 300 sorties of which 249 were successful. Forty-four of these sorties involved picking up or landing agents in France and all but eight of these missions succeeded. Some 139 agents were landed for the resistance and 221 were evacuated.[5] Some Hudsons were fitted with radars which enabled the guerrillas on the ground to guide the aircraft to the landing place but the guerrillas had to carry a great deal of radio equipment and many refused to do so. Apart from supporting SOE and other resistance groups in Europe, Hudsons and Lysanders also helped MI9 evacuate pilots who had been shot down over the continent.

France

More supplies were dropped to the French *Maquis* by the British and Americans than to other groups, partly at least because this was logistically easier. The French, under Jean Moulin's guidance, were also well organized to receive support though, as elsewhere, the situation was vastly complicated by the existence of rival groups of guerrillas. General de Gaulle's Free French denied the right of SOE to operate in France without their prior agreement. Nevertheless, according to one account, 198,000 Sten guns, 128,000 rifles, 595,000 kilograms of explosives, 2,700 bazookas and 285 mortars were dropped to the French during the war.[1] The great majority of these supplies were dropped in the last few months when the US Army Air Force was involved. Of 7,500 successful sorties between 1941 and 1945, 6,750 took place after January 1944 and 94 per cent of all supplies were dropped during the same period.[2] Throughout the war SOE would have liked the British effort to have been on a far larger scale. It put forward a plan in 1941 which would have called for 8,000 sorties by RAF bombers. When this was rejected as impractical by the Chiefs of Staff, SOE put forward a second proposal which required 2,000 bomber sorties.[3] This was also dismissed and as late as 1943 *Maquis* units were often very short of weapons. Despite these and other difficulties and the terrible retribution which their actions brought down on the heads of the population, the *Maquis* had two great achievements to their credit: they delayed German supplies during the crucial weeks before the D-Day landings in Normandy and they restored French morale after the crushing defeat in 1940.

Yugoslavia

The Yugoslav campaign was by far the most interesting from the point of view of the use of aircraft to attack, supply and support guerrillas. In the early years, when the Germans, Italians, Bulgarians and Cetniks had the Partisans on the run, it was the Germans' use of aircraft to harry the guerrillas which was most significant. Then, in the summer and autumn of 1943, Allied supplies began to reach the insurgents. Finally in 1944 Allied aircraft came more and more to dominate Yugoslav airspace and a guerrilla force had the unique experience of being able to summon a devastatingly effective air force to destroy the conventional forces of the invader—perhaps the dream of every insurgent leader!

A *coup d'état*, backed by King Peter, unseated the pro-Axis government in Yugoslavia on 27 March 1941.[1] On 6 April Hitler was ready to deal both with this situation and with the arrival of British forces in Greece. The Germans bombarded Belgrade and, despite heroic resistance by the Third Yugoslav army and by the Greeks, the two countries were rapidly overrun. By 18 April the Greek Prime Minister had committed suicide and the British were considering evacuating their forces. Both the Yugoslav and the Greek Kings fled into exile and conventional resistance to the invaders came to an end. Nevertheless, insurgency began in Yugoslavia in July 1941 and the Allies infiltrated Captain Hudson into the country by submarine to liaise with the rebels.[2] However at that stage Allied methods of communication were still primitive and Hudson was isolated. In the early days, the Allies knew only of the Royalist resistance force, the Cetniks led by General Mihailovich. So savage were the German reprisals against the guerrillas that Mihailovich decided that resistance was not worthwhile. Instead the Cetniks cooperated with the invaders and British assistance to them was cut off at the end of 1943. It was left to the Communist Partisans led by Tito to continue the resistance.[3]

In late May 1943 two British officers, Stuart and Deakin, and four other ranks were dropped from a Halifax to make contact with Tito and assess the situation. Typically, their first attempt to land was aborted by an electric storm which forced the aircraft to fly so high that the officers lost consciousness. On the second occasion they were successful in landing and making contact with the Partisans.[4] They found themselves in the middle of one of the vast encircling campaigns which the Germans and their allies used to try to eradicate the Partisans, to kill their wounded and to butcher civilians who were thought to have given them any support. Deakin noted later that the daylight hours belonged to the Stukas, Henschels and Dorniers of the German air force. Stukas dive-bombed the last bridge over the Piva river which the Partisans needed to cross in order to escape their pursuers. Some managed to get over and to reach the high ground beyond where 'a sinister game was imposed upon us . . . the planes in low dives criss-crossed the wood in straight patterns, leaving on each run a neat pattern of bombs and at times, the smaller fry tossing grenades from their cockpits.[5] It was in these attacks that Tito was wounded, Deakin had his boot blown off and Stuart was killed. Partisan leaders and the British mission hid in a cave, where they were attacked both from the air and from the ground.

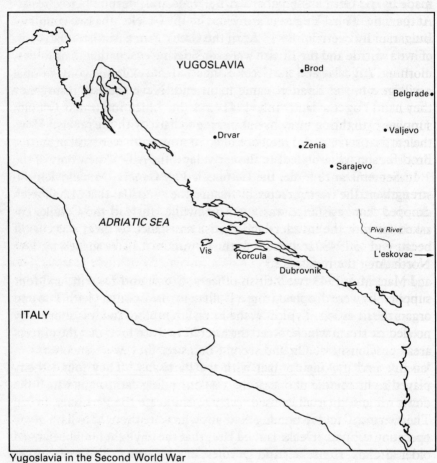

YUGOSLAVIA

•Brod

Belgrade•

•Drvar

•Valjevo

•Zenia

• Sarajevo

ADRIATIC SEA

Piva River

Vis

Korcula

L'eskovac →

Dubrovnik

ITALY

Yugoslavia in the Second World War

However some of the Partisans managed to escape through the encircling German forces during the night, leaving behind 2,000 who were hunted down by dogs, betrayed by spies and killed.[6]

On 17 June Deakin radioed for supplies of explosive to block the railways in the area and on 25 June the first successful supply drop was made by a Halifax bringing a spare radio set, bandages and explosives.[7] At the time the guerrillas were still constantly on the run from German, Bulgarian and Cetnik forces and from aircraft; 'On one occasion a battle of wits with a solitary German Fieseler Storch lasted throughout a morning, the pilot seeking for movement in the abandoned houses of a village street'.[8] Such pursuits made supply drops difficult because they had to be constantly rearranged and the Germans tried to disrupt supplies by lighting beacons of their own to decoy the aircraft. Nevertheless the partisans did receive enough British explosive to blow up the Brod-Sarajevo line in forty places and the Brod-Zenia line in seven.[9]

In September 1943 the British liaison group with Tito's forces was strengthened when Brigadier Fitzroy Maclean and a larger group was dropped from two Halifaxes. No sooner had they arrived than Tito asked for more supplies. Maclean explained that this was impossible because of 'our difficulties; lack of aircraft, lack of bases nearer than North Africa, the needs of our own forces'.[10] For these reasons Tito and Maclean agreed that the Royal Navy should be encouraged to bring supplies by sea. Maclean himself went to the island of Korcula to organize the landing. This was successful but far more support was needed as the Germans were gradually expanding their control over areas previously dominated by the Partisans. As Maclean recorded, 'enemy aircraft, against which they had no protection whatsoever, played an important part seeking out their positions and pinning them down while additional land forces were brought up to deal with them'. The Germans found aerial photography particularly useful in these operations. Furthermore just as the Allies could bring in supplies in older aircraft, so the Germans could use old aircraft against the insurgents; 'in other theatres perhaps the Stuka had had its day but for us, in our kind of warfare, without fighter support or anti-aircraft defences, it had kept its old terrors'.[11] Similarly the vulnerable Fieseler Storch— the German equivalent of the Lysander—proved ideal anti-insurgent aircraft because of their slow stalling speed and good visibility for the pilot.

Maclean left Yugoslavia to meet Sir Alexander Cadogan and other British officials in Cairo and to try to encourage them to give more support to the Partisans. This was becoming much easier as the Allies invaded Sicily in July 1943 and the Italians overthrew Mussolini. The Allies were to make their way painfully up the Italian peninsula, advancing air power closer to the Balkans. Maclean wanted to bring out Partisan leaders to discuss the situation with Allied leaders. However at this stage the RAF was unenthusiastic: 'They had, they said, far better uses for aircraft than smashing them up in futile attempts to bring out futile figures from the Balkans.'[12] Nevertheless, Maclean managed to find a Baltimore bomber and to persuade the American Lightnings to escort it. Unfortunately cloud prevented the Baltimore from landing and the Partisans tried to fly out in a small captured aircraft.[13] A German observation aircraft spotted their efforts and destroyed the aircraft, killing and wounding many of the Partisans. However Tito persevered and eventually his representatives were evacuated in a Dakota escorted by Lightnings.

Later Maclean met Churchill himself and a definite decision was taken to increase supplies for the guerrillas. The RAF built a runway on the Yugoslav island of Vis which greatly increased their ability to supply the Partisans and bomb the enemy.[14] A Balkan Air Force was also established under Air Vice Marshal William Elliott. Inevitably all this took time to build up and it was at this stage that Tito and his staff were nearly killed. Maclean had heard a number of rumours that the Germans were planning such an attempt. In May 1944 a German aircraft flew slowly over Tito's headquarters at Drvar, reconnoitring and photographing. Maclean was away at the time but the British mission was afraid that an attack was pending and moved some distance away. Three days later the Germans bombed the area heavily, then landed parachutists and troop-carrying gliders. Tito was pinned for a while in his cave and, even after his escape, the pursuit was very hot indeed.[15] Eventually Tito asked to be flown out and he and his staff were evacuated in a Dakota. The RAF had intended to evacuate him but Soviet pilots stole a march on them by arriving first in a British Dakota and evacuating the Yugoslav leader.[16] Tito was taken first to Italy and then to Vis in HMS *Blackamoor*.

The attack on Drvar was really the last German offensive before the scale turned decisively against them. Vast quantities of equipment reached the Partisans in 1944 including 100,000 rifles, 50,000 light machine guns, 1,380 mortars and 97 million rounds of small arms ammunition.[17] Inevitably some of the supplies went astray, some were decoyed by the Germans and some were dropped too high and drifted all over the countryside.[18] On other occasions supplies landed without parachutes or with the parachutes unopened, threatening the Partisans waiting for them below. But much still arrived. Vast Allied air armadas began to cross the country, derisively sweeping aside the Axis fighters. Contact between Balkan Air Force and the insurgents was close; 'it became relatively common for Beaufighters, Spitfires, rocket-firing Hurricanes to be rushed in the nick of time to the support of some hard-pressed Partisan outpost or prepare the way for a Partisan attack on some German outpost'.[19]

To hinder the German retreat, Tito and his British allies prepared a plan—Ratweek—to interdict German railroads. Partisans with support from Mustangs and other aircraft blew up the railway in numerous places. At first the Germans made frantic efforts to repair it but 'they had reckoned without the Balkan Air Force. Every time that we received reports of a breakdown gang at work we signalled its intention to Bari and within a few hours our fighters were on to it.'[20] Eventually the Germans abandoned the attempt and escaped on foot. Junkers which tried to bring officers out of Greece were also shot down.[21] Particularly strong German defences or concentrations of troops were attacked from the air. When the Allies heard that tanks were concentrating near Leskovac, fifty Flying Fortresses were sent to destroy them. Maclean and others 'watched [as] the whole of Leskovac seemed to rise bodily in the air in a tornado of dust and smoke and debris. When we looked up again the Forts, which were still relentlessly pursuing their course, were mere silvery dots in the distance . . . even the Partisans seemed subdued.'[22] Similarly, when the fortress at Valjevo proved particularly difficult to destroy 'a pair of rocket-carrying Beaufighters, summoned from Italy, administered the *coup de grâce* to the beleaguered garrison by swooping down and discharging their rockets at point blank range into the barrack buildings'.[23] One of the aircraft was shot down in the attempt and the crew killed.

Of course the Partisans always wanted more air support than the Allies could give. Early on they tended to suspect Allied treachery rather than the weather or other difficulties when supplies failed to arrive. They also felt the Partisan wounded were not evacuated because of Western anti-Marxism until Tito summoned Maclean and upbraided him.[24] As a result a stream of Dakotas flew in to the country and took out the casualties. It was an astonishing situation, air power and insurgents coming together for the first time to attack a conventional army. In the end Yugoslavia was overrun by Soviet ground forces but the successes achieved by the Partisans with Western air support had a very important, long-term political impact because they enabled Tito to negotiate from a much stronger position with the Russians and the Western allies.

Greece

Superficially, the situation in Greece seemed similar to that in Yugoslavia. Different bands of anti-Axis partisans were operating within the country and Allied officers were dropped to liaise with them. The bands spent much time attacking each other rather than the Germans. Although the Communists became the most important, they never acquired the dominance which Tito's guerrillas acquired further north, not least because they were much less willing to attack the Germans.[1] The first SOE group in Greece was landed from a submarine on the island of Antiparos and fell into Italians hands, together with lists of Greeks they intended to contact. Another group under Colonel Myers was parachuted in successfully from four Liberators in October 1942. Myers' group managed to blow up a key bridge despite its difficulties with the Greek factions.[2] The British subsidized the ELAS Communist movement and supplied them with equipment. In return the guerrillas built a landing strip which improved communications between the liaison officers and the outside world. In all, 1,072 agents were landed in 82 operations between 1941 and 1943 together with 5,000 tons of supplies and 1,000 tons of arms and ammunition.[3] Such supplies helped the guerrillas hinder German withdrawal from Greece, destroying 100 trains and 500 trucks in the process.[4]

Norway and Poland

If France was the easiest country in Europe to infiltrate from the air, Norway was difficult because of the weather and Poland because of the distances involved and Russian unwillingness to co-operate. Nevertheless by the end of the war a force of some 33,000 men had been armed in Norway and this was able to take charge as the Germans withdrew and pending the arrival of Allied forces.[1] Poland's fate was much more tragic. Overrun in 1939 by both the Germans and the Russians, Polish resistance gradually increased and a government-in-exile was established in London. The main Polish resistance movement owed allegiance to London and was armed with supplies captured from the Germans. The British began making plans to help the Poles in December 1940 but these were not feasible at the time because of the distance involved. Later a modified Whitley managed to drop three agents near enough to Poland for them to make contact with Polish resistance groups.[2] However it was not until 1943 that any number of supply drops took place and these always encountered great difficulty because of the range. Altogether the Poles asked for 1,300 operations; the Allies tried to respond in 858 cases and 483 of these sorties succeeded in dropping 345 agents and 600 tons of equipment.[3] The situation was greatly complicated because the Russians set up a group of Communist politicians in exile in Moscow as a government to rival the one in London. In August 1944, as the Russian forces advanced on Warsaw, the Polish Home Army decided to rise against the Germans and to seize the city.[4] The Germans were driven out but the Russians refused to help or, at first, to allow British and American aircraft to drop supplies to the insurgents and then to refuel in Russian-occupied territory. The Poles fought on for fifty days but they were eventually forced to surrender after 150,000 had been killed. Nothing but decisive intervention by the Russians could have saved the Home Army as the Germans were able to bring five divisions against them. However the inability of the British and Americans to supply the Poles adequately from the air hastened their destruction.

Malaya

In Malaya guerrilla units were even more isolated from the West than they were in Poland. In August 1941, SOE wanted to train guerrillas in Malaya to stay behind if the country were overrun by Japan. The army did not at that time believe such an outcome possible and turned the suggestion down. Nevertheless a guerrilla training school was eventually established and several hundred Chinese and others were given brief training. Some of the British officers involved, including Major Spencer Chapman, stayed behind after Malaya was captured. For a brief period Chapman did manage to attack the Japanese, derailing trains and cutting bridges. But what he could achieve was inevitably limited by his resources. Like the other British left in Malaya, he came to depend almost entirely on the Communist-led Malayan Peoples' Anti-Japanese Army (MPAJA) which sprang up amongst the Chinese living in Malaya at that time. Chapman's account shows that the guerrillas could achieve little against the Japanese because of their inadequate training, their lack of arms and the savage reprisals taken by the Japanese against civilians. When the MPAJA did stage attacks, Japanese aircraft flew over the area to prevent the peasants escaping;

then they sent in ground troops who killed all the young males, raped the women and took them off to army brothels.[1] Routine Japanese aircraft sorties prevented the insurgents growing much food in the jungle and one of the camps where Chapman had stayed was discovered by aircraft and destroyed.[2] Chapman noted how easy it was for a guerrilla to convince himself that aircraft passing overhead were particularly looking for him, even if they were on routine patrols. On the other hand, another British officer left in Malaya, John Cross, recalled the feeling of security which the jungle provided against observation and air attack.[3]

In May 1943 a small SOE team landed in Malaya from a submarine but the British officers involved were unable to move around the country because Japanese control was so tight. Contact between the guerrillas and the outside world, either by radio or by sea, continued to be tenuous. The theatre was beyond the range of aircraft and thus of effective supplies. It was not until long-range Liberators were based in Ceylon and India in 1944 that the situation began to change. Even then Malaya was at the limit of the aircraft's range and they had to carry 16,000 lb of fuel for 2,000 lb of men and equipment. Generally the weather and mechanical problems created greater difficulties than Japanese aircraft and of the twenty-seven aircraft lost by Nos. 357 and 358 SD Squadrons in India, only one was shot down by fighters. From November 1944 onwards the MPAJA was receiving substantial quantities of supplies and by July 1945 SOE had dropped 300 men into the country and some 7,000 Communist guerrillas had been armed.[4]

Conclusion

The extent of the support which the guerrillas in turn provided for the Allied war effort is still a matter of great dispute. Some historians, such as Walter Laqueur, A. J. P. Taylor and Sir Basil Liddell Hart, have largely dismissed the insurgencies.[1] The Allies would have won in any case, the Germans only used weak divisions against the insurgents and ones which needed to recuperate after the much more severe fighting on the Eastern Front, whilst the Japanese found it easy to contain the MPAJA. On the other hand, the historian of SOE, M. R. D. Foot, argued that the Allies would have been better advised to use more of their aircraft in support of the *Maquis*, the Partisans and so on rather than for strategic bombing.[2] The argument cannot be easily resolved; certainly the strategic bombing campaign was immensely expensive in aircraft and crews. However many would have been lost supporting the guerrillas if the Western powers had concentrated on such an effort. Moreover, whilst strategic bombing caused tens of thousands of casualties amongst German civilians, insurgency brought down terrible retribution on the heads of the Yugoslavs, Karens, Malayans and others. The most one can say is that guerrilla warfare did handicap the Germans and their allies and make their task more difficult. It also restored the self respect of the conquered peoples.

On the other hand, the wartime insurgencies made life more difficult for the West when the Axis was defeated. From Greece to Malaya and from Yugoslavia to Italy one problem that caused confusion amongst the Western Allies was the political complexion of the guerrillas whom they were supporting. In some cases, such as Yugoslavia and Malaya, the democracies supplied Communist guerrillas because they were operating most effectively against the Germans. In other cases, such as Greece, they were more hesitant. But, as the German menace receded everywhere the politics of the governments which would succeed them became more important. The Second World War ended with Spitfires attacking Communist insurgents in the streets of Athens and Mustangs and Spitfires strafing the nationalists in Indonesia.[3] The postwar world saw the spread and intensification of guerrilla warfare in every continent. There were many reasons for this development. Not only had the Allies encouraged guerrilla movements but the defeat of France and The Netherlands in 1940 and the conquest of Singapore in 1942 had for ever destroyed the myth of Western invulnerability and vastly encouraged the growth of Asian nationalism. Finally Mao Tse-tung's achievements in China suggested that a poor man's form of warfare had been discovered which could negate the material superiority of the West.[4]

Thus the colonial powers found, when they sent their forces back into Malaya, the East Indies and the Philippines, that the situation had changed dramatically over the previous four years. There was simply no comparison between the sophistication of the insurgents whom the colonial powers encountered after 1945 and most of the groups which they had dealt with in the 1930s. The balance of power tipped very rapidly against the metropolitan states. The British Labour government wisely moved quickly to give independence to Burma, India, Pakistan and Ceylon. Guerrilla warfare broke out in the East Indies, in Malaya and in Indochina. Even in Africa, which had been much less affected by the Second World War, the Mau Mau insurgency began against British control in Kenya.[5]

Changes in military technology were not for the moment assisting governmental forces. Rifles, mines and machine guns had been spread through the world as a result of the Second World War and the ideological divisions of the Cold War intensified this trend. We have already seen that the march of technology before 1939 meant that aircraft were less suitable for anti-guerrilla operations. Not only were Spitfires and Hurricanes less helpful than the biplanes which they replaced but the jet aircraft which superseded the planes of the Second World War were still faster, less reliable and less robust. Thus the only technical developments which were of advantage to governments fighting guerrillas in the early postwar years were the very gradual introduction of helicopters for evacuation of casualties in Malaya and Indochina and the use of trainer aircraft in the attack role. The Harvard, the standard trainer of the war years, was used by the British or their allies to attack insurgents in Greece, Malaya and Kenya and by the French in Algeria. In terms of counterinsurgency, it was by far the most important aircraft of the period from 1945 to 1955. Of course, in time, helicopters were to dominate the war against guerrillas but this did not happen until the second half of the 1950s.

Finally European populations were losing their imperial ambitions and pretensions. They were more concerned after 1945 with improving their own conditions than with the 'romance of empire'. They had lost, or were losing, their confidence that they had the right to dominate non-European peoples. They faced criticism from the United States and the Soviet Union for their colonial activities and these criticisms were taken up by India and other states as they became independent. A world public opinion was growing up which would be ready to attack any use of military power by the Europeans that it considered excessive and, particularly, the employment of aircraft. Consequently many factors were moving against the Europeans and in favour of anti-colonial guerrillas. The insurgents themselves were becoming highly educated and they were acquiring more modern weapons. On the other side, modern technology was making aircraft less suitable for counterinsurgency, and public opinion was becoming more sensitive to the use of aircraft against guerrillas.

3

Harvards, Marxists and Nationalists 1945–54

The Greek Civil War

Commentators sometimes suggest that aircraft have only been used to attack non-white guerrillas, but this is an illusion born of the fact that most insurgencies occur in the Third World. As we have seen, aircraft were used in Yugoslavia and elsewhere during the Second World War to attack guerrillas; they were also used very extensively against guerrillas during the Greek Civil War from 1944 to 1949, first by the RAF and afterwards by the Royal Hellenic Air Force (RHAF) with the active encouragement of British and later American advisers. The war was important for the RAF because it showed that new methods would have to be evolved if aircraft were to play a part in countering insurgencies. 'Air policing' would no longer work against sophisticated and ideologically-motivated rebels. The war also demonstrated that most of the aircraft developed for fighting during the Second World War were far from ideal for attacking guerrillas.

The British armed forces landed in Greece in October 1944 when the German empire was being rolled back.[1] Initially welcomed with great enthusiasm as liberators, they found terrible hardship amongst the Greeks and little prospect of improvement; the 1945 wheat crop was expected to be only 53 per cent of the 1938 level and there was not much the British could do to improve food supplies.[2] British troops occupied Athens itself but most of the countryside remained under the control of the guerrillas who had been fighting the Germans.[3] The most important group of insurgents was the Communist-dominated ELAS organization and its political wing EAM. An all-party government, including EAM, was formed in October and some hoped that the political situation might eventually be resolved peacefully even though massacres of one group by another were continuing.[4] The British tried to

69

remain neutral though their forces in the Peleponnese and elsewhere were involved in disarming the Greek Security Battalions, who had maintained order under the Germans, and in handing their arms over to ELAS. Many were subsequently murdered as old scores were paid off.[5]

Although they were nominally members of the same government, Right-wing forces and EAM deeply distrusted each other and each suspected the other of plotting a coup. In November the government, including its EAM members, ordered all volunteer forces to give up their arms within a month. The Left wanted the Right-wing Mountain Brigade and the Sacred Battalion of royalist officers disarmed; the Right wanted to see ELAS deprived of its weaponry.[6] At the beginning of December 1944 the government began to break up as its EAM members resigned. Violence increased though direct conflict between the British and ELAS did not really begin until 15 December.[7] Some 700 British army and RAF personnel were concentrated in the RAF headquarters in the Cecil and Pentelikon Hotels which were isolated from other units. The British knew they were vulnerable but feared the loss of prestige which would have followed the withdrawal of the headquarters.[8] They were also reluctant to provide the 148 vehicles necessary to remove them. On 17 December, two days after open strife between the British and ELAS had broken out, the Communists opened fire on the hotels. A Halifax attempted to drop supplies to the garrison but they fell outside the perimeter held by British forces and bad weather prevented aircraft providing close air support.[9] Shortly after midnight on 19 December ELAS launched an attack with 1,000 men. The west wall of the Pentelikon Hotel was dynamited and both hotels were subsequently overrun. Forty-five officers and 550 other ranks were taken prisoner. It was a most inauspicious beginning to the involvement of the RAF in postwar insurgencies.

The capture of RAF headquarters was a considerable blow to British morale but it was essentially a sideshow. Aircraft continued to give support to army units which gradually forced ELAS out of Athens.

> During the period of the full moon, Beaufighters of the night intruder squadron were employed in strafing ELAS motor transport which moved mainly by night . . . In reviewing the damage inflicted on the enemy which was considerable . . . it must be borne in mind that there were no enemy aircraft and no organized anti-aircraft except unco-ordinated small arms fire. Nevertheless results were impressive in view of the small number of

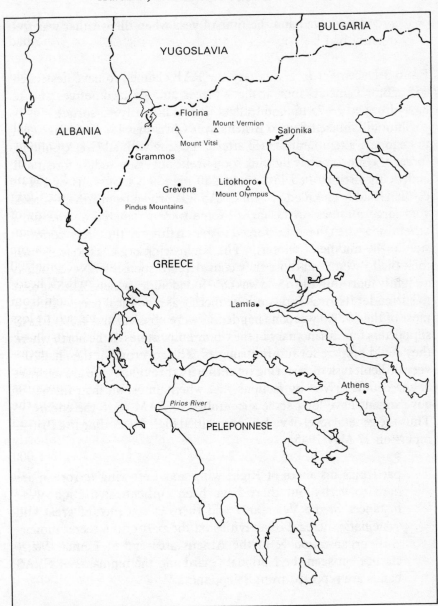

The Greek Civil War 1946 -1950

aircraft involved and the time of year when the weather was frequently bad.[10]

From 3 December to 15 January the RAF claimed to have destroyed 455 motor vehicles, four artillery pieces and six locomotives and to have dropped 23.75 million leaflets. It had flown 1,665 sorties.

Churchill himself flew to Athens over Christmas 1944 and managed to negotiate a temporary truce after a meeting with all Greek political forces.[11] Unfortunately fighting soon broke out again and, before it had ended, the British had lost about 250 men and thousands of Greek civilians had been killed. When ELAS was driven from Athens it took very large numbers of hostages. Some were butchered on the spot, others died when they were forced to march through the Greek countryside in the middle of winter.[12] The Right-wing organizations in turn took their revenge on those they considered responsible. Nevertheless a slightly more durable peace was concluded under which ELAS agreed to surrender its arms and continue merely as a political party—though most of the 40,000 weapons handed in were obsolete and 4,000 ELAS supporters found sanctuary in the Communist states to the north where they could prepare for future struggles. The government then had 'the very difficult task of restoring its authority throughout the greater part of the country riven by factions . . . when almost all instruments of government have long since succumbed to EAM or to the enemy'.[13] Thus the general level of violence remained high. According to a British report on 27 May 1945,

> particular instances of Right-wing and Left-wing terrorism are hard to verify but there have been authenticated Right-wing instances in the Velos area and there is evidence of great and systematic increase of activities on the part of the secret monarchist organization X in the Athens area and at Lamia. Many clashes between the National Guard and the remnants of ELAS bands are reported from Peleponnese.[14]

The British wanted free elections to be held, the demobilization of any remaining irregular forces and the establishment of a representative and stable government. Elections eventually took place on 31 March 1946 against the objections of Premier Sophoulis. They were boycotted by the Left-wing parties and thus the monarchists won 49 per cent of the vote. A Right-Wing government under Tsaldaris came to power and King George II returned to Greece on 28 September 1946 for the first time since the war. The elections and the king's return reflected the polarization of Greek politics and probably encouraged the slide into civil war.[15] Because they had suffered from the clash with ELAS forces in December 1944 and they had seen similar insurgencies develop elsewhere, the British seemed less complacent about the situation than the Greek government. They were already training the RHAF for operations against insurgents.[16]

The Communists later dated the onset of the civil war from their attack on Litokhoro at the end of March 1946. Some sixty guerrillas captured the town, burned down the police station and killed six soldiers and gendarmes.[17] However the first real clashes between the Communist Democratic Army and the government's National Army took place in July 1946. At that time the Communists may have been trying to establish a base area in Grevena in southern Macedonia although they were still far from clear whether they wanted to wage a full-scale civil war. On its side the government tried to clear rebel bands out of Mount Vermion and Mount Olympus in July by using tanks and RHAF Spitfires. Communist newspapers described this drive as ineffective and the historian C. M. Woodhouse has supported this judgement. He also described the RHAF as useless at this time.[18] Certainly the guerrillas easily escaped to attack the town of Naoussa on Mount Vermion. Gradually the situation deteriorated and in autumn virtually every road in Western Macedonia was cut while even in Athens secret Left-wing organizations could assassinate anti-Communists.

The Chief of the British Imperial General Staff visited Greece in December 1946 and warned the government that it could easily lose the civil war.[19] The Democratic Army had many advantages on its side including the experience of its own fight against the Germans and the benefits of Yugoslav experience in the same struggle. It had friendly countries to the north where Marxist regimes were in power. From these it could draw supplies and send its own bands over the frontier for training and recuperation. It could also use these territories to move its troops from one part of Greece to another in safety. The Democratic Army had the support of perhaps a quarter of a million Greeks who saw ELAS as a patriotic force and as a movement against rapacious landlords. It could operate in both town and countryside and it had many sympathizers inside the government's forces.

The technical balance was nothing like as favourable to the government as it had been in guerrilla wars in the 1920s. Guerrillas in Greece were able to keep in touch with Yugoslavia and elsewhere by radio. Apart from the possession of artillery, which was anyway very difficult to move in the mountains, and of aircraft, the government's forces were no more heavily armed than the guerrillas. Communist aircraft dropped supplies to the insurgents near the Albanian border and guerrilla marksmanship was such that they shot down a number of Spitfires and damaged one Harvard. Thus guerrilla warfare spread across the whole of Greece. The Democratic Army was led by Markos Vaphiades, a former trade union official who had served with ELAS in Macedonia. At first it operated mainly in small bands. It was not until 1949 that the Communists made the crucial mistake of challenging the army in battle.[20]

Though they have subsequently been bitterly criticized by commentators for their inertia, the British had been trying since their occupation of the country to build up the Greek army and air force. Three RHAF squadrons, which had been operating with the RAF in the Middle East, returned to Greece in November 1944. The Greeks were trained in RAF methods and tended to use English in their communications, a fact which became important later when the Communists argued that RHAF aircraft were being flown by British pilots since they had overheard English used in their radio conversations. By the following April the RHAF had twenty Spitfires, five Harvards and four Austers and by June 1946 one historian describes it as having fifty-eight 'obsolete' aircraft and 291 pilots.[21] In fact it was not so much the age of the aircraft which was important as their suitability for anti-guerrilla operations. RAF officers in Greece quickly became convinced that the Spitfires were not ideally suited to the conflict;

> here the reconnaissance pilot is not looking for tanks, guns or vehicles or even for fairly large bodies of infantry but only for small parties of ragged men armed with rifles and perhaps accompanied by mules. These men will be moving in broken wooden (*sic*) country and will almost certainly have seen or heard the aircraft in time to take cover.[22]

In any aircraft such groups would be difficult to see but spotting them was easier in the Harvard than the Spitfire. The Harvard trainer was able to turn faster than the Spitfire and could carry an observer in the rear seat. Harvards had a cruising speed of 170 miles an hour and they were robust aircraft which were easy to fly.

Other types of aircraft including Austers were also available to the Greeks. Some 1,500 Austers had been built during the war for artillery spotting and light communications. On the face of it their slow stalling speed should have made them very useful in irregular warfare but the wind currents in the mountains made them too difficult to control; in such circumstances 'it is extremely difficult to fly a light aircraft let alone to use it for a military purpose'.[23] The ineffectiveness of the Auster was unfortunate because despite the fact that 5,000 Harvard trainers had been built for allied air forces in the Second World War, the Air Ministry in London claimed that Harvards were in short supply. It tried to persuade the RHAF that the Martinet was an effective substitute. The Miles Martinet was designed for towing targets; however the Harvard's range was greater, its stalling speed was lower and it was easier to maintain. The last point was vital as there were few RHAF engineers.[24]

The Palestine insurrection in 1936 and the Second World War had broken the tradition of imperial policing and there seems to have been no suggestion by the RAF that the Greeks should operate in this way. Public opinion would anyway have protested against such measures. When British pilots serving in Africa at this time argued that guerrillas should be bombed in Eritrea, 'this was held by civil authority to exceed the level of force justified and was too reminiscent of Mussolini's peace-keeping methods'.[25] In any case air control depended on the idea that guerrillas operated in the vicinity of their own village and therefore that the village was responsible for the guerrillas' actions. Clearly the Democratic Army was active all over Greece and no individual village could be held responsible for attacks on government forces.

At first the idea was that aircraft should be used primarily for reconnaissance and for guiding the Greek army to the guerrillas. However 'it soon became obvious that aircraft could be used not only for reconnaissance but could take offensive action with cannon and machine guns against guerrilla bands, though great care had to be exercised to avoid killing the civilian population'.[26] Thus the Harvards were used to guide the Spitfires to their targets. This proved inefficient and in the end the Harvard itself was armed so that it could attack the Democratic Army, despite a certain amount of resistance in London to this very significant change.[27] The RHAF with British guidance set a fashion for using training aircraft to attack guerrillas which was to be followed in almost every succeeding guerrilla war from Malaya and Kenya to Vietnam and the Dhofar. Further squadrons of Spitfires and Harvards were sent out to Greece once Whitehall realized how serious the situation had become. The Greeks also acquired a squadron of Wellington bombers, though these were later changed to Dakotas as the ability to move troops around quickly seemed more important than bombing.

Where the Greeks showed themselves considerably more conservative than the French armed forces, who were fighting guerrillas in Indochina at this time, was in their apparent indifference to parachutists. The Greeks used motor transport in the plains but in the mountains they had to rely on mules and thus they were no faster than their enemies. The British advisers encouraged them to establish forty specialized commando companies for hunting down the guerrillas. However, an American marine colonel who analyzed the war concluded that the effort involved had not been worthwhile and that they could move no more quickly than regular army units.[28]

RAF officers wanted their Greek counterparts to consider themselves the main striking arm against the insurgents, leaving the army to 'mop up' afterwards. But the RHAF tended to see itself merely as an auxiliary and to leave most of the fighting to the army. National Army officers believed that the guerrillas could be caught if they were penned against the Akeloos and other rivers. The British rightly pointed out that the insurgents would simply escape across such obstacles. Thus they felt that aircraft alone were fast enough to prevent them from dispersing. In any case close co-operation between the two Services was vital. Yet, there were communication problems as the mountains often prevented radios operating effectively. More seriously, an RAF officer reported, 'the discord which exists between the RHAF and Greek National Army at Field Headquarters has to be seen to be believed'.[29] It was not, therefore, surprising that on one occasion it took the RHAF six to eight hours to respond to a request for help from the army. To try to improve the situation, British officers toured the country telling the National Army of the need for air support. To emphasize the message, they arranged a lecture in the presence of the Greek King and for a time this seemed to improve matters. But in fact there were continuing problems.

Finding the right equipment and choosing the best tactics were by no means the only problems. Morale in the army and RHAF was extremely low. RAF officers noted their Greek counterparts sitting around drinking coffee when they should have been flying; 'the general attitude seems to be that the bandits were far too strong and efficient and that it was little good to fight against them. Pilots would fly if ordered into the air but they did so unwillingly and with the obvious hope that the weather would provide an excuse for an early return.'[30] Politics may have played a part in forming these attitudes. Before the civil war broke out, the British had hoped that recruits for the Greek armed forces would be chosen according to their qualifications rather than their political views. But Major General Smallwood commented in April 1945, 'there was little doubt that discrimination against ex-ELAS members on political grounds was to be observed in medical examinations for recruits to the regular army'.[31] On the other hand former ELAS supporters were certainly not excluded entirely; General Scobie, the Commander of the British troops in Greece, believed that there were 200 of them in the Corinth brigade alone and the situation was the same in the RHAF.[32] On one occasion during the civil war there was an attack on an RHAF bus and the British suspected that it might have been carried out by government forces since most of the casualties were Left-wing and two were known Communists. One Spitfire was blown up by a time bomb and there were other cases of sabotage from within the RHAF. In July 1947 British liaison officers said that up to 20 per cent of RHAF officers might be covert sympathizers with the Democratic Army. About a dozen officers in the Athens area planned to defect taking their aircraft with them.[33]

The year 1947 was particularly difficult for the Greek government's armed forces as the insurgents' estimated strength grew from 14,000 to 20,000 men. In March there was a note of optimism in British reports, one RAF officer commenting, 'Some of our hints have been taken to heart; aircraft have been scrambled more quickly and more initiative has been shown generally. The result has been that bandits have been hit more often and successes have been exploited.'[34] But in April British liaison officers reported that the guerrilla forces were operating in such small groups that they were very difficult to observe from the air. Lack of co-operation between the army and RHAF was continuing to hamper the first major operation designed to sweep the insurgents from central Greece and up towards the north.[35] In May there was a guerrilla attack on the RHAF base in Salonika during which three officers were killed and five or six wounded. The British liaison officers consoled themselves with the thought that this might have 'tended to correct the Left-wing sympathies of many officers and men'.[36] Moreover in the same month a reconnaissance by a Harvard and two Spitfires discovered a party of 200–300 guerrillas beyond the Pinios river. Six Harvards and fourteen Spitfires made attacks on them and, even though the army only followed up the attacks very slowly, forty guerrillas were killed and ten taken prisoner.[37] In June the situation deteriorated again, with guerrilla groups infiltrating back into areas which the government believed to have been cleared. Frontier garrisons withdrew in case they were overrun.[38]

The RAF believed that, if ground forces were withdrawn, the RHAF should become more active in the region to compensate. But the reverse was usually the case as RHAF officers convinced themselves that everything was hopeless. Part of the problem was simply exhaustion: 'The fatigue of pilots who have now been in operation for a very long time is now beginning to tell. Morale and initiative were high when offensive operations began but have dropped off'.[39] Pilots felt that senior officers were incompetent and discipline was lax; 'After being briefed, pilots would often go to the canteen for a drink or smoke before taking off and would follow the same practice on landing and before reporting for interrogation'.[40] Not surprisingly it was taking 45–90 minutes to scramble aircraft. The Greek army had planned to clear the Mount Olympus area but had to abandon the idea and rush forces to Florina near the Yugoslav frontier in case the Democratic Army should declare it an independent state. Many civilians fled to the towns or were deliberately driven from the villages by the insurgents, who wanted to increase the government's economic problems.[41]

The arrival of the first US aid in August 1947 gave a brief boost to morale and eventually three Greek divisions out of eight were armed with American weapons.[42] The United States had been inclined to leave Britain to control Greece and it was only as the Cold War intensified and Britain's economic position weakened that Washington became prepared to assist. Historians are agreed that US aid did not tip the scales against the guerrillas, but without it the situation would have been parlous indeed. Civilian morale was hit when government forces abandoned the villages they had been protecting and went on drives against the guerrillas. The army itself was tired and its operations were slowing down even though the British did not think its casualties were very high. RAF liaison officers were often more pessimistic than their army equivalents. Air Commodore Gray, who had played a major role in RAF attacks on the 'Mad' Mullah in Somalia in 1920, headed the RAF Mission in 1947–48. He told his army equivalent, Major General Rawlins, 'I consider the recommendations you make are half measures which will be unlikely to bring about stability in Greece. You know only too well my views on the matter.'[43]

September 1947 seemed to be the low point as far as air operations against the guerrillas were concerned. An RAF report of 5 September spoke of the 'disastrous decline in the morale and initiative of the RHAF'. The sortie rate had dropped to only a quarter of the July figure.[44] Major General Rawlins toured the country with the Greek King. He concluded that the RHAF needed to seal off the frontiers so far as possible to prevent guerrillas coming and going. The National Army would also be much more effective at fighting in the mountains if it were to carry the war to the enemy. Guerrilla intelligence was good while the National Army suffered from lack of information. Troops were badly led and thus units sometimes blundered into and attacked each other whilst too much time was spent inactive behind barbed wire.[45]

During the winter of 1947–48 operations tended to grind to a halt. Wing Commander Kemp RAF reported 'with the exception of the RHAF national forces of Greece were almost inactive during the past winter'.[46] The authorities in Whitehall were warned that Greek morale would collapse if the war went on much longer. Thus 1948 was an unsatisfactory year as far as government forces were concerned, despite the increase in the size of the army from 132,000 to 147,000 men and the steady flow of US aid and weaponry. On June 29 government forces attacked the insurgents' base in the Grammos area with 50,000 troops. After two and a half months the guerrillas withdrew into Albania, only to reappear near Mount Vitsi. Government troops failed to drive them out of that region and the insurrection also began to spread in the Peleponnese. During the winter the Democratic army even re-established itself in Mount Grammos and the situation for the government looked gloomy indeed.[47]

In fact, however, salvation was much closer than the British could foresee. General Papagos, who was appointed to command the Greek armed forces early in 1949, at last managed to restore their morale and galvanize them into action. The British had fretted not only about the freedom of the guerrillas to use countries to the north as sanctuaries but also that government frustration with this situation could produce 'some frontier clash which might provide the other side with an excuse for more open aggression'.[48] However in June 1948 the Cominform expelled Yugoslavia and a year later Tito cut off aid to the guerrillas. Perhaps this encouraged the guerrillas to stand and fight for their mountainous base areas rather than to avoid a conventional clash. Whatever the motives, the decision proved fatal because the government's forces could bring all their firepower to bear. Thus the end of the war came very quickly indeed after the key battles of August 1949. Government forces took three days to clear Mount Vitsi and only a little longer to overrun Grammos. The insurgents had divided their men between the two bases which could not reinforce each other and they faced much more heavily armed government troops. The National Army blasted roads up Mount Grammos so that it could bring up heavy artillery and the RHAF could field three squadrons of Spitfires, three flights of Harvards and a squadron of Dakotas. It was also reinforced at the last minute by forty-nine American Helldivers. US advisers were reluctant to let the Greeks employ these as they were so unused to flying them but the commander of the RHAF begged them to let him do so. As *The Times* commented afterwards: 'Both in the breakthrough and in the pursuit, the Air Force gave invaluable aid, the Helldivers in particular destroying resistance and breaking up fleeing columns'.[49]

Like the Communist states to the north, the Greek Communists had already started to fall out among themselves. In January 1949 Markos had been sacked and replaced by the Secretary General of the KKE, Zachariades. The new leader had tried to restore morale by capturing the town of Florina only to lose 2,000 men in the attempt and 'the retreat became a rout as the air force sprayed the struggling mob with bombs, bullets and flame'.[50] In May 1949 the Peleponnese were cleared of guerrillas and the National Army believed that guerrilla casualties were running at 15,000 a month. By January 1950 the fighting was almost over. Some of the 650,000 refugees were starting to return to their villages. The RHAF was now primarily involved in watching the frontiers to see that infiltration did not begin again. The British believed that there were still some 5,500 insurgents in Bulgaria, 1,500 in Yugoslavia and 6,000 in Czechoslovakia but, owing to change in Soviet policy, they were not allowed to return to the fray.

This was one of the key factors in the war. Stalin had been reluctant to aid the Democratic Army from the beginning. Nevertheless, until the split between Yugoslavia and the Cominform in June 1948, Greek insurgents had been able to use the Communist states as their base. The loss of this source of support and safety was devastating. Almost as important was the incompetence of the guerrillas' leaders who had alienated the population by conscripting unwilling villagers, kidnapping children to have them indoctrinated in the Communist states and carrying out random killings. US and British military aid also played a vital role. Given the low state of morale in the Greek armed forces and among the public as a whole, it is difficult to believe that they would have won without outside assistance. Nevertheless the achievements of the government's forces should not be entirely dismissed. The RHAF had carried the war to the enemy even when the weather and the state of the National Army's morale had brought other operations to a standstill. It also provided airborne artillery support in regions which were inaccessible to the army's guns. It played an important part in gathering intelligence through its reconnaissance flights, in weakening Communist morale and in hampering the movement of the insurgents in the daytime. One American commentator noted later, 'the air effort immeasurably exceeded the return from any comparable effort on the ground'.[51] The RHAF's manpower had never risen beyond 7,500 against a maximum of 150,000 in the Greek army. Moreover, most of its aircraft had been obsolete and thus its material costs had been low. Against this the same American observer believed that it could have been used far more effectively, particularly to increase the mobility of the ground forces, and that maintenance of aircraft was poor.

From the point of view of air power in general, the civil war had shown that air policing methods were out of date in the new conditions. They could not deal with insurgents who were motivated by nationalism or Marxism, sceptical of what aircraft could do and willing to operate right across the country. The war had shown that trainer aircraft could play an important role in discovering and attacking insurgents. Indeed they would often be more effective than more advanced aircraft, though greater firepower would be needed if the enemy stood and fought as the Democratic Army did in 1949. The Greek Civil War also underlined the vital importance of close co-operation between ground and air forces. The guerrillas whom they had to combat were far more sophisticated than their prewar predecessors. Future events were to confirm how close the balance between insurgents and government forces had become.

The Malayan Insurgency

Whereas RAF officers were only involved in the Greek civil war as advisers after 1945, during the Malayan insurgency the RAF experienced its first prolonged contact with modern guerrillas in terrain which made air operations particularly arduous. Most of Malaya was covered by dense jungle or by rubber plantations. The weather often made flying dangerous and the guerrillas moved in small groups or camped in huts which it was difficult to find or to destroy from the air. Some of them already had battle experience because of their efforts against the Japanese in the Second World War and they also had weapons dating from that period. The RAF, for its part, was going through a period of rapid contraction and great technical change. To combat the guerrillas it made use of almost every type of service aircraft from Sunderland Flying Boats to Austers and from Dragonfly helicopters to

Spitfires. But most of the aircraft involved were far from ideal for counterinsurgency and they became increasingly less suitable as jets were introduced.

The RAF went in to the Malayan emergency still believing that aircraft could play the predominant part in the offensive operations involved. It came out of the war convinced, in the words of the last AOC, that 'the main killing weapons were the ground forces, supported by the air with both always acting in concert with the political objective'.[1] Indeed the pendulum perhaps swung too far the other way and there was a tendency to suggest that bombing attacks on the guerrillas had been totally useless because of the difficulty of locating them. There are enough comments by captured guerrillas to suggest that this was not the case. The point was that such attacks could only be a part of a concerted political, economic and military effort.

In March 1947 RAF squadrons in Malaya had just finished dropping extensive supplies to Karens in Burma to try to prevent them starving. Subsequently squadrons were occupied in carrying VIPs around the country, demobilizing men for return to Britain and spraying DDT on the Singapore docks and other areas.[2] Squadrons had been testing the new Meteor jets to see how they stood up to tropical conditions and, before they were crated up to return to Britain, they gave a flying demonstration before 5,000 people in Kuala Lumpur. Vampire jets were also sent to Malaya in January 1948 to test their effectiveness in those conditions.

This leisured change to peacetime conditions was played out against a steadily deteriorating political background. Undoubtedly the former members of the MPAJA who were now running the Communist party, hoped that the country would drift into their hands as a result of strikes, demonstrations and other disturbances. They also knew that Britain's commitment to its empire was declining rapidly, hence its withdrawal from Burma, India and Palestine. The British formulated constitutional proposals in Malaya which were rejected by sections of the population and, in the general ferment, a weakened police force only maintained order with difficulty. Nevertheless the Communists became sufficiently pessimistic about the possibility of a peaceful takeover to transfer the struggle to the jungle. They had handed over some of their weapons when the MPAJA was officially disbanded in December 1945 but they had hidden many of the most effective ones.[3] In June 1948 the uprising began with attacks on rubber plantation and tin mine managers. The aim of the 4,000–5,000 guerrillas was to drive the Europeans from the countryside, thereby wrecking the economy

The Malayan Insurgency 1948 - 1960

and confining government control to the towns. In the end the attempt was to fail but the disruption caused was still considerable. On 7 May 1949 the *Malayan Tribune* reported that all prospecting for tin had ceased since June 1948 and that some mines had closed. Nevertheless many other mines and plantations remained open and profitable, particularly after the outbreak of the Korean War in 1950 which lifted commodity prices.

In June 1948 the British had some twelve battalions of troops in Malaya. Many were, however, under strength and training had been severely disrupted by the rapid process of demobilization. As one typical signals regiment reported, 'on account of the heavy commitments and the rapid breakdown of manpower due to the speed up of the release programme, any form of collective training has been impossible'.[4] The RAF maintained 28 and 60 Squadrons with Spitfires, as well as some Austers and a Dakota, together with the Far East Flying Boat Wing with Sunderlands, in the region.[5] The Austers were called upon to reconnoitre areas where the guerrillas had struck and the Spitfires, Beaufighters and other aircraft, which were sent to reinforce them, were summoned to attack any who could be identified but not dealt with by ground troops. Despite the long years of 'imperial policing' before 1939 and the advisory rôle in Greece, the air force had to feel its way towards the best use of its resources in the new circumstances. Even if informers gave away the very approximate position of the insurgents hiding in the jungle, they were still extremely difficult to spot and, if they were spotted, it was unclear whether RAF attacks had injured or killed them.

An advanced RAF headquarters was set up in Kuala Lumpur, separate from the headquarters for the whole region which did not move from Singapore to Kuala Lumpur until 1953. A number of experiments were also tried to devolve control of aircraft to match the dispersed nature of guerrilla warfare. In the end, however, the AOC preferred to retain control of all aircraft so that they could be moved rapidly to wherever the need was greatest. Requests for help from aircraft were channelled through a Joint Operations Centre in Kuala Lumpur where the Air Headquarters and Headquarters of the Army were next door to each other. The GOC and AOC also had adjoining offices. The RAF's initial aims were to help to restore order, to fly over isolated plantations and villages to boost morale and to try to prevent infiltration either from Thailand in the north or from over the sea.[6] The effects of 'showing the flag' over isolated areas were, of course, difficult to quantify though there were plenty of grateful acknowledgements from the European rubber plantation managers.

Most attacks on insurgents were carried out in conjunction with ground forces. For example, early in December 1948 the Queens' Own Hussars moved into Bruas where Communists were active. Four Malay and one Chinese gave information about the whereabouts of the insurgents' camp and preparations were made to attack it, including the summoning of twelve armoured vehicles. To try to preserve some element of surprise, rumours were spread that an attack was to be made on a quite different target some miles distant. At nine minutes past nine on the morning of 21 December, Beaufighters began the attack and Spitfires followed up at 9.34. By 11.30 a.m. the ground forces had arrived, though all but one of the guerrillas seemed to have fled from the camp. Then a second camp was discovered and two more arrests were made. One of the prisoners said that all the others had fled when the bombing began but the two had become so frightened when bombs fell only 150 yards away that they had hidden in a small cave until the arrival of the troops. Despite the disappearance of the main band, the RAF felt that the air attack had been justified since otherwise the guerrillas might have ambushed the ground troops or fled before their arrival.[7]

Sometimes air attacks were made when the army simply could not reach a particular area because conditions were so difficult, because there were not enough ground troops available or because a rapid response was necessary to guerrilla attacks. For example in Bahau the guerrillas were intimidating labourers on the plantations and forcing them to support the insurgency. The position of the guerrilla camp was given away in 1949 by a Chinese informer and local officials wanted to attack it before Labour Day in order to give the impression that the government was taking the initiative. A ground and air attack was planned but the troops were unable to reach the camp which was surrounded by deep swamp. Thus the RAF had to carry out the operation alone and the Spitfires were only able to make one attack instead of the three planned because of low cloud.[8] Similarly in the Kaki Bukit area guerrillas were entrenched in caves with a very good field of view so that they could escape if any troops appeared. Instead the caves were attacked by Spitfires and Beaufighters on 4 May 1949.[9] Guerrillas entrenched on the summit of Bukit Tumpgal were also attacked and subsequent reports suggested that

it was most stimulating for the local population and has raised their morale considerably. The air strike is still one of the main topics of conversation in the coffee shops and everyone is convinced that if the strike is repeated in future attacks the bandits will soon lose heart.[10]

Nevertheless the utility of air attacks on the guerrillas did not go unquestioned even at this stage. In January 1950 Air Marshal F. J. Fogarty in Singapore warned the AOC in Malaya that doubts about the utility of air attacks had been expressed in Britain and Australia.[11] As a result the officers involved in Malaya began much more systematically to try to discover the effects of air strikes. Captured guerrillas were particularly questioned on this point with varying results. One claimed in Pahang in May 1950 that bombing 'has very little effect . . . I myself experienced some days of continuous bombing for eight hours each day in the jungle . . . most of the bombs exploded in the tops of the trees.'[12] Yet another guerrilla from the same area commented a little later, 'immediately after the bombing we bolted for our lives . . . I was terribly frightened'.[13] Very probably the impact of air attacks was determined more by the state of mind of the individual guerrilla than by their destructiveness. This led some British army officers to emphasize the importance of air strikes; a Major in the Scots Guards commented:

> I hope it is explained to the pilots that, far from being a waste of time, this 'area' strafing is of *vital* importance in South Selangor where the troops are so thin on the ground that virtually the only hope of ground contact with the gangs lies in the successful denial to them of as many jungle portions of the area as possible. If they are disappointed that they cannot have pin-point targets and the satisfaction of killing bandits, they must be consoled with the thought that we on the ground have come to regard the killing of bandits as a bonus after months of seemingly fruitless activity![14]

Such reassurance was important because morale was a problem for bomber squadrons, one of which dropped 17,500 tons of bombs between 1950 and 1958 and was credited with killing only sixteen insurgents.

Surprisingly, considering the experience elsewhere, captured insurgents sometimes felt that general attacks on areas of jungle were more worrying than sorties against specific camps. As one report noted on 30 September 1949, 'the bandit suggested that bombing over a wide area, followed by intense machine-gunning before follow-up by troops, will produce more fear and despondency and consequent lowering of morale than concentrating on precise targets'.[15] Some insurgents also felt that 500 lb bombs were less frightening than larger numbers of 20 lb bombs and strafing from Sunderlands and other aircraft. Quite often attacks on the neighbourhood were enough to force guerrillas away from their camps. Abdullah Ben Arsad was captured by guerrillas in April 1949 but subsequently managed to escape. He reported that 'bandits are not afraid of bombing [but they] didn't much like gun and rocket attacks'. Arsad felt that guerrillas did not know when an air attack was going to occur but the security forces knew that they had developed a routine to deal with such events. Once the aircraft were heard, they would leave the camp and hide during the attack. Then they would return to collect their kit and make off as fast as possible before the ground troops arrived.[16]

The RAF strafed roads in areas where ambushes had taken place to try to deter future attacks on passing vehicles. For a time they also warned villages in the area that they would be attacked if the ambushes continued.[17] However there was considerable resistance to the prewar notion of allocating collective responsibility and to the threat to innocent civilians caused by strafing the jungle. One officer suggested that 'in combined operations the RAF should confine itself to dummy attacks, so that it would be possible to discriminate between bandits and others and unnecessary killing could be avoided'.[18] This was not accepted but the idea of attacking villages saddled with collective responsibility also appears to have been dropped. The police and Special Branch had to give permission before an area could be bombed so that civilian casualties could be avoided. This obviously slowed matters down considerably and officers disagreed among themselves about the importance of being able to mount air strikes rapidly. Some like Richard (later Major General) Clutterbuck, doubted whether it was of any importance at all and argued later that 'quick air strikes, also indiscriminate bombing, became very unpopular towards the end'. Others contended that the army would have found rapid air strikes useful but that communications and regulations made this impossible and thus reduced the value of aerial operations.[19]

Press hand-outs distributed in January 1950 claimed that the RAF had carried out a record number of attacks during the month—fifty-eight attacks and 328 sorties.[20] In the first three months of the emergency ten attacks a month had been normal; now fourteen attacks a week were becoming possible. The diversity of aircraft involved was considerable. The same report said that Spitfires, Tempests, Brigands,

Beaufighters, Sunderlands and Harvards had been used. Tempests had been in service since 1943 and in 1949 No. 33 Squadron armed with Tempest IIs had been sent from Germany to Malaya. This was a particularly important development as the Tempest could carry rockets or 2,000 lb of bombs. The Brigand was originally designed as a torpedo aircraft and was then converted to the light bombing role, replacing the Beaufighters of No. 45 squadron in Malaya where the RAF found it one of the most effective strike aircraft.

The ubiquitous Sunderland Flying Boat had been in service since 1938 but these aircraft proved a very useful, if somewhat eccentric, addition to RAF strength in Malaya because of their ability to carry large numbers of 20 lb bombs. As one pilot recalled later,

> the standard practice was to fly along a race-track pattern at about 1,700 feet above ground level to run along or parallel to the longer axis of the target area, roughly once every ten minutes, dropping a 2,000-yard stick of sixteen bombs. This phase of the operation lasted for two hours. Despite their small size, the bombs made a very impressive bang and, having a proximity fuse, would explode just above the ground, or sometimes in the jungle canopy, hurling shrapnel over a very extensive area . . . On conclusion of the bombing phase we would descend, literally to tree-top level and, following the same flight pattern, make a series of strafing runs . . . for up to another hour. Consequently, the occupants of the target area suffered our attentions for the best part of three hours. I am not sure that our efforts actually caused any casualties. However, I understand that these prolonged attacks could be highly demoralizing.[21]

In March 1950 RAF Malaya was further strengthened with the arrival of Lincoln bombers—the RAF's replacement for the Lancaster—and four months later these were joined by Lincolns from the Royal Australian Air Force.

In terms of numbers and payload, 1950 was the high point of the campaign as far as the RAF was concerned. The outbreak of the Korean war meant that some aircraft were transferred from Malaya to Korea. Sunderlands, for example, spent one-third of their time in Korea and two-thirds in Malaya. Moreover by the mid-1950s the piston-engined aircraft, which were in Group Captain Slater's words 'uniquely suitable for ground operations in Malaya', were replaced by jets. Slater justified the change on the grounds that jets were essential for general war and that the RAF could not maintain two distinct air forces, one for insurgencies and one for a war in Europe. Thus Canberra, Vampire and Venom jets replaced the Hornets and other aircraft, even though their payload was smaller, their stalling speed was far higher and their ability to loiter above the target was less.[22]

By November 1950 the RAF believed that it had killed 126 guerrillas in air strikes and wounded thirty-six. Another 137 guerrillas might have been killed by these attacks, whilst 509 insurgents had been captured in operations in which the RAF had been involved.[23] However, in retrospect we can see that that year was the turning point in the British approach to counterguerrilla operations and that the new tactics were going to put less emphasis on the RAF's bombing capacity. Tactical change thus paralleled changes in technology. In 1950 Lieutenant General Sir Harold Briggs was appointed Director of Operations in Malaya, to counter the steadily worsening situation. It was Briggs who emphasized the importance of controlling the Chinese squatters living around the Malayan towns and villages, because they formed the main body of recruits for the insurgents. He stressed the vital need to fight with political and economic as well as military weapons and to place more weight on the police. He did not entirely dismiss the importance of air strikes but he felt—probably rightly—that their impact on guerrilla morale was more important than the destruction they wrought. In particular, he believed that only two aircraft were required in each attack because their moral effect would be the same as when a greater number was used.[24] The AOC, Air Vice Marshal Mellersh, described these views as 'frightful' and 'disastrous'.[25] RAF squadrons in Malaya believed that they were already short of aircraft because increasing numbers were being sent to Korea and many felt that Briggs' views would worsen this trend. Yet, within a year, the RAF itself seems to have accepted many of Briggs' conclusions and reduced its stress on offensive operations. Mellersh told a lecture audience in London in March 1951 that the RAF's tasks in Malaya, in order of importance, were 'air supply for the Ground Forces; offensive operations on targets beyond the reach and resources of the Ground Forces; and intercommunication'.[26] This sudden change must have been made far easier for the RAF by the advent of a conventional war in Korea which was much more to the Service's taste.

At this time the RAF experimented with one other role which has become extremely controversial—the attempt to destroy insurgents' food supplies by spraying them with chemicals. At first the guerrillas planted their crops in rows which distinguished them from those planted by aborigines and made them obvious to RAF reconnaissance aircraft. Soon, however, they realized this was a mistake and began to disguise them. They were in any case often living with the aborigines and it was therefore impossible to distinguish guerrillas' crops from those belonging to the simple jungle dwellers. Yet, for a time, the RAF attempted to poison their crops from the air. As A. J. Short, the historian of the war, wrote subsequently, 'the destruction of aborigine allotments from the air with chemical sprays was not very well received by the communities with upturned faces below who had spent months clearing and planting the hillsides'.[27] At first sodium arsenate was used; later ICI suggested that Fernoxone might be effective. But in the end a mixture of trioxene and diesolene was employed both to kill crops and to keep the ground infertile. Whirlwind helicopters of 155 Squadron carried out most of the spraying after Austers had located the plantations. In view of what we now know about the effect of some types of sprays on the health of those in their vicinity, it was fortunate that shortages of helicopters and the indeterminate nature of the results limited attacks of this sort. Instead SAS teams came to operate with the aborigines in the jungle and to win them over to the government side thus stopping them supplying the guerrillas with food. Such teams were often supplied either by helicopters or if a landing strip could be built, by Pioneer light aircraft, though Valettas also dropped provisions by parachute. The SAS found aircraft useful in other ways; for example, on one occasion aborigines were flown to Kuala Lumpur to show the falsity of insurgents' claims about the collapse of the government.

The RAF carried out a massive propaganda drive to persuade guerrillas to surrender. Immense numbers of leaflets—which were supposed to be proof against tropical rain—were dropped over jungle where guerrillas were operating and sometimes they were read with effect. In July 1952, for example, two guerrillas who surrendered in the Kuantan area said that they had been harassed by security forces 'and had made up their mind to surrender after reading leaflets giving information of recent security forces' successes'. Similarly Wei Keiong, the platoon commander in the Selongor area, who surrendered in November 1952, ascribed his decision both to radio broadcasts and surrender leaflets.[28] In October 1952, experiments began with Operation Loudhailer, to test whether loudspeakers could broadcast propaganda from aircraft flying over the jungle. All sorts of problems developed. Coils burnt out and the noise of the aircraft sometimes spoiled the effect. Malayan was a more difficult language for broadcasting than Chinese or English because of its high pitched notes.[29] In the end, however, the technical problems were sorted out and recorded female voices proved the most effective. Valetta, Dakota or Auster aircraft with large loudspeakers slung underneath would be flown as slowly as possible at 1,000–2,000 feet. Wei Kong suggested that loud-speakers would be a great advance since guerrillas were forbidden by their commanders to read leaflets. During the tests themselves one guerrilla section commander, Wong Lo, surrendered as a result of the information he had been given.[30] Some 70 per cent of the guerrillas who surrendered said that their decision to do so had been influenced by the 'sky-shouters'.

Experiments were also made in 1952 with dropping SAS paratroops from a Valetta into jungle areas. At first no casualties were suffered but, given the nature of the terrain, the problems were obvious. Further experiments led to four SAS men landing in undergrowth, two of whom needed assistance to get out of their harness. Experience showed that about half of the troops dropped in any operation would in fact become caught in the trees and they were supplied with 250 feet of nylon webbing so that they could lower themselves to the ground. In July 1954, paratroops were used in Operation Termite in the Perak area. The RAF attacked guerrilla camps and the SAS then followed up the operation by parachuting into the jungle. The RAF kept them supplied by parachuting provisions into the area and evacuated casualties by helicopter. Casualties remained high and, according to one study of the SAS, 'the accumulation of casualties from this type of parachuting was such that no training jumps were permitted'.[31]

Thus apart from broadcasting and bombing, the RAF was also play-ing a key role keeping ground troops supplied. For example in Oper-ation Lemon in September 1949, Scots Guards, Suffolks and Jungle Police operated in the jungle for a month trying to track down Chan Sam Min and his band of 150 insurgents.[32] To feed the troops Dakotas dropped 89,345 lb of rations in twenty-eight sorties. Austers were also used for reconnaissance and Harvards and Beaufighters carried out strikes on suspected guerrilla positions. The following month the RAF was asking for three more Dakotas to keep supplies in the country flowing; existing transport aircraft were overstretched by Operation Watershed in the Sungei area, where 120 police operated in the jungle for two weeks while being supplied from the air. During 1950 alone the RAF dropped three-and-a-half million lb of supplies to such groups and by 1951 had parachuted down six million lb of supplies in 4,000 drops.[33] Furthermore, when the guerrillas withdrew deeper into the jungle in 1953, the need to keep their pursuers supplied increased.[34] The main problem with supply drops to troops in the jungle was that they gave away their presence. Thus according to one officer, 'there were regiments, especially Gurkha regiments, who had very high kill records. Their success was due to not taking as many air drops.'[35]

A development took place in May 1950, which was to have really momentous effects in the long run, when a casualty evacuation [Case-Vac] squadron was established with three Dragonfly aircraft. Based on the Sikorsky S-51, these were the first British-built helicopters to see service with the RAF. Over the next four years S-51s were to lift out 675 wounded or sick men from jungle clearings, to transport 4,000 passengers and 84,000 lb of supplies and to carry out nearly 6,000 sorties.[36] On one occasion in March 1952 a Dragonfly operated for ten hours with the same pilot in order to evacute sixteen Cameronians from a swamp.

The Bristol Sycamore, which began to replace the Dragonfly in 1955, was more serviceable and more effective though still under-powered and very difficult to fly in Malaya. As one officer wrote later, 'flying the Sycamores over the jungle was a real challenge mainly because of its limited power margin. The sheer hard work of moving the controls and the vibration of the aircraft made every hour worth five on a more modern helicopter.' During the campaign RAF Sycamores pioneered night flying operations and parachute dropping by rotary-winged air-craft. Casualty evacuation and parachute dropping by rotary-winged aircraft. Casualty evacuation was particularly helpful in the jungle where wounds could soon fester and the knowledge that soldiers could be lifted out quickly was very important for morale. It also enabled patrols to continue with their tasks rather than leave the jungle with the casualty. Of course, the helicopter force was tiny compared with what was to come, it was beset with constant mechanical problems and grossly overworked. As a result some wanted to base the helicopters in Singapore where servicing was easy. But this was too far from the battle and eventually all helicopters had to be based at Kuala Lumpur. Another problem for the helicopters was finding somewhere to land in the jungle. Sometimes clearings were simply hacked out of the forest though even the stumps of trees could cause damage. On other occasions river banks could be used or casualties could be winched up to the hovering aircraft.

When GHQ in the Far East first called, on 8 March 1949, for heli-copters to evacuate casualties, the RAF thought they would be too expensive.[37] Some RAF officers also argued that Austers had greater range and were likely to be more useful. Certainly light aircraft in general, and the Austers and Pembrokes in particular, played a very important part in evacuating casualties and transporting officers but there were many parts of the country where they could not land. Thus the army warned that certain operations would have to be cancelled if casualty evacuation were not possible and it was clear that it would take over this role if the RAF did not respond. Once the RAF had agreed to army demands, the main problem was to decide which sort of helicopter to procure. The issue was complicated because Fairey was developing an aircraft called the Gyrodyne which it claimed would be more suitable than American models. However, just as the army had decided that these would be ideal, the first prototype crashed and orders for the Dragonfly were rushed through, with strong backing from the government.[38] There was also bottleneck in the training of pilots which kept helicopter numbers down.

As in most future wars in which Britain was to be involved, helicopters were thus always in short supply. The Americans agreed to release ten S-55s and 848 Squadron of the Fleet Air Arm operated them in Malaya. These proved more effective than the heavy British copy of the same aircraft, the Whirlwind.[39] In theory the Whirlwind could carry ten passengers and a crew of two; in fact five armed soldiers was about the limit. One army officer noted before a discussion with General Templer (who was both High Commissioner and Director of Operations in Malaya from 1952 to 1954), 'you will know that the ten naval S-55s have completely revolutionized the conduct of operations in Malaya but more are needed and I would suggest that, if possible, the RAF should be persuaded to provide Malaya with more'.[40] Templer's general comment was that he wanted larger helicopters more quickly. One officer later suggested that 'without the very small force of helicopters we had in Malaya, four times as many ground forces would have been required'.[41] By 1955, 20,000 helicopter sorties had been carried out though, even two years later, there were still only twenty-six medium and fourteen light helicopters in the theatre.

As we have seen, by 1951 the RAF regarded photographic reconnaissance as its second most important role in unconventional warfare. Many of the available maps of Malaya were too old and on too large a scale: 'Rivers are frequently found to have changed their course, many of the smaller features are either grossly misplaced or entirely omitted and there still remain areas . . . which appear quite simply on the maps as "unexplored".'[42] Thus by 1951 the Army Photographic Interpretation Section in Kuala Lumpur had prepared maps covering 4,000 square miles from photographs taken from the air. Eighty thousand prints were made each month, despite the difficulties caused by the prevalent mist, and most crews of strike aircraft carried photographs to assist target identification. By the mid-1950s photographic reconnaissance was carried out mainly by Pembrokes, Meteors and Canberras. Tactical reconnaissance was performed by the Austers of 656 Squadron which had proved themselves so useful that some thirty-four aircraft were organized in five flights.[43]

Gradually the guerrillas were worn down by the terrible strain of living in the jungle and by the political and military measures begun by General Briggs and continued under Templer. In 1950 the government claimed that 650 guerrillas had been killed and this figure mounted to 1,100 the following year. Many surrendered because of the successes of the security forces and shortage of food.[44] By 1955 the number of guerrillas fighting the government had thus dropped from 8,000 to 3,000. Chin Peng, the guerrilla leader, offered to make terms but the negotiations failed. The number of surrenders continued to mount although it was not until 1960 that the war was effectively over, with no civilians or police killed.[45] Historians are agreed that the main reasons for the government's success were that many of the 500,000 Chinese squatters, who had been their main supporters, were moved to new 'model' villages where they had title to the land. They were thus cut off from the guerrillas and could not easily supply them with food. The government also concentrated on increasing its intelligence about the guerrillas and closely co-ordinated police and military operations.

Many of the histories of the Malayan insurgency were written during or soon after the US involvement in Vietnam and were strongly influenced by that conflict. Thus they tended to play down the importance of air power in guerrilla wars because it had not saved the Americans from defeat. Anthony Short wrote: 'Negatively perhaps the most important decision, *faute de mieux*, was that there would be no reliance on the illusions of air power; from the beginning to end military power had to go on foot.'[46]

Yet in 1956 alone 25,700 troops were lifted by helicopter, most movement was still by foot but air transport played its part and was to have an increasingly constructive role in anti-guerrilla operations as the years passed. In their history of air power, Air Vice Marshals Armitage and Mason noted:

> a total of 35,000 tons of bombs was dropped during the course of 4,067 air strikes . . . In terms of firepower delivered by air on to

terrorist targets . . . the meagre results were out of all proportion to the extensive effort engaged.[47]

They go on to quote Clutterbuck's conclusion that 'except for occasional successes with precision bombing, offensive air strikes were almost wholly unsuccessful in Malaya; they probably did more harm than good'.[48] Certainly accurate attacks were most effective as RAF Lincolns and RAF Canberras proved early in 1956, when they destroyed a guerrilla camp in Johore.[49] But even less accurate bombing raids could have a considerable effect on guerrilla morale as evidence from surrendered insurgents makes clear. The most that can be said with certainty is that aircraft only played a supporting rather than a central role as they had in the 1930s; nor did RAF want them to do more because the Air Staff was more concerned with re-equipping with jets for general war than with countering insurgencies.

Out of Malaya came the British view of anti-guerrilla operations as primarily dependent on politics—winning over the mass of the people, physically separating them from the insurgents and cutting off guerrilla supplies. But the guerrillas had also to be hunted down and the air force could support the army in such operations both by bringing in reinforcements and supplies and by helping to map the jungle. In Malaya aircraft harassed guerrillas when they could not be attacked by ground forces and assisted such forces when they were operating. Logistics came to depend more and more upon aircraft because of the difficulties of the jungle terrain. The air attacks and propaganda spread by aircraft undoubtedly effected guerrilla morale and increased the number of guerrillas who surrendered. But above all the use of helicopters for moving troops and evacuating casualties had shown the way operations were to develop in the future.

The Mau Mau Insurgency

Air power was just one of the many factors which enabled the British to defeat the Mau Mau insurgents in Kenya in the 1950s. The weakness of the guerrillas was as important as the strength of the colonialists. Mau Mau's greatest asset lay in the extent of its support amongst the Kikuyu tribe but it did not have any foreign help and thus the number of guerrillas was partly determined by the weapons available. The British were able to separate the mass of Kikuyu from the active guerrillas by moving people into new villages. They also destroyed the guerrillas' base in Nairobi, pursued them relentlessly in the forests of Mount

Kenya and the Aberdare mountains and harassed their supporters. It was in these operations that air power could play a part by bombing the insurgents, thereby lowering their morale, by supplying the ground troops and by distributing government propaganda. Of all the weapons used against the guerrillas, bombs were in fact what they feared most.

The Mau Mau revolt broke out in Kenya early in 1952. It was caused primarily by the growing frustration of the Kikuyu who made up 20 per cent of the five million Africans.[1] Their numbers had been increasing and they wanted to recover the land which they had abandoned and which had been appropriated at the beginning of the century. At that time their population had been decimated by disease, famine and drought, and the land which they evacuated was taken over by European settlers. Thus, in order to recover their land, some Kikuyu felt they had to expel the colonialists. The Kikuyu had set up a number of nationalist organizations in the inter-war period and in 1947 Jomo Kenyatta headed a new one, the Kenya African Union (KAU). The British regarded this as the political wing of the Mau Mau guerrilla movement when the rebellion broke out in 1952.[2] Trouble had been expected by the British for some years. In 1948 and 1949 RAF aircraft dropped leaflets putting the government point of view to the Kikuyu and in March 1950 the army was already preparing measures to deal with 'acts of violence or sabotage' and to liaise with the police in the event of an emergency.[3]

By 1952 the Mau Mau guerrilla movement had firmly embedded itself into Kikuyu society. Many of its leaders, including General China, had served with the King's African Rifles and thus had military training. They felt that they had not been adequately recompensed for the efforts they had made in the Second World War. Mau Mau activists persuaded or compelled people to swear oaths of loyalty to the organization and the government believed that 90 per cent of the Kikuyu had taken the first (and least extreme) of these oaths.[4] Mau Mau maimed or killed many Africans who refused to co-operate and boycotted the businesses of others. One particularly good measure of their success was the dramatic decrease in the number of Kikuyu attending Christian churches which the Mau Mau leaders regarded as a symbol of colonial power.[5] The government concluded that only one per cent of the Kikuyu was genuinely and fully on its side though many were against the methods rather than the aims of the insurgents. Mau Mau propagandists tried to spread the campaign to other tribes such as the Embu and Meru, though with only moderate success.[6] The movement also suffered from a divided leadership and the inability of its most charis-

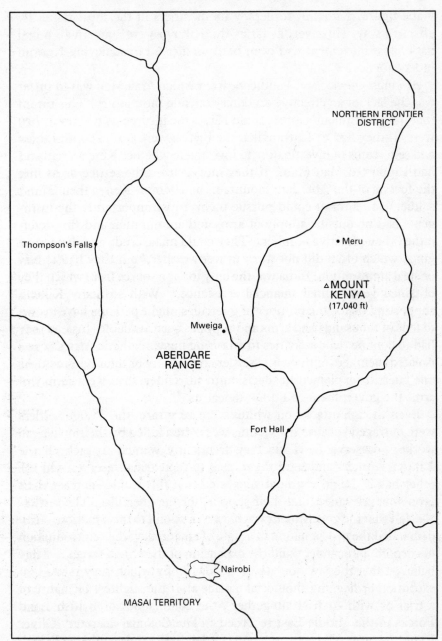

The Mau Mau Rising in Kenya 1952 - 1960

matic figure, Kimathi, to deploy its members in the most militarily effective way. However, as far as the Kikuyu were concerned, a real nationalist movement had been born, dedicated to achieving Kenyan independence.[7]

Amongst the decisive handicaps from which Mau Mau was to suffer was the lack of an effective sanctuary outside the country. This meant that the government's forces could harass the insurgents wherever they were. If they fled to Tanganyika, the British were also in control there and sent teams of investigators to investigate whether Kenyan refugees had supported Mau Mau.[8] If they moved from the settled areas into the forests of the Aberdare mountains and Mount Kenya then British soldiers and aircraft could pursue them. Most importantly the insurgents had no outside supply of arms and ammunition and this determined their effective numbers. They could make crude and dangerous guns, which often did not work in wet weather,[9] but they had to buy or steal ammunition. India was the only foreign source from which they obtained very limited financial assistance.[10] With so many Kikuyu supporting them, the number of guerrillas might perhaps have grown to tens of thousands had arms and supplies been available. Instead they had to confine their activities to attacking unsympathetic Africans and isolated members of the white settler community or their livestock. As one guerrilla explained his decision to surrender, 'had we a supply of arms the government could not defeat us'.[11]

Even though attacks on whites were very rare, the 55,000 settlers were outraged because the victims were often killed by their own farm workers or servants. Thus they frequently wanted to sack all the Kikuyu workers and send them back to their tribal reserves. On the other hand, the government suggested that this would increase their economic grievances and their support for the guerrillas. The settlers also felt that the government was slow to respond to the situation. They demanded the proclamation of a state of emergency, the reintroduction of corporal punishment and the expansion of the armed forces.[12] They believed that the law operated too slowly, 'by which they mean that execution or flogging should take place after the slightest formality of a trial or without trial altogether', the commander of British Land Forces in the Middle East recorded.[13] The Colonial Secretary Oliver Lyttelton was reluctant to grant settlers' demands and the British armed forces were under pressure in so many parts of the world that the government was unwilling to commit more troops to Kenya than was absolutely necessary.[14]

After the murder of one of the key loyalist chiefs, the British declared a state of emergency in October 1952. One hundred and fifty-eight of those suspected of organizing Mau Mau, including Jomo Kenyatta, were detained. The First Lancashire Fusiliers flew into Kenya in RAF Hastings and Valetta aircraft. The British believed that the Kikuyu were surprised by the sudden response and noted that the young men had disappeared from many of the villages. In some ways the army was disappointed by this: 'If they had assembled in force and been disorderly we could have hit them . . . as it is we have not yet had the opportunity to use the government's strength and to demonstrate that the government is much more feared than Mau Mau.'[15] Yet we now know that many joined the guerrillas out of fear of the government's measures.[16] The assassination of loyal Africans continued and so did the build-up of British forces; the Lancashire Fusiliers were followed in 1953 by battalions of the Buffs and Devons and later still by battalions of the Royal Northumberland and Royal Inniskilling Fusiliers. General Sir George Erskine was appointed in June 1953 to command all British forces in the area, including police and home guards.

As in all insurgencies, those opposed to the government could be divided into active rebels and the far larger group of passive supporters who supplied the rebels with food and information. In the countryside the government dealt with the second group by concentrating the people in villages. They took note of what had happened in Malaya and tried to improve on that pattern of resettlement. In particular they knew that some of the Malayan villages had been built with insufficient forethought in areas where there were inadequate water supplies or alternatively where they were flooded in the monsoon.[17] In Kenya the government built about 200,000 huts over a matter of months in 800 new collective villages, even though the Kikuyu were very reluctant to move to them because they contrasted so sharply with their normal pattern of living. As Erskine noted, 'the movement into villages was against all Kikuyu habits but the improvement in security which it provided and the increase in control which it gave the government enabled us to overcome opposition'.[18]

Government officers also liked to feel that the programme was in the long term interests of the villagers: 'Austere and squalid to start with, these villages rapidly improved as schools, churches, first aid centres and sports grounds were added. This revolution is one which may have lasting and beneficial results and a civilizing influence over the whole tribe.'[19] Many Kikuyu, by contrast, believed that those in the new villages and camps lived practically at starvation level. On the other hand, the government's measures did damage the guerrilla movement.

The insurgents had to leave the forests to find maize in the fields, where they were often ambushed by government forces. As one guerrilla recorded, 'in most cases our warriors met death while looking for food rather than in battlefields'.[20] The Mau Mau also had to expend scarce ammunition killing animals, many of which, like elephants, they would not normally have eaten.

The insurgents and their supporters were initially firmly entrenched in the capital, Nairobi, which 'was their main arsenal for supplies of arms, ammunition, clothing, money and recruits'. Some 30,000 Kikuyu had migrated to the city during the war, joining the 34,000 already there. Amongst these the government believed there were 300–400 insurgents who killed about two people each day. General Erskine put forward two plans to break their hold. The more drastic option was simply to remove all Kikuyu from the city and send them back to their tribal reservations where economic conditions were already hard. Their jobs would then have been given to members of other tribes and their economic situation would have deteriorated dramatically. The second, less drastic, plan was to divide the city into different areas and to search one area at a time, examining all Kikuyu to find out whether they had legitimate reasons for being in the city. Those who had not would be interned or deported to their reservations. In the event the plan chosen was close to Erskine's second option which he believed the least attractive of the two.[21] After the city had been divided into sections, 25,000 police and soldiers swept into it in April 1954 and began interning and interrogating the Kikuyu. By 8 May, 30,000 had been interrogated and half of these were interned. The guerrillas' presence in the city was never restored after these drastic measures which represented perhaps the only example of a British success against urban guerrillas in all their postwar operations.[22]

Erskine presided over a great increase in the size of the police and home guard forces which gave static protection to the population. He wanted to free the army and RAF from this duty and to use them in an offensive campaign against the insurgents. He created three striking forces, one made up of 39 Infantry Brigade and the Kenya Regiment, the second made up of the East African Armoured Car Squadron and a dismounted element, and the third made up of the air forces.[23] No. 39 Brigade and the RAF operated in mountainous and thickly forested areas near Mount Kenya and in the Aberdares. The government declared 820 sq. miles around the Aberdares and 780 sq. miles around Mount Kenya prohibited areas, where the security forces could attack anyone in sight. At first the army tried to move across the zones in lines of 'beaters', hoping to drive the insurgents before them. But this proved ineffective and instead small groups of soldiers began to operate in particular areas of jungle for long periods. Paths were driven deep into the forests so that camps could be established there and everything possible was done to make life difficult for the guerrillas.[24]

Aircraft had an important supporting role in these operations. Local pilots sometimes used their own aircraft to assist the government and, because of their knowledge of the terrain, this help was invaluable. The Police Reserve Air Wing, commanded by a retired RAF officer, gradually developed out of these *ad hoc* arrangements under the pressure of war. Originally it had only one Auster but by November 1954 it had ten Piper Pacers and a Cessna. The number of pilots involved grew to seventeen full-time and eight part-time. The Pipers were very useful to them because they could carry 300 lb of freight, fly for up to six hours and drop supplies at over 10,000 feet. The more powerful Cessna could fly even higher. Many of the aircraft were based at Mweiga, a 1,200-yard strip which was some 6,200 feet up in the Aberdare mountains. Piper Pacers and Cessnas carried out reconnaissance, maintained contact with ground patrols and dropped supplies to troops operating in small groups who did not need large supply drops. They were even given light weapons and achieved one of the first successes against the insurgents. According to Kimathi, one of the pilots saw smoke and 'dropped several grenades in the camp amidst the people. Nine were killed and eighteen injured. We then hid the smoke by day and fire by night.'[25] Kimathi went on to say that for some months afterwards aircraft had been ineffective. However they had some considerable impact if they simply prevented the guerillas lighting fires, because the cold was often intense in the mountains.

In March 1953 the government forces received reinforcements in the shape of a flight of the ubiquitous Harvards. These particular ones had been used for training in Rhodesia. Subsequently seventeen Harvards were maintained by the RAF in Kenya, two were usually being serviced and four were in reserve. They were armed with a gun and carried 450 rounds of ammunition. They also had bomb racks so that they could carry eight 19 lb bombs under the wings to attack the insurgents, whilst the Pipers and others concentrated on reconnaissance. In this their pilots' knowledge of the terrain was a great advantage and, if they had located a guerrilla camp which they could not destroy on their own, they could summon the Harvards to attack it. Many of the Kenyan forests were between 5,000 and 15,000 feet above sea level and this created special problems for the small aircraft which were constantly buffeted by the air currents. Often their sorties had to be flown at night, adding to the pilots' work load.[26]

It was the Harvards which achieved the next success for air power when they spotted a large guerrilla meeting just before it was about to break up. As one of the insurgents recalled, 'to my surprise I saw six Harvard bombers from Mweiga airdrome aviating directly to our camp . . . The airplanes started dropping bombs at the guards camp about a mile away.' Some fell within 100 yards of where he was lying and 'caused a horrible death hooting noise, earth tremors and much fear'. The Harvards left after devastating the huts but injured only one person.[27] This was in fact typical; their moral effect was often much greater than physical. On a later occasion Harvards spotted the clothes which some girl guerrillas had spread out to dry. Four guerrillas were injured and two of these were killed subsequently when they were pursued by ground forces.[28] Such ground and air attacks undermined insurgent morale and forced many to flee.[29]

Limited servicing facilities and the difficult conditions in the mountainous areas of the country contributed to the Kenyan authorities' surprisingly slow demand for helicopters. The Chiefs of Staff were planning to send two helicopters to Kenya by Bristol Freighter aircraft soon after the beginning of the emergency in November 1952. However in January 1953 the Governor said that the servicing difficulties in Kenya made it not worth sending in helicopters.[30] The situation did not change, despite pressure from the Prime Minister, Winston Churchill, himself to use rotary-winged aircraft to scare Mau Mau. There were further discussions about using the aircraft to evacuate casualties from the Aberdares in August 1953 but it was not until October 1954 that any helicopters actually arrived.[31] Then they began to evacuate casualties from the forest areas—two of the first to be brought out had been seriously injured by rhinoceros which were often more of a menace than the guerrillas. The main problems encountered by the helicopters were caused by the high temperatures and the height at which they had to operate. These meant that engine revolutions had to be kept higher than normal, that smaller loads could be carried and that casualties could not be winched aboard.

RAF Lincoln bombers from, successively, Nos. 49, 100, 61 and 214 Squadrons joined in the campaign from 1953 onwards and attacked the insurgents hidden in the forests. Initially two aircraft were deployed to the Eastleigh airbase but by the end of 1953 the number had been stepped up to six. The Lincolns had radar guidance and could keep the insurgents awake by bombing during the night. They could drop five 1,000 lb bombs or nine 500 lb weapons and used both their forward and rear turrets for strafing. During one peak period in September 1954, 214 Squadron carried out 159 day and seventeen night sorties and dropped over two thousand 500 lb bombs. The Piper Pacers usually marked the targets beforehand. Erskine felt that these attacks were useful even though it was difficult to show concrete results.

> In circumstances of this kind you have to be satisfied with indirect results such as an increase in surrenders, a drop in Mau Mau morale, prisoners' reports and similar evidence. It is seldom that you can expect actual casualties immediately after an attack. I am convinced that the air effort prepared the way for ground action.[32]

However the lack of visible results encouraged grumbling amongst the white settlers about the cost to the colony of aircraft operations.

The Lincoln's large bombs certainly had a much greater impact on guerrilla morale than the smaller ones of the Harvards. At first the Mau Mau simply imagined that the large aircraft 'with a protruding navel' were transports, then their bombs began to fall. 'Some thought that the airplane had crashed down upon us, others thought that this was the atomic bomb they had heard of . . . fear and the airplanes' speed did not give us time to think.'[33] When the aircraft left, the guerrillas found the bomb holes were twenty yards in diameter and thirty feet deep. Such attacks altered the insurgents' behaviour. Previously they had often left the forests to spend two days in the reserves; fear of the Lincolns made them extend these periods away to a week, even though this increased the risks of capture by the security forces.[34] Many gave up the struggle altogether, despite the fact that casualties were few. After one raid 'seven fighters . . . shouted goodbye to us swearing they would never again enter the forest and wishing to die in the reserve exchanging gunfire with the enemy rather than to endure the unassailable Lincoln bombers'. Similarly, after his capture, General China said the bombing was the most feared of government weapons.[35]

In Britain bombing had, however, become a very sensitive political issue. When the Air Staff considered the possibility of dropping 4,000 lb bombs from the Lincolns, the Colonial Office warned that there would be strong public objections.[36] In retrospect this seems very surprising since most of the public would not have known the difference between the two types of weapons, but it reflected official concerns. Operations outside the prohibited areas were also tightly controlled for the same reasons. Harvards and other small aircraft could drop 19 lb bombs in unpopulated parts of the reservations but they were not permitted to strafe and they were only supposed to drop bombs when they had air controllers on the ground. In fact these rules were breached on at least one occasion, though the goverment was very worried that news of this might reach the press.[37]

Photographic reconnaissance by Meteor and Canberra jets could sometimes help locate the enemy and assess the effect of attacks. Between August 1954 and May 1955 a quarter of a million photographic prints were produced. As General Erskine reported, 'from photographic reconnaissance resources we were able to identify terrorist hides in the forests and, with two radar stations established, the RAF was able to carry out accurate bombing in all weathers and by day or night over a wide area'.[38] Though the degree of accuracy actually obtained was probably less than this suggests, bombing did have an impact. The RAF helped the April 1954 operations in Nairobi by harrying the insurgents in the countryside with an intensive bombing campaign so that troops could be released to help in the urban struggle. Air and ground operations were co-ordinated by a Joint Operations Centre in Nairobi. For example, this arranged for ground forces to be removed from some sections of the Aberdare forest from August to December 1954 so that the Lincolns could bomb unhindered. In 1954 alone the Lincolns flew 1,118 sorties, the Harvards 3,316 and the aircraft of the Police Reserve flew 1,309.[39]

The government had to tread very carefully over bombing because it was itself 'bombarded' by parliamentary questions and by press reports suggesting that its forces were committing atrocities. It was determined that air actions should not add to these outcries. General Erskine admitted in 1955 that the security forces had used excessive pressure to gain information from captives and that he had tried to put a stop to this.[40] There were parliamentary protests against the 'collective punishment' of villages and widespread concerns about conditions in the various huge internment camps. The Christian Church helped to act as a brake on some of the excesses as missionaries published accounts of torture in the press, and these were taken up by Parliament.[41] But probably most of the outrages were committed by the African forces used by the government, whose capacity to deal with these was limited because in the early stages of the war it could only release soldiers for offensive operations by relying on African guards. Later on it wanted such guards to replace British forces in Kenya completely. Thus General Erskine was extremely concerned in January 1955 that morale amongst these forces would simply collapse if large numbers were prosecuted for torture or murder. In the event those involved were given an amnesty at the same time as one was offered to the insurgents.[42]

The guerrillas were already under increased pressure by the end of 1954 and had been forced to operate in smaller groups. Thus the air attacks on Mau Mau targets were gradually reduced. By May 1955 General Lathbury succeeded Erskine and he felt that all the Lincolns should be withdrawn.[43] The RAF was opposed to this as it believed that the insurgents were 'on the run' and that bombing in the prohibited areas prevented the guerrillas sleeping and lowered their morale. Some felt that 'Lathbury may have been swayed by the anti-air element who were kept in place by General Erskine. Also that he may not yet have had time to appreciate the limitations of the soldier in the forest.'[44] There was probably something in this explanation. Lathbury does appear to have been less impressed by air action than his predecessor and to have put greater emphasis on using surrendered insurgents against their former comrades. But the situation was also changing. In the autumn of 1955 the Harvards were released and the Police Reserve Force was deprived of all its offensive armament.

While this was happening, the Kenyan goverment was trying to find further 'sky shouting aircraft' to encourage even more Mau Mau to abandon the campaign. These had already been used extensively. The two Austers involved in this work had flown 138 sorties in 1954 and Pembrokes had also been employed. Now Lathbury thought the time ripe to extend the effort. However the Air Ministry said that it would take four months to convert aircraft held in store and the forces in Malaya claimed they wanted more rather than less aircraft of this sort and could spare none for Kenya.[45] The Kenyan shortage itself is surprising as it was easy to convert a Pembroke aircraft for this role by replacing its rear door with four Tannoy loudspeakers. How effective any further aircraft would have been is unclear since we now know that some of the insurgents tended to dismiss government calls for their surrender as a sign of weakness and this limited the impact of early efforts at 'sky shouting'.[46]

Nevertheless, as the insurgents were worn down, such appeals became more effective. In January 1955 the government had offered favourable surrender terms to the guerrillas, despite the opposition of the settler community,[47] and within six months nearly 1,000 had taken advantage of this. In November 1956 the army gave up operational command to the police but the state of emergency was not officially ended until January 1960. In all this the effort by the RAF and the volunteer pilots had been essentially supplementary to political measures and to ground action, though important for all that. They had supplied troops in the jungle and carried out reconnaissance in support. They had also harried the insurgents with bombs and propaganda and they had brought in reinforcements as these were demanded.

The insurgents had shown more originality than the British in the campaign. Their attempts to impose Mau Mau oaths of loyalty were certainly original though their campaign was undermined by organizational weaknesses and shortage of arms. On the British side the effort and originality employed was not comparable to the exertions made in Malaya. Most of the administrative and military techniques used— relocation of Africans into new villages, issuing of identity cards, use of surrendered or captured Mau Mau to attack the insurgents or to demoralize them by propaganda,[48] construction of physical barriers to hinder the flow of food to the insurgents, emphasis on intelligence— had already been tried in that theatre. As far as aircraft were concerned, two aspects stand out. First, the aircraft involved were strikingly different from those needed for a European conflict; Harvards, Pipers, Cessnas and obsolete Lincolns bore the brunt of the campaign. Seven Harvards, three Pipers and four Lincolns crashed, whilst some Lincolns were destroyed on the ground possibly by sabotage. Few jets were involved, while helicopters arrived late and were only used on a very limited scale. Secondly, the political sensitivity of bombing and strafing was underlined. The government simply could not afford suggestions that it was employing excessive force to defeat the insurgents or killing innocent civilians in air attacks.

The French Experience in Indochina

Whilst the RAF was struggling to make the best use of its aircraft in guerrilla warfare in Greece, Malaya and Kenya, the French armed forces were fighting insurgencies in Indochina and Algeria from 1946 to 1961. In both cases they faced far larger and more powerful groups of insurgents than those the British had to deal with and, partly as a result, they developed very different tactics. In Malaya, air power became increasingly the handmaiden of the army but in the French wars the process was almost exactly reversed. Despite the difficulty of finding the guerrillas in the jungle and the short range and unreliability of the aircraft available, assistance from aircraft was the only way the French found of saving ground columns from destruction in Indochina. It was also the most effective way of hunting down and breaking up groups of guerrillas in Algeria.

For much of the Second World War the French continued to administer Indochina even though France had been defeated in 1940 and the Japanese dominated the area. However in March 1945, in a last effort to humiliate the Europeans, the Japanese took direct control and killed or imprisoned the French soldiers and administrators. In the meantime the Vietnamese Communists and nationalists, led by Ho Chi Minh and encouraged by the United States, had begun to wage a guerrilla campaign against the Japanese.[1] When the war suddenly ended after the atomic bombing of Nagasaki, Ho Chi Minh proclaimed Vietnam's Independence and established a Vietminh government in Hanoi. There was then a hiatus before the Nationalist Chinese took over the northern part of the country and the British occupied Saigon. Subsequently the Chinese co-existed with Ho Chi Minh's government, whilst the British tried to maintain order in the southern part of the country before handing it back to the French troops who arrived in force in October 1945 under General Leclerc.[2]

From March to September 1946 the French and the Vietminh attempted to negotiate a compromise which would allow each of them some control over Indochina. However the talks broke down, the war started in earnest with Vietminh attacks on the French in December 1946 and it was not until February of the following year that the French had gained control of Hanoi. The Vietminh fell back into the jungle but they had established a firm hold over many of the villages and could stage guerrilla attacks wherever they chose. The French controlled the towns and could use some of the roads in the daytime but they could not destroy the insurgents. No French government was willing or strong enough to abandon the struggle, yet it was never fought with as much determination as the Algerian war would be later; by 1949, for example, they had only 150,000 regular troops in Indochina, compared with over half a million men in Algeria in the 1950s.

The situation seriously worsened from the French point of view when China was conquered by Mao Tse-tung in 1948–49. The Vietminh were then able to cross the frontier to refit, rearm and train their forces. In 1950 Ho Chi Minh and his military commander, Giap, were ready to seize the initiative. They fell upon the French bases at Cao Bang and elsewhere along Colonial Road 4 on the frontier with China and destroyed them one after another in October 1950.[3] Of the 10,000 troops who had been stationed on the frontier, 6,000 had been lost together with thirteen guns, 125 mortars and a mass of lighter weapons. The most distinguished French General, de Lattre de Tassigny, went to Indochina to save the situation. Subsequently, the Vietminh tried to seize the road from the Tonkin Delta to the Chinese frontier and to advance towards Hanoi and Haiphong. The French rebuffed these attacks in 1951 but only at the expense of straining their resources and stripping towns and villages of their protection.

De Lattre de Tassigny restored French morale but he thought in terms of conventional warfare and saddled the population with an immense chain of blockhouses manned by 80,000 troops. This was supposed to protect the Red River Delta, although the insurgents were easily able to circumvent it.[4] After de Lattre de Tassigny's departure in December 1951, General Salan had to withdraw forces from Hoa Binh, the last outpost seized, because it was drawing in too many reserves, although Salan had no better ideas for winning the war. The last French commander, General Navarre, tried to protect Laos and to lure the insurgents into a trap by occupying the valley of Dien Bien Phu near the Laotian frontier in November 1953. He believed that he had enough transport aircraft to keep the valley supplied and enough artillery and bombers to destroy any Vietminh who attacked the base. Both calculations proved completely incorrect; the siege began in March 1954 and Dien Bien Phu fell with the loss of 12,000 French troops fifty-six days later.[5] The surrender led to the end of the first Indochina war, the French withdrawal from the area and the establishment of a Communist state north of the 17th Parallel.

In 1946 the French Air Force was still recovering from the Second World War and it was equipped with only a few obsolete aircraft. In Indochina it set up tactical air headquarters in Saigon, Hue and Hanoi. It was handicapped by the torrential rain in the region from May to September and by the jungle which covered most of the countryside. It had between 46–60 Spitfires, 63 King Cobras, 35 Ju 52 transports and 20 C47 Dakotas.[6] To these the French navy could add only eight Catalinas and nine Sea Otters for reconnaissance, though later it tried to keep two carriers with their strike aircraft off the coast at any one time. Not all the aircraft available were very suitable; Bernard Fall, the French historian of the war, argues that the Spitfires rotted in the jungle.[7] The French Air Force inventory improved greatly as US aid grew from June 1950 onwards. In August 1950 a US mission under General Brick was established in Vietnam and two months later the US sent forty F6F Hellcats by Carrier to replace the ageing Spitfires. The French wanted more King Cobras with their 37 mm cannons but the US had no spares for these and instead it sent F8F Bearcats in February–March 1951, five RB26 reconnaissance aircraft in the following July and twenty-six B26 bombers in December.[8] The US loaned the French navy a carrier, the *Belleau Woods* and the naval Corsairs, Hellcats and Bearcats contributed to the French air effort in the later stages of the war. The navy also used Catalina flying boats to try to prevent junks running supplies to groups of Vietminh near the coast.

US assistance was delayed by the effort being made to win the war in Korea but Washington nevertheless sent twenty C47 Dakotas in 1952, a further twenty-seven the following year and later some more modern C119 Boxcar transports. To keep the aircraft flying, which the French found increasingly difficult, the US also sent American technicians to Vietnam in January 1953.[9] In any case the French took greater risks with their aircraft than the Americans would have done. They removed the rear doors from the Boxcars to make supply dropping easier and they frequently finished tying down the load when the aircraft was taxiing to take off. Because of US support, the French were able to push their sortie rate up from about 450 a week in 1950 to 930 in 1951. In that year they flew 85,000 hours of operations, 22,000 of these on ground attack sorties, 9,000 on bombing raids, 16,000 on reconnaissance, 27,000 on transport and 11,000 on liaison duties.[10] In 1949 the French dropped 834 tons of bombs; in the first seven months of 1954 alone they dropped 12,800 tons. General de Lattre de Tassigny claimed in July 1951 that US aircraft and napalm had arrived just in time to save the French position. The French High Command regarded napalm as particularly effective in the jungle compared with bombing or strafing, though Bernard Fall questioned this judgement.[11]

Despite the limited number of aircraft available at the start of the war and the great difficulty of locating guerrillas except when they operated in large concentrations, the French employed their planes in a number of innovative ways. The most important of these was the widespread use of parachutists to reinforce troops under siege, to attack the enemy and to cover retreats. When the first post on the Chinese frontier was assailed in May 1950 it was recaptured by the paratroops. In October the same year paratroops were dropped to cover the retreat from the other posts on the frontier. In 1951 parachutists were dropped at Laichau, Le Day, Mao Khe and Hoa Binh and they played a vital part in their defence.[12] When the French had to fall back on the Black River in 1952 they dropped Bigeard and his paratroops into the jungle to hold the village of Tu-Le while the other troops escaped.[13] Bigeard was able to carry out his mission though many of his soldiers were captured or killed.

On the other occasions the French resorted to ruses, dropping sacks on parachutes to simulate an air drop and then, when the Vietminh had congregated in the area, destroying them with bomber attacks.[14] They also developed methods—perfected later by the Americans— of covering an area with bombs and shells from aircraft before the parachutists landed. It is worth noting that General G. J. M. Chassin, who was appointed to command the air forces in Indochina at a crucial moment in July 1951, was a former paratroop officer.[15]

The lumbering French ground forces proved alarmingly susceptible to ambushes in the jungles of South-East Asia. Accounts from both the French and the Vietminh show that French columns were often saved from total destruction by the intervention of the air force.[16] In 1951 when the guerrillas made a feint attack against Bao-Chuc, they quickly enticed Colonel Vanuxem and his rescuing party into an ambush, Vanuxem only managed to extricate half his force with the help of intensive air and artillery bombardments.[17] Vietminh intelligence was excellent and they almost always knew what the French were planning, as one French soldier noted gloomily: 'The French were justly and universally unpopular and nearly every native was willing to pass on to the Viet the slightest piece of information, no matter now unimportant.'[18] Other accounts show that the French effort was so badly organized and incoherent that they even tortured their own spies.[19] Thus, when patrols left their posts to stage an attack, they were frequently forced to retreat in confusion or to call in air support. Bernard Fall described how the crack Force Mobile 100, which had acquired a very high reputation in the Korean war, was slowly demolished in a series of ambushes in 1954. Only when the guerrillas exposed themselves to air attack were the French able to defeat them and save a remnant of their force.[20]

Transport aircraft were particularly useful because the guerrillas controlled the roads, especially at night, and ambushed or mined vehicles during the day. Even had this not been the case, the very size of the country made transport by aircraft an attractive option—troops could make journeys in a matter of hours which would have taken days or even weeks by train or boat.[21] By November 1952 the French had managed to collect 100 transport aircraft which flew a total of 3,340 hours in one month, despite the difficulty of keeping them serviced.[22] Transport aircraft could bring men and supplies into besieged fortresses. During the siege of Lai Chau in the mountains there was an aircraft movement every two minutes.[23] Transports enabled de Lattre de Tassigny to concentrate as many men as possible in the northern part of the country in January 1951 for a massive offensive against the Vietminh. Then, when the French advance began, the transports complemented the fighter bombers in their attacks on the guerrilla forces.[24] The Vietminh lost 6,000 men at the battle of Vinh Yen, through napalm and other bombs. Transport aircraft also supplied the Montagnard tribesmen who were led by French regulars. These fought against the Vietminh guerrillas in what was arguably the most innovative and successful part of the campaign. By the end of the war they needed 300 tons of airborne supplies a month but they were holding down great numbers of Vietminh and more than justifying the effort expended.[25]

In contrast, as commanders of anti-guerrilla operations were to find later, many of the giant encircling campaigns in which parachutists and ground troops were involved often failed to find the insurgents and consumed far more resources than was justified. This was, for example, true of the massive concentration of forces which the French brought to bear on Route 14, the 'Street without Joy' in July 1953 and which only killed some 182 of the Vietminh 95 Regiment.[26] Weather and the difficulty of bringing air power to bear greatly hampered the government forces and most of the insurgents had fled the area long before the lumbering French regiments arrived.

It was also excessive faith in transport aircraft which led Navarre into the trap of Dien Bien Phu. He believed that aircraft could land in the valley and bring all the supplies which the French garrison would require, so blocking the Vietminh's advance into Laos. Thus by January 1950 twenty C-119s and fifty Dakota sorties were being made each day to keep the garrison fed and armed.[27] But the airfield was put out of action four days after the battle began for all but small aircraft and it was closed to these as well two weeks later. Thus the French had to drop the 170 tons of ammunition and 32 tons of food which the garrison needed each day and, as Vietminh artillery forced aircraft to fly at ever higher altitudes, more than half of the dropped supplies often fell into enemy hands. Two hundred aircraft flew round the clock to keep the garrison alive. Transport aircraft also dropped napalm and Lazy Dog cluster bombs on the Vietminh. However, the French insisted on using Lazy Dog against the AA guns rather than on the troops against whom the Americans believed the cluster bombs would be most successful.[28] The situation revealed the deficiencies of the old C-47s which had to overfly the valley twelve times in order to drop their 2½-ton loads, whilst the newer C119 Boxcars could drop six tons in one pass. The Vietminh anti-aircraft fire quickly intensified and forty-eight aircraft were shot down over the valley, fourteen crashed on landing and 167 were damaged. And still the besieged forces ran short of ammunition before the Vietminh broke in on their defences on 7 May.[29]

The exaggerated faith in the ability of aircraft to keep the Dien Bien Phu garrison supplied was compounded by French and American suggestions that the besiegers could be driven off if enough bombers were used against them. The Chief of Staff of the French Army, General Ely, visited Washington in March 1954 to try to persuade the US to participate in the war. The Commander of the Navy, Admiral Radford supported the French suggestions and argued that strikes by the 200 aircraft on the US carriers, *Essex* and *Boxer*, off the coast of Indochina, and from aircraft based in the Philippines could change the balance of forces. Fortunately the Army Chief of Staff, General Ridgway, believed that nothing but a massive effort by ground forces would make any difference. His opposition to Radford's suggestions and the scepticism of the British was decisive.[30]

Exaggerated faith in air power was partly the result of its successes in the campaign but French transport aircraft could not supply Dien Bien Phu, nor could American bombers alone find and destroy the Vietminh. Aircraft had other limitations, notably their vulnerability on the ground. Most of the airfields in the north were near Hanoi or Haiphong but there were about six others where C47s could land and around thirty which could take light aircraft.[31] The defence of these airfields proved a constant problem for the French. General Chassin reported: 'It requires blockhouses constantly occupied, day and night, by personnel always on the alert, a continuous belt with powerful lighting patrolled by sentries with highly-trained police dogs.'[32] Villages near to airfields were a permanent threat as they could harbour 'suicide volunteers' capable of invading the airfield and sabotaging equipment. At key moments the Vietminh were able to penetrate French airfields just as they occasionally penetrated American ones later. During the attempt to resupply Dien Bien Phu, some guerrillas made an epic journey through the sewers to blow up eighteen French aircraft; altogether at this period they destroyed thirty aircraft and 53,000 gallons of fuel on the ground.[33]

Thus the Vietminh usually held the initiative and their intelligence was nearly always better than their enemies', though the French air force did its best to counter these advantages. In 1953 the French had eleven Bearcat aircraft equipped for photo-reconnaissance and one squadron of light aircraft used for artillery spotting and liaison duties in North Vietnam.[34] Such aircraft tried to detect Vietminh movements and lead heavier aircraft into the attack, marking targets with smoke bombs. On average the French reckoned to fly one hour of reconnaissance for two hours of combat. Aerial reconnaissance seems to have worked better than one would have expected, given the jungle-covered nature of the country and the efforts by the Vietminh to hide their activities. Air force officers argued that the information it supplied was far more effective and up-to-date than information received from other sources.[35] Moreover Bernard Fall maintained that aerial reconnaissance allowed the French to calculate quite well the number of troops the Vietminh might bring against Dien Bien Phu. The French miscalculation concerned the quality of the Vietminh soldiers and particularly their ability to bring up artillery. The Morane 500, the French-built version of the Fieseler Storch, was particularly effective. In October 1952 they led the B-26s which destroyed insurgent columns at the battle of Nghialo. Unfortunately for the French, they could not operate effectively at night and General Chassin called for research into infrared techniques which might be of help.[36] But the French did experiment with dropping flares from Dakotas over forts which were under attack and these sometimes enabled the B-26s to bomb the insurgents during the night.

Evacuation of casualties always presented the French with problems; in the jungle rapid evacuation was essential if men were to survive. At first they relied mainly on the ubiquitous Morane 500 whenever a landing strip was available.[37] In 1950 two Hiller helicopters arrived in Indochina—though with little in the way of spares. Later Bordeaux and other French towns raised money so that helicopters could be bought and sent to Vietnam for evacuating casualties. By the end of the war between nineteen and thirty-six Hiller and Sikorsky helicopters were available.[38] The Hiller had a range of some sixty miles but this could be extended by carrying jerrycans of fuel. It could carry a stretcher on either side of the fuselage though the engine was always overloaded in tropical conditions when two casualties were carried. Helicopters helped to evacuate casualties, yet they were clearly insufficient for the French to adopt the system of rescuing more than a few of the pilots who had been shot down which was later adopted by the Americans. Indeed the French pilots called their aircraft 'traps' because there was so little chance of their surviving if they were hit. Thus, altogether French air arms lost 650 men including sixty-one officer pilots.[39]

There were some doctrinal divisions inside the French forces about the use of aircraft. According to Bernard Fall, 'there were many voices amongst air force personnel who averred that a greater concentration on strategic targets (rear depots, bridges, ordnance plants) of the enemy would have helped the war effort more than a constant 'babying' of the ground troops who—in the view of these pilots—finally expected the air force to do what their own artillery or mortars could probably do just as well'.[40] General Chassin himself appears to have supported the views which Fall was attacking. He condemned ground troops who protested when the air force gave greater priority to interdiction than ground support since 'cutting the Vietminh supply of arms and ammunition from China is of greater effect on subsequent operations than an attack on a fortified village in the district'.[41] But the French lacked the aircraft for sustained interdiction operations and the Vietminh was always able to bring up the supplies which they needed, as the Vietcong were to do against an immensely more powerful air force in the 1960s.

Despite these controversies, relations between the army and air force seems to have been good on the battlefield. The air force developed a very high idea of its importance in the struggle but this was partly justified. According to Chassin, 'the air force always plays a predominant part and it can be said that in the majority of cases, it is they who swing the balance in our favour'.[42] Thus Chassin's great fear was that aircraft might fall under the army's control as they had in France in 1940. The air force invited army officers to courses to show them what aircraft could and could not do. One limitation, which was obvious to the men on the ground, was the inadequacy of radio contact between ground and air. During the retreat from the frontier forts in 1950 the commander of one French force struggling through the jungle, complained: 'if only we had a Morane to guide us!' At one moment a Morane did pass overhead but the pilot did not understand what was happening and simply dropped bales of English cigarettes to the demoralized troops.[43]

Forward air controllers from the air force accompanied the troops to try to ensure that the best use was made of air power, though the French sometimes fell into the temptation of trying to avoid casualties amongst their own men by sacrificing civilian lives—a fatal error to make on any scale in countering insurgency. Bernard Fall recorded visiting a Foreign Legion regiment which decided to summon up the air force and to destroy a village rather than to suffer losses. He also watched the air force napalm a village because stray fire had come from its approximate vicinity.[44] We now know how civilian casualties produced recruits for the Vietminh. As one guerrilla recorded later, 'when the planes went away we came out [of the bunkers]. My best friend Huu was lying on the ground, burned by napalm. She wasn't dead but she was dying. We sat around her at night watching her. Her body glowed with phosphorous.' When he was himself wounded by an aircraft and had to lie still for two months, he spent his time thinking about 'killing the French . . . Everybody thought about that, all the young people at least. That's what we would do when we grew up—kill the French.'[45]

Not only did the French forces make widespread use of parachutists and exploit what helicopters were available; they also hoped to develop aircraft specifically for guerrilla wars. Many air force officers argued that what were needed were slow aircraft which could locate and attack guerrillas. As General Chassin put it, 'the only aircraft that can see anything clearly is the small, slow machine such as the Morane 500 Criquet'.[46] The Moranes were able to call up attack aircraft but in the half hour to two hours that it took them to arrive the Vietminh had often fled. On other occasions the guerrillas took care to be out of the area when the ground attack aircraft came up to support the French, then returned to destroy them once the aircraft had left. Thus Chassin wanted new aircraft which could fly at a minimum speed of fifty miles per hour and carry two machine guns and rockets. Similarly Lieutenant Colonel Jacquard argued that the Bearcats and B-26s were too powerful for pacification and that the French should 'follow the American lead' in arming light aircraft.[47] Such views make an interesting contrast to the ideas of the last British commander of the RAF in Malaya. When Americans suggested that a specialized aircraft might be produced for attacking guerrillas he replied: 'This is the sort of argument that makes the average airman shudder.'[48]

French aircraft did make a major contribution to staving off defeat until 1954. They rescued innumerable columns from what would otherwise have been total destruction in the jungle. Parachute drops enabled the French to withdraw in less disorder than would otherwise have been the case and sustained bombing helped de Lattre de Tassigny to defeat Giap's armies in open warfare in 1951. Aircraft attacks increased the problems of the Vietminh forcing them to move by night or to pay great attention to camouflage. On the other hand, exaggerated faith in transport aircraft was one of the factors leading to the disaster at Dien Bien Phu and excessive faith in bombers almost brought the Americans in to the war at the same time. In any case, air power could not defeat an insurgency of the sort which sprang up in Vietnam after 1945, particularly in such terrain. Above all it could not compensate for the hostility felt by the great majority of the Vietnamese towards French occupation, for the half-hearted support for the French war effort in the Metropolis and for the terrain which was so suitable for guerrilla operations. After 1950 the Vietminh had an open frontier across which to bring supplies and they had the heartening example of the Chinese to show that a Communist insurgency could be victorious. They were also fighting against an army which frequently showed gross incompetence at winning over the peasantry. An Englishman who fought with the Foreign Legion in Vietnam commented afterwards, 'I had fondly imagined that the Indochina war was an all-out effort to protect an innocent people against the unwelcome attention of the Communists . . . The men of the Foreign Legion were first-class soldiers, but they had nothing whatsoever to do with a mission of pacification and political re-education.'[49] A Frenchman who served with the parachutists was equally disillusioned. Murder, rape and looting were commonplace.[50] Technology and courage were no compensation for such errors.

4

Helicopters and Insurgents 1954–88

The Algerian War

The use of aircraft by the French in Indochina was circumscribed by the limited numbers available and the difficulty of finding the Vietminh in the jungle. During the Algerian insurrection, which broke out within months of the end of the Indochina War, the French government and people were willing to provide far greater resources and the terrain enabled aircraft to be more effective.[1] As in Vietnam, the French armed forces showed ingenuity and imagination in making the best use of the material available. Thus they employed helicopters in Algeria on a far larger scale and in more varied ways than any armed force was to do before the American intervention in Vietnam. They utilized them not just for evacuating casualties but also as gunships and as assault vehicles for carrying troops right into the battle. They made great use of photo-reconnaissance aircraft and of radar. Relations between their air force and the army appear to have been close and this enabled air support to be provided very rapidly for the ground troops.

The French had occupied Algeria since 1830 and regarded it as an integral part of France. Of its nine million inhabitants in 1954, one million were Europeans who were determined that it should remain French, whatever might happen in the rest of France's African colonies. France also had a very large economic stake in the country which increased when the oil resources of the Sahara were exploited in 1957. Not surprisingly, therefore, a writer in the highly-regarded *Revue de Deux Mondes* argued in the same year that 'the Mediterranean unites more than it divides. Algiers could become a second capital' for the French state.[2] On the other hand, there had been stirrings of nationalism amongst the Moslem population in the 1930s and these led to a brief rebellion in Setif in 1945. By 1954 over 600,000 Moslems had fought for France in the Second World War and in Indochina;[3] they knew therefore that the French were far from invincible and had observed the Vietminh's success with interest. They also watched the neighbouring colonies of Tunisia and Morocco become independent. Consequently they began to demand the same opportunities but they knew that only force would persuade the French to grant Algeria its freedom.

The nationalist movement, the *Front de la Liberation Nationale*, (FLN) and its guerrilla army, the FLA, began the rebellion on 31 October 1954 when they attacked some seventy different places. In the beginning the insurgents were strongest in the Aures Mountains in Eastern Algeria and the Kabylia area, where the poverty of the villagers was worst, but by 1955 they had spread across the whole county. With military precision they divided Algeria into six *Willayas* or military districts, each with a guerrilla colonel in charge. Beneath the *Willayas* came smaller *Nahias* under the command of a guerrilla captain; at their peak the guerrillas usually operated in companies of 140 men.

Estimates of the initial strength of the guerrillas vary between 700 and 3,000, but there were much larger numbers of auxiliaries. The guerrillas suffered very high casualties and lost most of the first group of their leaders in the early months of the war. In three years of fighting they lost 30,000 killed and 13,000 captured. Yet their numbers increased as the FLN spread its influence throughout the Moslem peasantry and townspeople. At their maximum the insurgents numbered perhaps 40,000 and had the support of 80,000 auxiliaries.[4] In 1954 only half the guerrillas were actually armed and their weapons usually dated from the Second World War or earlier. But more modern Czech arms gradually replaced these.[5] Those Moslems who would not willingly back the guerrillas were coerced. Severe tests of loyalty were laid down. Any Moslem caught smoking, and thus supporting the French tobacco monopoly, had his nose cut off as a warning to others. By 1958, 12,000 Moslems who had supported the French had been killed and many more mutilated. The French found themselves surrounded by a sullen, hostile or frightened population. At the same time the FLN tried to terrorize the European settlers by killing some 2,000 and mutilating or threatening others. One of the most spectacular incidents occurred on 20 August 1955 at the El Halia mining centre, near Philippeville, when about 110 European men, women and children were killed and mutilated, provoking the French to kill over a thousand Moslems.[6]

After initially responding rather slowly, French governments showed their determination to win by steadily increasing the forces they committed. Some 54,000 were deployed in 1954 and this had risen tenfold by 1959 if the large numbers of Algerian *Harkis*, or self-defence

The Algerian War 1954 - 1961

forces, are included.[7] From the French army's point of view, the insurrection went through four phases; the first year of the war when the guerrillas were expanding and consolidating their position; secondly, the period from October 1955 to 1958 when French troops were spread across the country defending the towns and villages and when the guerrillas in Algiers were destroyed; this was followed by a third phase from 1959 to April 1960, when General Challe created mobile teams which hunted down the insurgents in the countryside and forced them to operate in much smaller groups; finally, there was the political phase of the war when General de Gaulle negotiated to give Algeria independence despite the efforts of rebellious army officers to prevent this by overturning his government.[8]

To defeat the insurgency, the French had to separate the mass of the population physically or emotionally from the guerrillas. They tried to do this both by removing perhaps two million people to areas which they could control and by using 300,000 troops in static defensive roles. They also established Special Administrative Sections (SAS) in the countryside in which military officers set up schools and other facilities and so attempted to win the support of the people. One man, who visited the soldiers involved in 1955, described them as élite units and contended that they were often highly successful at convincing the villagers both that the French were in Algeria to stay and that they would be able to protect them from the insurgents; later commentators have been much more sceptical.[9] In a single area the army had 600 military doctors and 250 nurses undertaking an average of 950,000 consultations a month. In the same area the army ran 750 schools with 1,000 soldiers acting as teachers for 60,000 Moslem pupils.[10] The army even hoped to 'brainwash' suspects interned in camps into giving their support. They utilized the techniques which had been employed against their own forces by the Vietminh.

French forces had to prevent the newly-independent countries of Tunisia and Morocco from becoming effective guerrilla sanctuaries, sources of supply and reinforcement or recuperation areas, as China had been for the Vietminh or Yugoslavia and Bulgaria for the Greek Communists. In the end they achieved this by building massive fences of barbed and electrified wire protected by mines along 3,000 kilometres of the frontiers. The most famous of these fortified lines was the Morice Barrage which stretched 200 miles along the Tunisian frontier from Bone to south of Tebessa. Already strong, much of it was doubled later by General Challe[11] and one French officer calculated the cost as about half a million US dollars for every forty kilometres. The

PLATE 1. Samawah in Iraq in 1923 showing the aircraft used by the British against the Beni Huchcim tribe. However, the scene could have been anywhere in Iraq, Aden or Jordan in the 1920s where the RAF maintained order with aircraft and armoured cars after the withdrawal of the army. *(Public Record Office, AIR/5/344)*

PLATE 2. The Beni Huchcim tribe refused to pay taxes to the British or to stop its attacks on travellers. RAF attacks, illustrated in this photograph, forced them to obey the British with what the RAF claimed was the minimum of casualties. However, the attacks did cause concern particularly in the Labour party. *(Public Record Office AIR/5/344)*

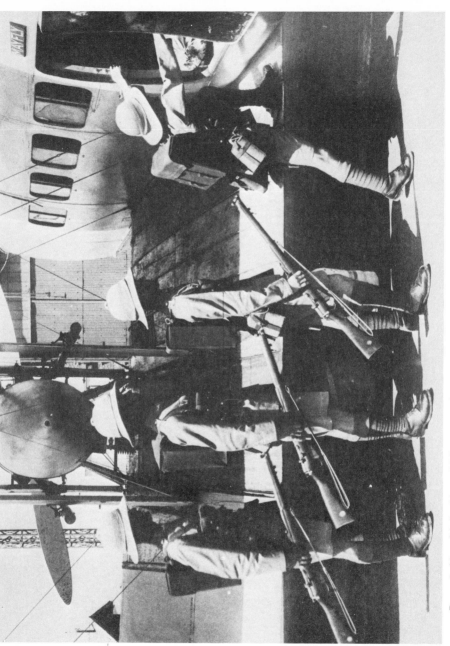

PLATE 3. Aircraft helped imperial forces to retain control not only by attacks on rebels but also by transporting troops to scenes of disorder in Cyprus, Palestine and elsewhere. This photograph was taken in 1934 to inform British soldiers how to embark.

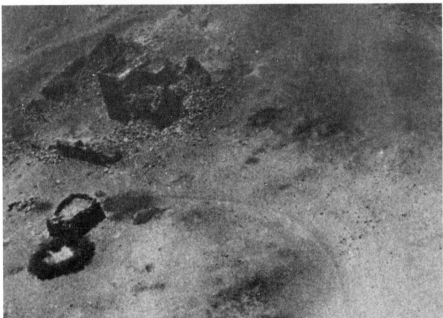

PLATES 4 and 5. Air control was maintained by the RAF longer in Aden than elsewhere. In 1948 the Ahl Yehia tribe refused to obey government orders. The photographs show their fortress at Dar Hashus before and after the 34 sorties carried out by Tempests from RAF Khormaksar. The British believed that only one Adeni had been injured in the attack which, typically, was intended to damage property, not to inflict casualties. *(Public Record Office AIR/23/8370)*

PLATE 6. As the speed of combat aircraft steadily increased in the 1940s armed forces were compelled to make use of trainer aircraft in the anti-insurgent role. The British first encouraged the Royal Hellenic Air Force to use Harvards against communist guerrillas in the late 1940s but the Harvard trainer also saw combat in Kenya and Algeria. Photograph shows a Harvard at the *Imperial War Museum, Duxford*.

PLATE 7. The fertility of US technology was demonstrated by the development of the fixed wing gunship for use in Vietnam. The idea of having rows of cannon facing at right angles to the aircraft and providing massive firepower was simple but no one had tried it before. This photograph shows an AC-130 Hercules gunship over Vietnam. (*US Air Force Photograph*)

PLATE 8. The British used Lincoln bombers against guerrillas in Malaya and Kenya and the Americans employed B-52s on a massive scale against guerrillas in South Vietnam. They had a devastating effect on guerrilla morale but they also turned many Americans against the war. Here a B-52 drops bombs over a guerrilla stronghold only 18 miles north of Saigon. (*US Air Force Photograph*)

PLATE 9. The Americans used B-52s against targets in Laos and Cambodia as well as against North Vietnam. Attacks on Laos and Cambodia hindered but did not halt guerrilla supplies along the Ho Chi Minh trail. Bombing raids around Hanoi were amongst the most controversial military enterprises in the war but they did not force the North Vietnamese leadership to abandon the struggle. (*US Air Force Photograph*)

PLATES 10, 11 and 12. The helicopter revolutionized every struggle against guerrilla forces from Malaya to Afghanistan. Even in Northern Ireland they have found a major role transporting troops safely away from mined roads and observing activities in urban areas. (*Wing Commander N. G. Fox*)

French moved all civilians away from the area which became a 'free-fire zone' where anyone who moved could be attacked. They guarded the fence with mines and with radar to detect any attempt to cross. Occasionally the FLN made such attempts but they were costly and ineffective.[12] Groups who tried to circumvent the barrage by making their way through the Sahara to the south were often detected by aircraft and intercepted. The French air force and navy also kept watch on ships which might be delivering arms. They trailed 600 of these vessels and boarded about sixty of them.[13]

The war was an urban as well as a rural struggle because the FLN managed to establish themselves amongst the Moslems of Oran, Tlemcen and Algiers. In the capital itself the French believed there were some 4,500 guerrillas and auxiliaries who caused fear and confusion by planting bombs in public places such as coffee bars and railway stations. They also demonstrated their power by calling strikes. Nevertheless by October 1957 Colonel Massu and the French paratroops had won the Battle of Algiers by using torture and execution to break down the guerrilla organization. 30–40 per cent of the population of the Moslem Casbah were arrested and 'interrogated' at some time or another.[14] However the paratroops' methods increased the bitterness of the conflict and made some Frenchmen doubt the wisdom of the struggle.

When the war began, French air strength in the country was said to have been limited to eight Junker transport and one helicopter.[15] Shortly afterwards they persuaded the American forces in Germany to supply them with eight Sikorsky helicopters and many more were bought in the United States or produced in France so that 110 transport helicopters were available in 1957.[16] By 1959 the air force had built up a very extensive helicopter force which flew 40,000 operational hours, evacuated 7,500 casualties and carried 48,000 passengers and 1,200 tons of freight. The army had the Bell H13 and Sud Aviation Alouette II light helicopters and the Sikorsky H19 and Vertol CH21 for transporting troops—about 100 in all, plus 120 light observation aircraft. The air force had the Sud Aviation Alouette II and Sikorsky CH-34 which was the 'workhorse' of their transport fleet carrying 12–16 men for up to three hours. The air force had 130 Mistral jets comprising over half the total number of these British-designed Vampires built by *Sud Est* under licence for the French air force. It also had twenty-four P47s, twenty-two B26s, over sixty transport aircraft, 122 helicopters and a number of light aircraft including the ubiquitous T-6 or Harvard, making a total of over 800 in all.[17] They flew over 144,000 missions in

1959 alone. Apart from the helicopters, the equipment available was hardly very advanced but it was adequate for the purpose.[18] It was not necessary, for example, to accompany ground convoys with the most modern aircraft; very few were ambushed when they were watched over by even the most antiquated planes.

One of the most important of the air force's roles was reconnaissance. This was much easier in the sun-blasted desert areas of Algeria than it had been in the jungle-covered hills of Vietnam. Nevertheless a good deal of Algeria was rocky and mountainous and this caused problems for reconnaissance aircraft. The FLN were masters of camouflage and troops could pass within feet of their hides without noticing them. The weather was also unpredictable. Sandstorms in the Sahara in the south quickly put helicopters out of commission while storms could rise in the Kabylia area within hours and make observation from the air impossible. Yet if the difficulties were obvious, so were the advantages which air reconnaissance alone could give. As a result the air force carried out 34,500 reconnaissance missions lasting 73,000 hours in 1959. Once the barrages had been built along the frontiers these had to be patrolled by aircraft to make sure that no breaches occurred. This was vital because the insurgents had ten battalions in Morocco and twenty in Tunisia, some 25,000 men in all, who were just waiting for the opportunity to enter Algeria and to bring in new supplies of weapons.[19] Even at night the barrage was patrolled by Aeronavale Neptune aircraft equipped with flares. Ground radars were also built and these could vector bombers to the targets if they picked up any suspicious movements in the darkness.[20] Bombs may rarely have hit their targets but they were a deterrent.

The air force found even its Vampire jets useful for reconnaissance. The insurgents would hide if they heard an aircraft coming but they were unable to escape so easily when fast low-flying jets were used. Key areas were constantly watched and photographed so that any strange events could be recorded. As a result the French knew when the peasants were not working normally in the fields or even when strangers had arrived in the area. They could detect when the villagers became afraid of the aircraft and thus were probably harbouring insurgents. Aircraft could pick up the smallest detail. On one occasion Colonel Bigeard found and destroyed an important guerrilla band in the Sahara area simply because an aircraft had reported an unusual type of shrub growing out of a sand dune.[21]

If guerrilla bands were located by aerial reconnaissance or intelligence they could be attacked by ground forces. But the French found that they had melted away long before their forces arrived, even if they sent them in lorries. The FLN stationed guards on the roads who would light fires when they saw the French vehicles approaching and warn their colleagues. Thus many accounts of the war describe the apparently endless and futile efforts to follow an elusive enemy across dry and very difficult country where temperatures sometimes rose to 45° Centigrade in the shade. One paratrooper recalled afterwards: 'whole days were wasted climbing up and down from one *djebel* (mountain) to another'.[22] The helicopter transformed the war to the delight of the army and air force alike. Not since aircraft had first been used in guerrilla wars in the 1920s had technology suddenly produced so dramatic and important a change. The helicopter enabled the French to become more mobile than the guerrillas whose main means of transport was on foot. The helicopters could easily stage surprise raids, landing troops within a village and rounding up the inhabitants before they had any idea that they were threatened.

The helicopters were vulnerable even to small arms fire from the ground but the air force gradually found ways of minimizing the danger. They flew to the landing areas at 1,500 feet or more which minimized the risk. Before making a landing which might be opposed, they used B26s to bomb the guerrillas with cluster bombs or napalm, and then strafed the ground with T-6s or Vampires. Of all the fixed-wing aircraft it was indeed the B-26s and Harvards which they found most useful and they particularly praised the B-26 for its robustness and reliability. One in every five of the helicopters was also armed with a 20 mm gun or SS-II missiles and these could attack any guerrillas who emerged to opposed the landing. Finally the troops would try to land two minutes after the strafing ceased. The idea of arming the helicopters was itself an innovation and they had trouble preventing the recoil causing excessive vibration until this problem was solved by a mounting invented by a naval pilot. They were uncertain whether the guns should be mounted to fire forwards or sideways but decided that the latter produced better results. The guns were simply bolted on to the helicopter so that more aircraft could be converted rapidly into gunships if needed. They also experimented with armouring the helicopters but found that this made them too heavy and instead protected the two pilots with thick pieces of nylon capable of stopping bullets up to 8 mm.[23] They concluded that gunships should keep 2,000 feet from the target rather than closing, as many pilots were inclined to do.

The helicopters carried 'élite' troops, paratroops, Foreign Legion or the parachute commandos who were swamped with volunteers when they were established in 1956 and went into action about a year later. Because so many helicopters were avilable, in contrast to the situation in Indochina, the paratroops rarely jumped from aircraft to assault the enemy although they were dropped from Noratlas aircraft from time to time and retained their reputation for dash and effectiveness. According to one commentator, 'it was the paratrooper, racing the length and breadth of Algeria, often carried to the assault in helicopters, who fulfilled the romantic image of war as an enterprise of danger'.[24] When they were not on operations some of the airborne forces were retained on 15-minute alert so that they could be rushed to any area where they might be needed. If major operations were planned, helicopters would be sent from major rather than subsidiary bases so that the insurgents would find it more difficult to guess which area the French would attack. At the same time the network of subsidiary bases was built up so that there were 200 in the Sahara region alone. The air forces also established fuel dumps in as many regions as possible to increase the range or payload of the helicopters. The insurgents naturally appreciated the importance of the airfields and frequently mined them during the night but this only temporarily handicapped the French effort.[25]

All the French airborne operations required effective radio control. They built VHF stations on stretches of high ground across the country and used both air force and army units to protect them against the guerrillas. Ground troops could radio for assistance and the air force claimed that they would respond rapidly. In theory the troops' demands were passed through the army commanders to the air force which had control of all air assets. In practice the air force was listening in to the same appeals and frequently had its aircraft on the way to the troops before the army had made its official demands.[26] Tactical air headquarters were co-located with army corps headquarters to increase the level of co-operation between the two services.

Despite their technical proficiency, French helicopter operations in Algeria had their critics. Bernard Fall claimed that,

in spite of the fact that the barren hills of Algeria made aerial surveillance a great deal easier than the jungle-covered terrain of Vietnam, the results of 'heliborne' operations were not overly successful. The Algerian nationalists soon learned the foibles of the lumbering and noisy craft and quickly developed effective techniques for helicopter baiting and trapping.[27]

But the French armed forces flatly denied these claims or that guerrilla opposition caused them much difficulty when their methods were perfected.[28] In 1957 sixty-two helicopters were hit by enemy fire; in 1959 thirty-five were damaged. In 1957 nine helicopter crew were killed; in 1960 none were. Much more serious objections were raised by members of these élite forces themselves, who believed that the brutality of their methods often alienated the villagers and undid the work of the Special Administrative Sections. The villagers found themselves in the usual predicament of those caught in the fighting—'tools of the FLN, the peasants in their clumsiness seemed to ask for trouble. And the repression, in this general state of tension, became increasingly brutal. Fear engenders cruelty; cruelty, fear.' If such accounts are accurate, the paratroopers frequently looted, raped and murdered innocent bystanders as well as those suspected of sympathizing with the enemy.[29]

The French armed forces could argue by 1960 that, because of their tactical and technical efficiency, they had greatly reduced the power of the FLN and avenged their own defeat at the hands of the Vietminh. In the air in particular they had demonstrated a level of ingenuity which was a far cry from the conservatism of the French armed forces in the 1930s. They had had to overcome the problems of terrain and climate where the temperatures even at 7,000 feet could rise to over 100° Fahrenheit and where sand constantly reduced the life of engines and airframes. They had used helicopters on a scale which they had only been able to dream about in Vietnam. Despite the great courage of the insurgents and the support which many of the population gave to them, despite their willingness to accept massive casualties and their military training, the rebels were ground down by the technical and numerical superiority of the French forces. They were cut off from their natural base areas in Morocco and Tunisia and increasingly separated from the Moslem population as a whole. In purely technical terms the French armed forces could have done little more to keep Algeria part of France. The situation was perhaps epitomized by their successful effort to prevent guerrilla forces in Tunisia and Morocco from participating in the struggle. Technically the military answer was effective but it would not end the war because the guerrillas could not be destroyed on neutral territory.[30] Thus, in the end, Algerian powers of resistance outlasted the French and Algeria became independent in 1961.

The British in Four Wars

Introduction

The British did not employ air power in their anti-guerrilla operations in the 1960s and 1970s in the same way as the French or Americans. Above all they did not generally make use of helicopters as gunships but rather for transporting troops. Employed in this way helicopters were, to use the modern jargon, force multipliers, enabling relatively small numbers to do the work which would otherwise have stretched the resources of far more.

The country which had utilized air power most intensively and imaginatively in unconventional warfare between the world wars had become technically conservative; the air force which insisted more than any other that it could fight unconventional wars on its own and that it was not simply a troop transporter had become just that. One of the reasons was that the combined politico-military approach to defeating guerrillas had been so successful in Malaya. Sir Robert Thompson's analysis of this campaign became standard and obligatory reading for all staff officers in the British army and Thompson believed that the usefulness of helicopters could be exaggerated.[1] Another reason for British conservatism was that the helicopter was the victim of inter-service disputes about operational priorities.

As early as August 1945 the War Office had begun to study the application of helicopters in warfare. The Royal Army Medical Corps (RAMC) were particularly excited by the possibilities they presented in the field of casualty evacuation. Light aircraft had flown 700 casualties out of Burmese airfields in two months during the campaign there and the primitive helicopters available had even managed to bring out about twenty.[2] However few funds were provided for new military equipment in 1945 when such massive stocks of old equipment were available. Moreover the British helicopter industry was fragmented and lagged far behind its American counterpart.[3] Thus little progress was made until the campaign in Malaya in 1948 showed the vital importance of helicopters for evacuating casualties and moving troops in the jungle.[4] In their haste to have helicopters on the battlefield, the British then had to buy American helicopters or build them under licence.

Once small helicopters had established themselves in these roles, despite the indifference of the RAF, the army's attention turned to larger transport helicopters. Many army officers were worried about the vulnerability of roads to air attack and wondered whether some or all of their wheeled transport could not be replaced by large helicopters.[5] However, as the Vice Chief of the General Staff was reminded in December 1952, the RAF was 'not really interested' in transport helicopters and would never give them any degree of priority.[6] Instead the Executive Committee of the Army Council set up a committee to study the problem in February 1953, taking care that no RAF officers should be included to put a damper on the proceedings.[7] The committee concluded that fifty large helicopters flying three sorties a day over 150 miles might replace 1,000 lorries. Helicopters would never entirely take over from wheeled transport, as they were not suitable for every operation and they were too expensive, but they would make a very important contribution. The RAF believed that the committee's calculations were far too optimistic and that it would take 900 helicopters to supply an army corps, not ninety-six as the committee had suggested. Helicopters would also be extremely vulnerable to air and ground attack.[8] The army still wanted to proceed as fast as possible and proposed to set up its own establishment for evaluating helicopters. In the end a joint army–air force Experimental Helicopter Unit was formed at the instigation of the Minister of Defence.[9] At first it had six Sycamore aircraft and later six Whirlwinds.

Many of the RAF's individual objections to the schemes put up by the army may have been technically justified at the time but it is, nevertheless, remarkable how each debate should have taken the same form. The army would conceive some new scheme for which helicopters might be suitable and the RAF would dissent. It is also notable that in Malaya, in Aden and in the Confrontation with Indonesia much of the work had to be carried out by Royal Navy helicopters because RAF helicopters were either not available or were ineffective for the purpose. The point was that the RAF did not want to spend money on helicopters itself but neither did it want the army to develop them on its own. It wanted to control all aircraft but it also wanted to concentrate resources on fixed-wing aircraft capable of fighting the Soviet Union. The Royal Navy was free from the Air Staff's dead hand in this respect and thus invariably came up with better equipment. As one army officer put it succinctly in August 1953:

Owing to the present system we are failing increasingly to make proper military use of helicopters, already assessed at their proper value by the Royal Navy, civil operators and the American services. The helicopter would probably be of greater value to the army than to any other service or organization. The light aircraft for operational use is not of interest to the RAF and the situation is unlikely to change.

Even six years later the other services felt that Britain was lagging behind in this area, despite the key role helicopters were playing in Algeria.[10]

The RAF no longer existed on sufferance as it had in the 1920s. It was not the cheapest of the three Services as it had been in 1927 when it had cost £14.5 million against £49.9 million for the Royal Navy and £35.8 million for the army. On the contrary, it was now very often the most expensive and, as the custodian of the nuclear force, arguably the most important. It no longer needed to prove its efficiency in unconventional warfare even though—with the exception of Korea, Suez and the Falklands—every war in which it was involved after 1945 took this form. The Air Staff were naturally much more concerned with preparing for general war against Soviet attack than with guerrilla warfare. For this purpose it needed the 'V' bomber force and air defence aircraft to protect the homeland not cheap, slow aircraft for use against insurgents. Something of a compromise was reached with the army in 1957 when the Army Air Corps was formed and took over aircraft weighing less than 4,000 lb, such as the Auster, but this left the helicopter force still divided between the two Services.

All this helps to explain why helicopter development in Britain was much slower than in the United States, which had the resources to develop all sorts of aircraft, or in France which devoted much more effort to guerrilla warfare. Nevertheless, the British did manage to defeat the Indonesians and to help the Omanis destroy the rebels in Dhofar. If the British lost in Aden this was because of government policy rather than military failings, and it was largely urban guerrilla warfare which frustrated them in Cyprus rather than rural campaigns for which helicopters were most suitable. Thus, in the event, the British armed forces did not greatly suffer from their technological conservatism; indeed ironically they probably benefited from it. Had they used helicopters as gunships on a massive scale this might have increased the unpopularity of the conflicts in which they were engaged. Finally, thanks to Sir Robert Thompson and other writers, they gradually developed a very clear idea about the importance of defeating guerrillas by a combination of political and military means.

Cyprus

The Cyprus campaign in the mid-1950s illustrated both the political and the technological situation clearly. As the growth of Arab and Jewish nationalism threatened Britain's position in Palestine, Egypt and Iraq, so the British put more emphasis on their bases in Cyprus and Aden. In 1952 Whitehall was planning to expand the airfield on Cyprus for use as an advanced bomber base.[11] In 1953 it was working on a joint headquarters for Middle East Forces at Episkopi in Cyprus.[12] Yet Cypriot nationalism had been growing since the 1930s. The Head of the Orthodox Church in Cyprus, Archbishop Makarios, was determined that Cyprus should not become independent as a secular state accommodating the views of both the Greek majority and the Moslem Turkish minority.[13] Makarios wanted Cyprus to become part of Greece—the process known as *Enosis*—so that the Church's position should be confirmed and a poll held in 1950 showed that 96 per cent of Greek Cypriots were in favour of this policy.

The man chosen to achieve this end, George Grivas, had offered to help the Germans in 1943 against the British but his offer had been rejected. Later he became prominent in the Greek civil war as the leader of the Right-wing guerrilla movement 'X' and had failed abysmally afterwards as a politician.[14] He was determined, ruthless and politically uncompromising. He was not a natural leader of the Greek Cypriots whose largest political body was the Communist party. Yet so strong was the force of nationalism becoming in the area that he managed to rally many Greek Cypriots to his cause and to terrorize the others into silence.

After 1945 Makarios may have hoped that Cyprus would slowly and inexorably fall under Athens' control as Britain withdrew from its empire. But the removal of British bases from the Middle East to Cyprus belied his expectations and on 28 July 1954 Henry Hopkinson, the Minister of State for Colonial Affairs, told the House of Commons that Cyprus would never become independent. On 1 April 1955 the EOKA (National Organization of Cypriot Fighters) guerrilla movement, led by Grivas, began a guerrilla campaign by planting bombs in the broadcasting station[15] and other targets in Nicosia. Subsequently Grivas organized demonstrations by students and school-children and the killing of Cypriot policemen who were too efficient or loyal to the British. The conflict gradually spread to the whole of the island, with attacks on British officials, servicemen and their families and especially on the Greeks who worked for them. The British then tried to find

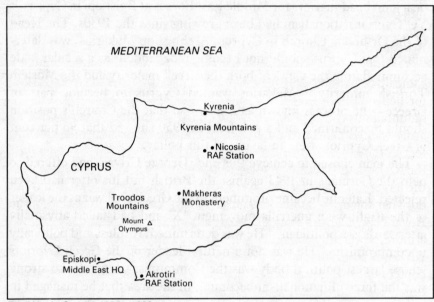

The War in Cyprus 1955 - 1960

a compromise solution and to involve Turkey by calling a tripartite conference of the British, Turkish and Greek governments in London in August 1955, to settle the Cyprus problem. However anti-Greek riots broke out in Istanbul and the conference broke up. In September 1955, as the situation continued to deteriorate, London appointed Sir John Harding as Governor. Harding had presided over the defeat of Mau Mau as CIGS but he initially tried to find a political rather than a military solution and to separate Makarios from EOKA by offering independence free from Britain and Greece. Since this was precisely what the Archbishop did not want, he refused to take the bait and the British exiled him to the Seychelles in March 1956.[16]

The question of the role which air power could play in the campaign came up rather belatedly in June 1956. The authorities in Cyprus asked for helicopters to evacuate casualties and move troops in the rugged mountainous countryside which forms the backbone of the island. The army wanted helicopters there which could pick up four men at 4,500 feet in the hottest Cyprus weather.[17] Apart from its small Sycamores, the RAF was at this time replacing the Sikorsky S-51 or Dragonfly with the larger S-55 or Whirlwind. However Whirlwind Mark IIs could not do what the army wanted because of their limited performance. The Royal Navy had the Mark III version of the same aircraft and this had a more powerful Cyclone engine which could fulfil army needs. The RAF was planning to use 750-horsepower Leonides engines in its helicopters but these were not available. Yet, as RAF officers noted at the time, 'the time factor is all important and to be effective these helicopters are required in Cyprus within the next month to six weeeks'.[18] Sir John Harding was particularly pressing about the need for as many helicopters as possible, pushing the Chiefs of Staff Committee for small helicopters for reconnaissance and larger ones for troop transport. Two Sycamores were rushed out to Cyprus from Abingdon in a Beverly transport and the Air Staff also sent balloons by sea, in the hope that they could carry out some of the reconnaissance Harding wanted.

Sycamores of Nos. 284 and 103 Squadrons subsequently played a significant part in the conflict. Following up experience gained in Malaya, they pioneered night-flying and dropping troops in mountainous areas. In two years on the island they carried out 16,000 sorties, landed 3,500 troops and 113 tons of food, ammunition and supplies and they evacuated 200 casualties. To take one of their most notable successes; five Sycamores dropped forty-one troops near Makheras Monastery early in 1958.[19] Like many of the other eighty monasteries on the island, Makheras, 3,000 feet up in the Troodos mountains, was an EOKA stronghold. The troops searched the monastery and discovered the whereabouts of an EOKA hiding place about half a mile away. As a result Gregorius Afxentiou, Grivas's Chief of Staff, was killed. The British drove Grivas from the mountains and forced him to hide in Limassol, where he remained the brain behind the organization but was unable to take part in actual operations.

Grivas himself was obviously impressed by the effect which helicopters could have on guerrilla movements. He wrote later:

> I wish to stress the importance of the helicopter in guerrilla warfare. In my opinion they will play a very effective part in future operations of this kind . . . The British employed helicopters but on a limited scale and not always in the proper manner, mostly for carrying out reconnaissance against guerrilla bands in the mountains and over inhabited areas where operations were proceeding.

EOKA was, nevertheless, forced to carry out most of its ambushes at night 'because night hampers the enemy's movements and in particular makes difficult intervention by the enemy air force'.[20] On the other hand, Grivas was unimpressed by large-scale ground and air operations which he claimed rarely led to the capture of his men: 'Instead of ostentatious army and air force operations, it would have been better to have organized special "manhunting" parties, continually on the move, and capable of putting up the game from its hiding place.'[21] Above all Grivas believed that aircraft could not locate the hiding places which he had carefully prepared underground before the war began— as the Vietcong were to do later. These contained enough food for those inside to survive for a month and so they could also outlast British 'search and destroy' operations. On the other hand, the British believed that aircraft could locate caves and other hiding places.

Grivas's memoirs are critical of the way the British used their aircraft but unspecific about how they could have improved upon their tactics. It may be that it was simply that they did not use them as much as EOKA would have expected; when helicopters did transport troops 'these did not trouble us much [though] on many occasions when we found ourselves in a tight corner under pressure from the British, we came to realize how serious things would have been if proper use had been made of the helicopter'.[22]

Perhaps 'proper' here simply described the intensity of helicopter operations but this was partly determined by the numbers available. A further problem was the climate; for example in one operation in January 1959 the British planned to land sixteen observation points by helicopter yet only two could be landed because of the weather. The British were also still experimenting with the best way to co-ordinate ground and air operations. As the report on the January 1959 operation put it:

> we started with the Duty Officer in the Operations Room trying to run the air net and air requests in addition to his other duties. It was quickly apparent that this was impossible. We therefore borrowed the Ground Liaison Officer and set up a proper Air Office from which the GLO controlled the aircraft and planned the next day's sorties and requests. This developed quickly and easily into an efficient process, and we found that we could reduce the number of sorties required.[23]

In 1958 General Sir Kenneth Darling became GOC and Director of Operations in Cyprus. Darling was an expert on airborne operations having commanded the 5th and 16th Parachute Brigades and the Airborne Forces Depot. He made increasing use of helicopters and other aircraft to blockade villages which were suspected of harbouring guerrillas; 'a number of helicopters would fly low over the whole village while another helicopter landed inside the village to proclaim the curfew'.[24] Again, however, Grivas denied that this was effective. On the one hand, he maintained that all Greek Cypriots backed EOKA and so the blockading of villages to root out suspects was inevitably ineffective. On the other hand he implied that his active units could sneak out of the villages at night without being caught. What is difficult to assess is how accurately Grivas's memoirs reflected the real situation and how much they were simply written to trumpet EOKA's invincibility and what he described as the 'daring, resourcefulness, cunning, persistence' of its leader.[25]

The question of whether the armed forces should bomb the EOKA guerrillas in the mountain areas came up in June 1956. The CAS received a telegram from the Commander in Chief in Cyprus on 18 June suggesting that the acting governor felt that aircraft attacks could be very helpful, particularly for lowering guerrilla morale. They would only be 'used in limited areas which will have been declared danger areas. Intensive publicity both on the ground and using sky-hailing aircraft will precede their use.' Twenty-pound bombs could be dropped from Austers 'with a very small margin of error' and thus could be used

on ambush sites near roads. Venom aircraft could also fire rockets in
the mountains without danger to civilians and with good effect. The
Commander in Chief warned the acting governor that important political issues were involved. In any case the question of operational
responsibility would have to be decided first. Austers were flown by
the Royal Artillery officers but who would control them if they were to
be used in this way?[26]

The Air Ministry in London insisted that any bombing must be done
by what it termed 'professionals', meaning, presumably, RAF officers.
Ministers discussed the issue informally the same day and decided
not to rush a decision. The Colonial Office was unenthusiastic about
bombing and the Commander in Chief of Middle East Air Force argued
on 21 June,

> neither Keightley [C-in-C Middle East Land Forces] nor I are
> keen to start the use of offensive air power in Cyprus unless the
> operational advantages are greater than they appear to be at
> present. The air is making a very useful contribution in terms
> of reconnaissance, communication work and *casevac* [casualty
> evacuation].[27]

This well reflected how far opinion had moved since the 1920s and
particularly since the beginning of the Malayan emergency. It was not
because the Cypriots were Europeans that bombing was frowned upon;
after all the RAF had encouraged the RHAF to use aircraft offensively
against the Greek guerrillas in the 1940s. The point was that bombing
would have been highly visible to journalists covering the campaign.
There would have been protests from the Labour Party and the war
would have become even more controversial. Only very powerful military arguments could outweigh these disadvantages. Thus the light
fixed-wing aircraft available in Cyprus—Austers, Chipmunks and
Pioneers—were used primarily for observation and, in the case of the
Pioneer, for dropping supplies rather than for attacking the guerrillas.

In the event, the issue was not very important because enough firepower was already available to the British army to defeat Grivas and
his forces if the guerrillas could be found outside the towns. Intelligence
and observation were thus the key to victory. Originally Grivas had
imagined that most of his activities would take place in the Olympus
and Pentadactylos mountains. However the British gradually drove his
forces from these areas and into the towns and lowlands, even though
Grivas regarded British efforts with contempt. He believed that Hard-

ing had no plan and that 'the officers lacked initiative and judgement and the other ranks lacked training, dash and personal courage'. EOKA had only about 100 automatic weapons and 500 shotguns and so they were no match for British firepower, with or without air support.[28] But in the towns they proved particularly difficult to deal with and although Grivas had less than 300 guerrillas he managed to hold down thousands of British troops. He struck hard at British intelligence agents and most Greeks were far too fearful to give information to the British. As a result the authorities resorted to collective punishments for villages and towns suspected of harbouring insurgents or in which killings had taken place. Some commentators have argued that curfews and other measures of this sort simply alienated the ordinary Cypriot. Grivas's propaganda constantly accused the soldiers of mistreating innocent civilians, destroying food and crops and taking revenge for EOKA attacks. Later in the campaign he maintained that troops pretended to discover bombs in Greek Cypriot property to give themselves an excuse for blowing it up and also encouraged Turks to attack the Greek island [29]

Despite their claim in 1954 that they would never grant Cyprus independence, it was clear to the guerrillas' leaders that British resolution was not very strong. The Suez expedition drew soldiers away from the island and enabled EOKA to extend its operations. After Suez, Britain's position in the Middle East was weakened generally and the incoming Macmillan government in Britain was determined to reduce its imperial commitments. Lord Radcliffe had been sent to Cyprus to evolve a compromise solution in the summer of 1956. He proposed that the British should give Cyprus independence with a network of constitutional safeguards which would have enabled the Turks to veto *Enosis*. To encourage acceptance, Makarios was released from the Seychelles and allowed to return to the island while Harding was replaced as Governor in December 1957 by Sir Hugh Foot. The government hoped to reconcile Greek opinion by these changes but Grivas himself had some respect for Harding and nothing but contempt for Foot and his liberal policies.[30]

In fact the Greek Cypriots were not prepared to compromise early in 1958 because the British had not defeated EOKA and they still hoped for *Enosis*. Grivas, in particular, regarded all compromise proposals as little short of treachery and organized a boycott of British goods and sabotage of RAF and other British establishments. On one occasion four Canberra bombers and a Venom fighter were blown up by a Cypriot who had been working for the RAF.[31] In the meantime, how-

ever, the Turks had been arming themselves as they feared that no
constitutional safeguards would protect them against the Greek
majority in an independent Cyprus. They formed a secret organization,
Volkan, to take revenge for EOKA's attacks on Turks. Makarios suggested that the Greeks should throw a few grenades into Turkish demonstrations[32] and the relationship between the two communities rapidly
deteriorated. On 7 June 1958 the Turkish government's information
office was bombed in Nicosia. As a result, the Turks living in the
city rioted and burnt Greek property. Five thousand troops and their
associated equipment were rushed to Cyprus in Beverley, Comet, Hastings and Shackleton aircraft, 180,000 lb of freight were airlifted to
the island between 14–17 June alone. The operations demonstrated
both the versatility of aircraft—since the Coastal Command Shackletons were used to carry thirty-one troops—and the course the future
was likely to take because the Comets managed three journeys in the
time the other aircraft took to reach Cyprus once. As the danger of a
full-scale civil war grew, both the Greek and Turkish government
became concerned about the situation and agreed to informal talks
which began in Zurich in Feburary 1959. Talks followed at Lancaster
House in London and Cyprus became independent in 1960, despite
Grivas's bitter opposition to the compromises involved.[33]

Nobody had achieved their full aims. The British had quickly been
forced to abandon the idea of maintaining total control over Cyprus.
Despite the effort they brought to bear, involving 28,000 men,
armoured cars and helicopters they had been unable to defeat EOKA.[34]
On the other hand they maintained their sovereignty over the bases of
Episkopi, Akrotiri and Aghios Nikolaos, ninety square miles of territory which represented their main real interest in the island. Makarios,
Grivas and the other EOKA members had failed to achieve *Enosis* and
were to continue to fail to do so in the future. The Turkish Cypriots
had not allowed themselves to fall under the control of Greece but their
future was to remain precarious until the island was partitioned by
Turkish forces in 1974.[35]

From the military point of view the war showed the difficulty that
the British found in defeating even very small urban insurgencies.
Although they had driven Mau Mau from Nairobi and kept the
Communist guerrillas out of the towns in Malaya, they had not
destroyed the Stern gang and other Zionist organizations in Palestine
in the 1940s and they were to fail in the 1970s to defeat the IRA in
Northern Ireland. In Cyprus the arguments over the number of helicopters available, or whether offensive air power should be used, were

essentially peripheral. They showed more about the way in which bombing had become politically unacceptable and the importance of the very small helicopter force available than about the Cypriot campaign. The British could and did drive most of the EOKA guerrillas from the mountain areas even without bringing modern fire power to bear in the way the French had done in Algeria. On the other hand, they were dealing with a much smaller area and far fewer guerrillas.

Confrontation

By the early 1960s, when the British became involved in another major counter-insurgency, they had far more helicopters than they had deployed to Cyprus. They found, just as the French had in Algeria, that these could transform the campaign. They vastly increased the mobility of the ground forces and made it possible for a relatively small number of troops to protect thousands of square miles of jungle against a rather inefficient guerrilla force.

In 1961 the Malayan leader Tunku Abdul Rahman called for the establishment of a federation of Malaysia made up of Malaya, Singapore, North Borneo, Brunei and Sarawak—the South-East Asian states which had been dominated by Britain.[36] However the radical Brunei Party *Rakyat*, led by A. M. Azahari, was determined to wreck 'Malaysia', perhaps because Azahari himself had hoped to dominate the region and did not want it to be controlled by Kuala Lumpur. In preparation for this struggle, Azahari began to train guerrillas in Indonesian Kalimantan and the North Borneo National Army (TNKU) was born. With Indonesian backing, he sent small groups of TNKU guerrillas, numbering perhaps 2,000 in all, into Sarawak, North Borneo and particularly into Brunei in December 1962 to force the collapse of the plans for federation.

Although Singapore and Malaya were now independent states, the British still had very large numbers of troops, aircraft and ships based in Singapore as one of the main elements in their 'East of Suez' policy. They had some warning of what Azahari was intending and within twenty hours of the outbreak of Confrontation, following an appeal by the Sultan, Beverley transport aircraft had begun to pour forces, including three Sycamore helicopters, into the Sultanate of Brunei.[37] The rebels had attacked the Sultan's palace, the power station and other key targets in the capital but they were quickly driven out or killed. They had also captured other key towns such as Seria. This was retaken in a classic 'air–land assault'. Ninety troops were loaded into a

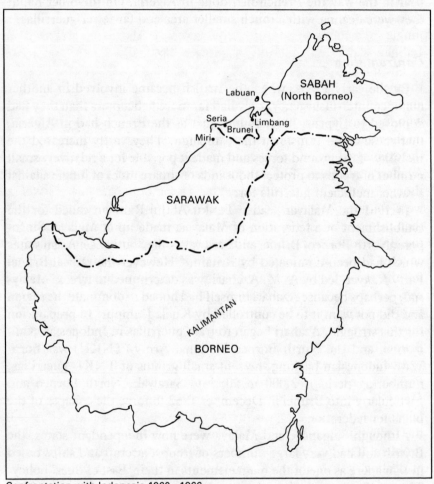

Confrontation with Indonesia 1960 - 1966

Beverley, which made a swift landing on Seria airfield where the troops leapt clear. It then took off before it had suffered more than a few hits from bullets.

Limbang in Sarawak was retaken by the Royal Marines after a landing from small boats; Bekenu was seized from shotgun-toting guerrillas by the 1st Green Jackets, who found the swamp more of an incubus than the enemy, and thus the rebels were gradually forced back into the jungle.[38] Headquarters for the army and air staffs were established on Labuan island, five miles off the North Borneo coast.

The main problem for British forces was not, in fact, the quality of the men the rebels sent into the country, nor the extent of their support amongst the villagers. They were far inferior to the seasoned guerrillas who fought in Vietnam and Algeria and they never established a hold on the minds of the local people, many of whom were quite happy with the existing situation and wanted neither federation with Malaysia nor Azahari's guerrillas. The war was clearly instigated from the outside, though some of the Chinese working in the Sultanate and elsewhere were won over to their cause. It was strictly a guerrilla conflict rather than in any sense a peoples' revolutionary war. The main problem for the British forces was the nature of the theatre itself. Dense jungle covered Brunei's 2,226 square miles where its 136,000 inhabitants lived for the most part in scattered villages.[39] Nevertheless the guerrillas were gradually hunted down as intelligence of their whereabouts improved and the helicopters moved the troops to positions from which they could launch their attack. By the end of December the threat to Brunei had almost disappeared.

Azahari had ceased to be a factor but Sukarno, the unpredictable President of Indonesia, now came out in open and bitter opposition to Malaysia. Sukarno and his fellow Javenese in the government may have felt the need for an external enemy and a new foreign triumph, while the Indonesian armed forces wanted to justify their size and cost. The problem facing the Malayan and British forces became mainly one of dealing with Indonesian infiltrators in Sarawak and Sabah. These territories covered 47,000 and 29,000 square miles of tropical rain forest respectively. Yet the Commonwealth forces opposing the guerrillas never numbered more than 17,000. The problems which this situation presented could only be solved by using helicopters to the full, to move troops into the jungle and swamp to wait for the enemy. They also resupplied the bases used by infantry companies which were set up close to the border with Indonesia and permanently manned to intercept the guerrillas who were crossing into Malaysia.

The trouble began on 12 April 1963 when thirty Indonesian regulars crept over the border and killed some policemen. On 23 April another police post was attacked and further incidents followed.[40] The early attacks were often made by TNKU irregulars but after September 1963 Indonesian troops were usually responsible. The Indonesian aim seems to have been to set up camps in the jungle and then to stir up the inhabitants to oppose the formation of Malaysia. But, as the British increased their forces to seven battalions in Sarawak, the Indonesians abandoned the idea of setting up camps inside Malaysian territory. Instead, after April 1964 they confined themselves to brief raids across the frontier. The British answer to the various threats was to build up the Sarawak Constabulary to give some protection to the villages. At the same time the British commander, General Sir Walter Walker, was determined that the counter-guerrilla campaign should be waged offensively. British Gurkha, Australian, New Zealand and Malayan soldiers would be flown into the jungle by helicopter; they would then wait near the trails, which led to the Indonesian frontier, for the infiltrators to approach and cut off their escape. Small groups were really intended as an early warning screen rather than as ambush parties, though they often carried out ambushes against an enemy armed with medium mortars, anti-personnel mines and rocket launchers.

Despite the threat presented by Indonesian anti-aircraft fire, supplies were dropped into some forward bases by Hastings, Beverley and Argosy aircraft. The Hastings had been in service since 1948 and could carry fifty troops or supplies. The Argosy was a much more modern aircraft which had come into service in 1962 and it could carry sixty-nine troops or 29,000 lb of freight. No. 215 Squadron, which was based at Singapore, flew Argosies throughout Confrontation, whilst the Royal New Zealand Air Force flew Bristol Freighters.[41] Tactical fixed-wing transport was provided by the Twin Pioneers belonging to 209 Squadron RAF and to the Royal Malaysian Air Force (RMAF). These had been introduced into the RAF between 1958 and 1961. They could carry up to nine paratroops or stretchers for evacuating casualties; 209 Squadron also had the older single-engined Pioneers which had been much used during the Malayan insurgency for supplying jungle forts. On this occasion the Pioneers and the Army Air Corps' Beavers proved invaluable for landing on small airstrips.[42]

Helicopters were used extensively to support outposts where even the Beaver and Pioneer could not land. They vastly increased the mobility of the ground troops and artillery. Howitzers were moved by helicopter into the infantry's forward bases to support operations along the borders. Other guns were kept back as a reserve, ready to be rushed forward by Belevedere or Wessex helicopters in an emergency. 225 and 110 Squadrons of the RAF operated turbine-engined Whirlwinds, which replaced the Sycamores, in Borneo. These were still limited in payload, though far superior to the early makes which had been used in Malaya in the 1950s. They had 10–14 aircraft to supply, reinforce or evacuate troops. The normal supply technique was to send food and ammunition as far forward as possible by road and to fly them the last few miles by helicopter. Pilots were specially trained for jungle operations but the weather for much of the year caused grave hazards. Often it was necessary to evacuate casualties by night or in bad weather, even though the Whirlwinds had no special equipment for this purpose. In one year alone 225 Squadron carried 40,000 troops, two million pounds of supplies and evacuated 630 casualties.[43]

The Wessex Mark I helicopters of 845 and 846 Squadrons from HMS *Albion* and *Bulwark* were in many ways more suitable than the Whirlwinds. Their empty weight was almost twice as great and they could carry a much greater payload—up to 4,000 lb as against 1,000 lb, Lieutenant-Commander G. J. Sharman, commanding 845 Squadron, deliberately based his aircraft as far forward as possible to cut journey time and to speed up the response to emergencies. The main base was at Sibu and a forward base was established at Belaga. However this was difficult for the RAF to keep supplied by parachute and another base was cut out of the jungle at Nangga Gaat which could be provisioned by boat. There were also very few areas in the jungle where a helicopter could land if it had mechanical problems, except for the shingle banks of rivers and the clearings which were hacked out of the jungle with so much difficulty. The Wessex was able to make a rolling take-off with eight fully-equipped troops and to carry enough fuel for a 60–80 mile journey. Between December 1962 and 1965, 845 Squadron flew over 10,000 operational hours, carrying 50,000 passengers and six million pounds of stores, and evacuting 500 casualties. Over the period, its aircraft were able to respond to 88 per cent of the requests received, despite the difficulties involved in maintaining them in the jungle. The Squadron's main casualties occurred between February and April 1965 when five aircraft crashed killing three pilots, two aircrew and eleven soldiers.

Apart from the RAF and Royal Navy, the army also had Sioux and Scout helicopters of its own. Each battalion had three Sioux aircraft to use as command posts and for observing the fire of the artillery's 105 mm howitzers and, more rarely, of the battalion's own 3 in mortars.

They also acted as communications aircraft, used 'homing devices' to locate army patrols in the jungle and resupplied and reinforced troops, sometimes by carrying light loads slung beneath the helicopter. The army used the larger Scout for artillery spotting, casualty evacuation and reconnaissance. They had a range of 315 miles against 215 miles for the Sioux and could carry four rather than two passengers. The RMAF had Alouette III helicopters which carried out much the same role as the Sioux and reinforced the allied effort.

With so many helicopter forces in operation there was inevitably some friction between the Services over the way they should be operated, particularly in the early phases of the campaign. One army officer argued,

> the difference in operational attitudes between the RAF and the Royal Navy . . . was most marked. Naval pilots would do, within sensible reason, almost anything which was asked of them. The RAF's pilots struck rigidly to the rule book, referred all decisions back to the air staff at Labuan (or Kuching) and virtually brought the war to a halt.[44]

Another army officer suggested that the problem was partly caused by 'the fact that the helicopters were initially under Transport Command and the pilots were generally accustomed to flying "air-liners", in which role the possibility of risk taking was never considered'. The Air Officer Commanding at Labuan was also 'too far from the front line to have any real feel for weather conditions or operational necessities of the situation'. Many RAF officers dispute these contentions but they reflected common opinions in the army.

Despite such disagreements, the invaders were gradually defeated and there was always the danger that Sukarno would respond to this by turning to conventional warfare. On 1 February 1963 the Indonesian Army Chief of Staff, General Jani, said that his forces were simply waiting for the order to move and a large Indonesian build-up was reported at the end of 1964. Indonesian forces had been built up over the years with Soviet help and the army had in theory over a quarter of a million men under arms. These were equipped with PT-76 tanks and other weapons even if they were not very well trained. The air force had Tu-16 bombers and MiG 21 fighters, whilst the navy even incorporated one Sverdlov class heavy cruiser. British forces in the area were increased accordingly. The aircraft carriers *Victorious* and *Centaur*, the Commando ships *Bulwark* and *Albion*, RAF V bombers and Javelin fighters of 60 and 64 Squadrons were all stationed in the region. Thus, though their infiltration campaign was steadily being defeated, the Indonesians never challenged the British to a conventional war.

Nevertheless Djakarta did decide to land paratroopers and Malayan – Chinese sympathizers in Malaya itself. On the night of 1–2 September 1964 they sent three Hercules aircraft loaded with paratroopers across the Straits. One apparently crashed in the sea and the other two dropped the troops over a very wide area. Most spent the next few weeks wandering around looking for their comrades, before being captured. Later raids were made by smaller groups mainly composed of volunteers rather than regulars, though a party of eighty regulars did land north of Singapore of 9 March 1965. As Sir Robert Thompson, the expert on counter-insurgency, wrote later, these attacks were 'an overt military act of aggression which might have prompted retaliatory action by RAF V bombers'. In fact there were rumours in September 1964 that the British were considering an air attack on Indonesia. An aircraft carrier *en route* to Australia was diverted to the region but it did not pass through the Sunda strait, which the Indonesians claimed, and thus did not challenge Djakarta directly. In any case a British attack would only have raised a storm of protest at home and abroad and consolidated Sukarno's position.[45]

Thus the Indonesian campaign gradually failed, above all because it had never won substantial support amongst the Malaysian people and remained a guerrilla struggle rather than a 'peoples' conflict'. Internal events in Indonesia also helped. In October 1965 the Indonesian Communist party attempted a coup, only to be put down by the army. Six months later the army, led by General Suharto, took power itself, unseating Sukarno and killing or imprisoning perhaps half a million suspected Communists. In August 1966 the Tunku flew to Djakarta for peace talks and the war came to an end. Its main interest from the military point of view was the role which it showed that helicopters could now play. As two of the commentators put it, 'the helicopter was the real battle-winner of Confrontation; without it it would have been impossible for the security forces to control such a vast area against the guerrillas'.[46] They calculated that a helicopter could move men further in an hour than they could move in the rain forest in five days on foot and that a battalion with helicopters was worth as much as a brigade without. Thus, even though there were never more than 100 helicopters available, they had transformed the war. Fixed-wing aircraft had also played their part, rushing forces from Singapore to the trouble spots,

supplying posts deep in the jungle, carrying out reconnaissance, sometimes strafing the enemy and deterring intervention by Indonesia's
main forces.

Aden

   As we have already seen, Aden and the Aden Protectorate were controlled by the RAF from the 1920s until the 1950s. Lord Lloyd, the
Minister of State at the Colonial Office, claimed in 1956 that the British
government could not 'foresee the possibility of any fundamental relax-
ation of their responsibility for the colony'. Nevertheless, the British
hoped to give the inhabitants a greater role in government and to form
some parts of the Protectorate, including perhaps Aden itself, into a
Federation which had some prospect of standing on its own. However
the Yemen continued to claim some of the Protectorate and, after the
1962 coup against the new Imam, Sana'a was dominated by anti-British
groups influenced by Nasser's Egypt. Indeed by the mid-1960s Nasser
had 40,000–60,000 troops in Yemen fighting the Imam's forces. He
also provided training there for insurgents willing to help 'kick the
British right out of the Arab world' as he put it in April 1964. Radical-
ism grew in Aden town itself and infiltrators crossed the frontier from
the 'sanctuary' of the Yemen into the Protectorate.[47]
   When trouble broke out in the Aden hinterland in the 1960s, many
asked why Britain did not continue its time-honoured method of dealing with unrest in the region by bombing the guerrillas. But, as we
have seen, air policing was not used in Greece, Kenya or Malaya. In part
this was because it was not suitable for the terrain and the insurgents in
those regions; however, it had previously worked in Aden. On the
other hand, it had already been under attack in the 1950s from the
British press and from Labour members of Parliament such as Philip
Noel-Baker. In May 1958 British newspapers criticized the government
for using aircraft when a British political officer in the Aden Protectorate was besieged by tribesmen and for using them to repel attacks from
the Yemen.[48] On 17 July of the same year, Philip Noel-Baker asked for
a White Paper on the subject and pointed out that the radio station
Voice of the Arabs claimed that Britain was using 1,000 aircraft and
150,000 troops to repress Arab nationalism in Aden and the Gulf. At
this stage, however, the government was still prepared to defend air
policing methods since 'in an area of great size, with incidents widely
scattered, bombing after due warning is obviously a most effective
means of dealing with tribes. The wisdom of the policy has been proved

by its effectiveness.'⁴⁹ Noel-Baker was unconvinced and in July 1959 told the House of Commons: 'In repeated messages from Oman and Aden, responsible correspondents have said that bombing as a routine weapon is obsolete, that "the use of modern aircraft against primitive tribes is disquieting".'⁵⁰

British practice was in any case changing. In a lecture in London in 1960 Air Vice Marshal Heath argued that military tactics were being adapted in response to new conditions. Previously the RAF had been able to keep the peace on its own 'because the troubles were sporadic and local, but the supply of more sophisticated equipment by Russia, Egypt and Saudi Arabia and the support given by these countries to the Yemen and to the subversive elements in the Arab states under protection, changed this position'. *Cairo Radio* was also constantly encouraging ferment in the area. As a result the RAF alone could no longer control the area and the army was called in and Joint Headquarters British Forces Arabian Peninsula was set up in 1957, with Heath as Commanding Officer.

Not everyone was agreed that it was a good idea to involve the army however. When revolt broke out in Aden in 1964 the Federal Ministers for Defence and Internal Security in the Adeni government both argued that

> ground action would be less effective, more wasteful and probably more dangerous than air action, that the presence of British troops in Radfan could well excite far greater opposition than would otherwise be the case, that the casualties which they would almost certainly incur would delight our enemies and cause doubt and dismay in Britain.⁵¹

The High Commissioner, Sir Kennedy Trevaskis, who quoted these sentiments in his memoirs, added 'in every respect they proved right. Eventually, air action had to be taken'. Other experts on Aden, such as Dr Bidwell, have concurred.

Trevaskis does not mention the growing opposition by Noel-Baker and others to the use of aircraft, nor the fact that air policing methods had not been used in insurgencies since 1945, but gives other reasons why this course was rejected; the Middle East Command had forgotten both the traditional ways of dealing with insurrection by tribesmen and the difficulty of defeating them on the ground. To these reasons Bidwell adds the death or retirement of many of the knowledgeable political officers. At the same time, as a result of the rundown of the rest of the

British Empire and the expansion of Aden as a base, it 'now swarmed with army officers anxious to win their spurs and to justify their existence at a time when defence cuts were in the air . . . the military authorities in Aden yearned for what one of the Brigadiers called a "tactical exercise with tribesmen" and to test training and equipment'. On the other hand, in his official history of the use of air power in the region, Air Chief Marshal Sir David Lee supported the new policy and argued that air policing 'clearly had its limitations when it came to maintaining security along a closed frontier or countering subversion in a populated area such as Aden state'.[52] What is really significant is that politicians in Britain and the armed forces, including the RAF, took one view whilst local political leaders and Arabian experts took another.

On 10 December 1963 nationalists tried to assassinate the High Commissioner and the government proclaimed a state of emergency. The insurgency spread quickly with roads being mined and ambushes laid, particularly in the Radfan area forty miles or so from Aden. The Qutaybi tribe there were once more causing trouble after the return of their leader from helping Republican forces in Yemen. According to Bidwell, 'in the past such incidents would have been put down by an experienced political officer, some Government Guards and perhaps bombing'. But in January 1964 government forces staged 'Operation Nutcracker' to clear the insurgents from the Radfan. They hoped to demonstrate that government forces could operate in the area and also to make it possible for the Royal Engineers to build a road through Wadi Rabwa so that the Radfan could be more easily controlled. British and Federal (Adeni) forces were supported by Hunters and Shackletons and transported by RAF Belvedere and Wessex helicopters of the Royal Navy. In terms of fixed-wing aircraft, the RAF was well represented in the area with three squadrons of Hunters for attack and one for photo-reconnaissance, one squadron of Shackletons and numerous transport aircraft.[53] It was the dearth of helicopters which was to cause problems. The terrain could hardly have been more of a contrast with that confronting British forces in the Far East but, for different reasons, movement on the ground was difficult in both cases. In Malaysia tropical rain forest covered the battlefield; Aden combined mountain, desert and the urban problems of Aden town itself.

The operation began with Belvedere and Wessex helicopters lifting Federal Regular Army (FRA) troops to the high ground above the Wadi Rabwa. Problems developed when a Belvedere was hit five times by rifle bullets which penetrated one of the fuel tanks. This demonstrated the vulnerability of the large aircraft in such conditions but, after some hesitation, the operation went ahead with Belvederes lifting 105 mm guns for the RHA up to the high ground, a new experience for 26 Squadron.[54] Snipers continued to give problems because they were so difficult to see. Once found they could be quickly killed or driven away by the Hunters or by ground fire. Nevertheless, the operations progressed and the area became sufficiently peaceful for the Royal Engineers to build a road through it with the help of local labour.

Operation Nutcracker was a success in that the guerrillas were driven out or killed. However, because the area was not garrisoned, the insurgents quickly returned and Egyptian radio and the insurgents were able to claim a victory against the imperialists. Thus the exercise had to be repeated by 'Radforce' under Brigadier Hargroves a few months later. This was made up of 45 Commando Royal Marines, a company of the third battalion of the Parachute Regiment, Royal Horse Artillery (RHA) with 105 mm guns and Royal Engineers. The first plan on this occasion was to carry 45 Commando directly by helicopter to one of the peaks dominating the area, nicknamed Cap Badge. However with only four Belvederes, two Scouts and four Whirlwinds, Hargroves decided that there were not enough helicopters and they were considered too precious to risk in this way.[55] In any case the Whirlwinds were painted and equipped for air-sea rescue duties and were little use for moving troops. Instead, a small SAS group was flown into the area by Scout helicopter to reconnoitre and to mark a dropping zone for a larger group who were to parachute from Beverleys. In the event the SAS failed to establish the dropping zone. They were surrounded and only saved during the daylight hours by the constant support given by Hunters which fired 127 rockets and over 7,000 rounds of ammunition. They escaped during the night, leaving two dead behind them.

The plan was then changed and eventually 45 Commando managed to seize Cap Badge with little difficulty.[56] However, when the paratroops were pushed further forward, they were bitterly opposed and advanced only with the help of the Hunters' fire power. During the advance RHA guns were also carried 4,000 feet up the mountains by the Belvederes, often flying far above the ceiling permitted with so large a load. Wessex helicopters became available with the return of HMS *Centaur* on 25 May which eased the problems for the other rotary aircraft. Meanwhile the Third Battalion of the Parachute Regiment managed to find a way up Bakri Ridge where about fifty tribesmen were concealed in caves and ridges. These were only dislodged with difficulty and with the help of constant attacks by the Hunters. Subsequently the guerrillas made the mistake of standing and fighting at

Shaab Sharah rather than running from superior forces. As a result government troops were able to inflict heavy casualties and the crucial 5,500 foot mountain, Jebel Huriyah, was taken without opposition. The operation had been a success; the problem was once again to prevent the guerrillas from returning.

As in the Malaysian Confrontation with Indonesia, commentators were convinced that helicopters had been vital in the Radfan.

> The helicopters were the key to the mobility and speed of the campaign. They could reduce the time it took a picquet to get into position on a mountain top from three hours to three minutes; they could move soldiers, weapons, radios, food in about a fraction of the time it took to do it on foot. Tactical mobility depended directly on the number of helicopters available.[57]

At the start of the campaign the Army had two Scout aircraft, later increased to five. The RAF had the Belvedere and the Royal Navy had Wessex in the theatre for part of the time. The five Scout pilots made no less than 7,200 high altitude landings, whilst the Belvederes carried out over a thousand sorties and carried more than 1.1 million lb of freight; 'had it not been for the few [helicopters] there were, the Radfan campaign would have been back to the old North-West Frontier style with a vengeance'.[58]

There was some friction between the army and RAF over control and employment of helicopters, as there was in Malaysia. The army believed that all aircraft should come under its control and that they should be used more aggressively. One officer recalled later 'I had the Scout converted into a rough and ready gunship but was not allowed by the RAF to use the Beaver in a bomber role although it was fitted with bomb racks.' Army officers felt that the helicopters should be based further forward than the RAF believed desirable from the maintenance point of view. They constrasted RAF operating procedures with 'the Royal Navy [who were] superb when a carrier was in Aden. They would move their helicopters alongside mine up country and really mucked in with us.'[59] Furthermore the RAF emphasized the vulnerability of helicopters, and particularly of the Belvedere, to small arms fire. Only twenty-six of these large helicopters were ever in RAF service. They had been developed from the Bristol 173 and 192 and they were the first twin-rotor machines to be built in Britain or to see service with the RAF. With a speed of 138 mph and a range of 75 miles, they could carry 6,000 lb or eighteen fully armed troops. But they were vulnerable and difficult to maintain since they sucked sand into the engines and at one stage were wearing out two engines a week. Spreading oil on the landing grounds helped to some extent, but the aircraft remained unreliable in the prevailing conditions and in November 1965 26 Squadron was disbanded and its Belvederes were sent to the Far East to participate in the last months of Confrontation.

Of course fixed-wing aircraft also played a major part as mobile artillery. The Hunters could bring heavy fire power to bear on the insurgents and respond very quickly to requests for help. They intimidated the guerrillas and made it difficult for them to move in the daytime. During the period from 30 April to 30 June 1964 the Hunters and Shackletons flew 527 and 85 sorties respectively.[60] Sioux and Scout helicopters and Auster aircraft of the Army Air Corps operated with P.R. Hunters of the RAF to provide useful intelligence since little information came from the local people at the start of the campaign. Ground-air co-operation was achieved *ad hoc* but methods improved as time went on. Interestingly enough, the mountains caused problems with radio communication as they had done in Greece during the civil war.

An element of the old air control methods was introduced into the Radfan at this time;

> the Shackleton flew over low in daylight to scatter leaflets warning the tribesmen that those guilty of attacks on the government were being punished and all who failed to leave the area must expect attack. The area was under proscription which involved crop burning, removal of livestock, and demolition of fortified buildings.[61]

At night they dropped flares and bombs to prevent dissident tribesmen from issuing out of their caves and cultivating their lands. One by one the tribes in the region made terms until finally the Ibdali, the last opponents of the government, sued for peace on 18 November 1964. Some rough order now prevailed in the Radfan but the outbreak spread to other areas with attacks in 1965 on British camps in many parts of the Protectorate.

The British response was by no means only military. Large sums of money were belatedly poured into Aden to assist economic development. The government also tried to win over the villagers by building schools, roads and wells in the Federation. Beverleys and other aircraft dropped hundreds of tons of cement, pumping machinery and equipment. No less than seven hospitals were built in the hinterland and roads were constructed. Electricity and water was provided for the first time in many of the villages, though the insurgents did their best to reduce the effectiveness of this tardy effort to win over 'hearts and minds'.[62]

In Aden town the guerrillas waged a typical urban campaign, involving intimidation of those sympathetic to the government and random bomb attacks against the British and any Arabs who supported them. In particular they killed five members of the Special Branch in six months, thereby reducing the amount of information available to the government. The main problem from the RAF point of view was to defend the crowded airfield at Khormaksar which occupied two to three squadrons of the RAF Regiment and many airmen who already had their hands very fully occupied keeping the aircraft flying.[63] Even in Aden aircraft found a use though nothing like as important a one as in the countryside;

> Another new technique was the increasing use of aircraft, and particularly helicopters, in support of these anti-terrorist operations. They were used to give early warning of crowds forming or massing and to watch out for terrorist movement such as mortar or bazooka teams positioning themselves.

In some cases army helicopters could follow and stop suspicious vehicles in order to search for arms or insurgents. A helicopter was also employed to transport the abortive UN mission which visited Aden in April 1967 to seek a peaceful solution to the conflict. The officials apparently did not enjoy the experience and 'after the mission was fired upon in a British Wessex helicopter . . . it refused to fly in the aircraft again on the grounds that it was smelly and had poor vision through the windows'.[64]

Aircraft from Yemen penetrated Adeni airspace and attacked villages on a number of occasions during the conflict. Early in 1964 an armed helicopter and two MiGs crossed the frontier and strafed the village of Bulaq as well as a frontier post and tents in the area. In response eight Hunters destroyed the Harib fort in Yemeni territory. Yemen then took the issue to the UN which called on both parties to exercise restraint and, more seriously, part of the Labour party and the British press criticized the action. Denis Healey later claimed that this was, as a result, the greatest mistake the authorities made and Sir Kennedy Trevaskis decided that he may have been right. In June 1965 two MiGs attacked the village of Marquad and a nearby frontier post, killing two women and injuring three other villagers. Pairs of Hunters subsequently had to patrol the frontier. However in July 1966 MiGs again crossed the boundary and attacked the house of the Amir of Beihan at Naqub, injuring several people. Hunters were then based at Beihan and they may have deterred further attacks. However Britain's failure to retaliate against the guerrillas' sanctuary further weakened local faith in its determination to remain in the area.[65] London was caught either way: if it retaliated it was criticized by 'progressives' in Britain, while, if it failed to do so, it lost the support of the Adenis who depended upon it.

Thus not only did the guerrillas have a secure sanctuary but the struggle was much closer to a peoples' revolutionary war than the Confrontation with Indonesia. The insurgents had more support and promised to revolutionize Aden's economy and society. However this was not the immediate reason the British failed; the campaign was doomed by their political decisions. The Defence White Paper issued in February 1966 announced that all British forces would be withdrawn after a certain date, whatever happened. This was in dramatic contrast to the policy of the previous Labour government which had announced, during the Malayan emergency, that independence would only be given when the insurgents were defeated. The members of the Federal government, which the British had established, were horrified. Their morale and that of the Federal police and armed forces collapsed as they desperately tried to make peace with those they had been fighting.

Thus the insurgency continued to spread and the British abandoned the colony to the strongest guerrilla organization, the Marxist National Liberation Front (NLF) on 29 November 1967.[66] It was perhaps fitting, given the role that air power had played in Aden, that British forces should have been evacuated in the weeks before independence by VC 10, Belfast, Britannia and Hercules aircraft. A Royal Naval task force, including the carrier, *Eagle*, provided air cover for these operations and flew the final 875 men out of Khormaksar by helicopter. The port, which had in 1958 been the second busiest in the world, was left to become a backwater.

The Dhofar War

Next to Aden, and deeply influenced by events in the colony, was the Sultanate of Oman. Sultan Said bin Taimur, the ruler of Oman, had been protected by British forces both against Saudi Arabian incursions and against his own over-mighty subject, the Imam, in the 1950s. RAF Venoms had been involved and Pembroke aircraft had evacuated casualties from amongst the ground troops, carried out reconnaissance and broadcast propaganda to the rebels. Thus for a time the situation was stabilized; however the Sultan was opposed to all aspects of modern society from cameras and music to the establishment of schools and refused to spend money on 'improvements', even after large funds from oil exports started to pour into the country in 1967. A rebellion against this state of affairs began in a very small way in 1962, spread from 1965 onwards and was vastly encouraged by the success of the NLF in Aden in 1967. By 1969 much of the Dhofar area, which lies some 600 miles from the capital Muscat and close to the frontier with Aden, was under the control of the Popular Front for the Liberation of Oman (PFLO).[67]

In 1970 the Sultan's son, Qaboos, staged a coup, took over the government from his father and began to modernize the state with the help of the funds he was earning from oil. Above all he built up the Sultanate's Armed Forces (SAF) to deal with the insurgency. His forces were officered by Britons and British, Jordanian and Iranian forces came to his assistance. Here, as in Aden, the *Adoo* or insurgents were often natural guerrillas; as one of the Royal Marines involved in countering the insurgency said later, 'their personal mobility was superb and their eye for ground was faultless. Whenever we moved they seemed to be watching us and waiting for a tactical mistake to exploit. If the opportunity came they pounced. Often it was only our superior firepower from guns or aircraft that enabled us to extract ourselves.'[68] The insurgents used the familiar Soviet AK47 rifle, the RPG7 anti-tank weapon and the 122 mm Katyushka rocket which could hit targets at 11 km distance. The rugged, roadless terrain dominated by mountains reaching up 7,000 feet was also similar to that in Aden, with difficult country ideal for small groups of men to stage ambushes and attacks, enabling them to have an impact out of all proportion to their numbers.

By the early 1970s the SAF had been virtually driven from Dhofar by some 2,000 rebels supported by 3,000 part-time militia. Government forces returned only for brief periods. Once the British SAS had become involved, however, they began to raise forces from amongst the Dhofaris to fight for the government. These were often composed of men who had fought for the *Adoo* but had been alienated by their methods or Marxist ideology. These *firqats* slowly grew in size and together with the SAF managed to re-establish a governmental presence in the area. The Omani government and the SAS did not neglect the political dimension of the struggle. The SAS and the Civil Aid

Department ministered to the health of the villagers and the government started to establish schools and drill wells for water. By 1975 some thirty-five wells had been sunk and 150 miles of road built; a year later there were twenty-nine schools, nine new government centres and fifty-four bore holes.

To reduce the mobility of the insurgents and to make it more difficult for them to receive supplies from the PDRY, the government began to build barriers across the Dhofar just as the French had used the Morice line in Algeria. The first of these to be set up in 1972 was the 35-mile long 'Hornbeam line' of barbed wire and mines which was also patrolled by helicopters.[69] This was sometimes penetrated by guerrillas on foot but seriously hampered their supplies. A further barrier to guerrilla movement was provided by the Imperial Iranian Battle Group which, from 1973 onwards, opened up and defended the Midway Road right across the country from Salah to Thumrait connecting it with the Gulf States. The Iranians also established a second barrier across the country known as the Damarand line. Thus *firqats*, SAF and their foreign allies began to wear down the various guerrilla bands whilst the new roads through the desert enabled Land Rovers and other vehicles to move troops rapidly. It was only towards the very end of the campaign in 1975 that the Omanis decided to make limited strikes against the sanctuaries just over the border in Aden. The anti-government forces had been firing continually at Sarfait from there. The 5.5 in guns brought into this fort by Iranian Chinooks and Hunter ground attack aircraft joined in the counter-bombardment.

The Sultan's father had established an air force (SOAF) following an agreement signed with Julian Amery in 1958 under which the British agreed to provide assistance. SOAF's aircraft were flown by British pilots under contract. The piston-engined Provosts were used for rocket-firing whilst the Beavers evacuated casualties and dropped parachutes.[70] In 1969 SOAF bought Strikemaster aircraft, which were equipped with 7.62 mm machine-guns and could carry 500 lb bombs or rockets. As a development of the Jet-Provost trainer, they were the natural successors of the Harvards used to counter insurgents in Greece and elsewhere twenty years earlier. Later in the campaign the King of Jordan gave the Sultan some Hunters to increase SOAF's fire power because the Royal Jordanian Air Force had replaced them with more modern aircraft. The Hunters were then flown by Jordanian or British pilots. SOAF bought four Short's Skyvan transports, which had the strength and versatility to land on the desert airstrips and carried about fifteen passengers. SOAF used them whenever possible to evacuate casualties as they were so much cheaper to run than the helicopters.

These included some Wessex Mark II and Augusta Bell 205s (which could carry 12–13 troops). There were also two smaller Augusta Bell 206s which could carry up to three passengers and were used for command and liaison work.[71] Some key government outposts, such as Sarafait, could only be supplied by helicopter and that with a great deal of difficulty:

> mortar and RLC weapons made fixed-wing operation virtually impossible and helicopters, to be safe from small arms fire, had to approach at 6,000 feet above the sea, and descend in a fast, sickening spiral, drop their load quickly and then climb laboriously back up to a safe height before departing.[72]

Trained and equipped by the Americans, the Iranian Air Force sent helicopter gunships to support their ground forces. Major General Perkins, the British officer in command of the operations, remarked later on the courage of the Iranian pilots but argued that 'although helicopters were useful for the engagement of specific targets, they were of little value on search and destroy missions when, in the thickly wooded terrain, enemy presence was often first manifested by a burst of machine-gun fire through the floor'. Consequently Perkins discouraged such roving missions but the Iranian Air Force also sent Chinook helicopters which greatly simplified the allies' logistic problems. They even lifted 5.5in guns into Sarafait so that the troops could reply to shells from the PDRY.[73]

Temperatures in Oman frequently reached 125°F and so parts of the aircraft which were likely to be touched had to be padded to avoid burns. Powerful upwards thermals added to the difficulties of flying and the Monsoon sometimes prevented helicopters evacuating casualties. On one occasion this meant that a soldier had to be carried for fourteen hours after an ambush and that he died in the process. By the early 1970s SOAF was divided into four sections, strike, air support, helicopters and the Viscount transport force.[74] All aircraft came under the control of the ground forces in contrast to the position in Malaysia and Aden and this arrangement worked perfectly satisfactorily. Servicing was carried out by a civilian firm but the facilities were spartan and aircrew frequently carried out their own repairs.

What could have been a turning point in the war occurred on 19 August 1975. A Strikemaster hunting for some guerrillas, who had fired a Katyushka rocket, was shot down by a SAM 7.[75] For the first time the guerrillas demonstrated that they had a weapon which could hit all the government's aircraft. It was also the first time aircraft piloted by Britons had had to face this particular threat. SAM 7s proved a particular danger to the helicopters; if they flew at low level they were vulnerable to the AK47s and heavy machine-guns; if they flew higher they were threatened by the missiles. On the other hand, evasive tactics were developed and exhaust shields gave some protection against the heat-seeking missiles. Although the SAM 7s undoubtedly made life more uncomfortable for pilots and passengers, they were far from decisive. Altogether twenty-three SAMS were fired during the campaign; only two more aircraft were hit, including one of the other Strikemasters.[76]

Despite this accession to the guerrillas' strength, by the end of 1975 the Sultan was able to proclaim that the war had been won. A few groups of insurgents remained active but these could not cause major problems. A British officer who served in the campaign listed airpower and particularly helicopters as one of the six major factors leading to the government's success, alongside the Sultan's reforms after the coup, winning the support of the population, joint civil-military control, interrupting the enemy's supply line (thus negating the advantage which he derived from the sanctuary in Aden) and establishing good intelligence.[77] Similarly the commander of the SAS talked of the 'war-winning Huey helicopters' and of the 'magnificent support' provided by the Sultan's air force whenever it was asked for help.

Conclusion

By now the pattern of British anti-insurgency tactics was clear. The old 'air policing' methods might play some part in the campaign in Aden but extensive use of bombing would have provoked growing complaints in Britain and elsewhere. They were also less feasible when operations were so much less localized. The new strategy meant that every effort had to be made to alleviate the political grievances of the population and thus to separate the 'fish from the sea'. The new tactics depended upon inter-Service co-operation and, as we have seen, there were disputes between the Services as to how this could best be achieved. In Indonesia and Aden control of aircraft was divided between the RAF, Royal Navy and Army; in Dhofar it was the ground forces who were in control. In many ways this seems the best arrangement when guerrillas alone present the problem and there is, therefore, less conflict between target priorities than there would be in a conventional war.

However the forces were organized, the method was the same; the helicopters would move the troops into contact with the enemy while the artillery and fixed-wing aircraft would supply fire power. The British eschewed the Franco-American example of using helicopters as gunships. Helicopters enabled them to move small numbers of highly-trained, professional soldiers rapidly on the battlefields. The operation should be as precise and cause as little damage to innocent civilians as possible, thus minimizing political objections in Britain, in the UN and elsewhere.

Before 1939 the British were more innovative than other nations in the use they made of air power in irregular warfare but after the Second World War the opposite was true. This was largely because they did not believe that helicopter gunships and heavy firepower could achieve the precision they wanted. But part of the explanation lies in the relationships between the Services. The RAF needed to emphasize 'air control' between the World Wars in order to preserve its independence. The discovery of innovative uses for the helicopter would not have served army or RAF purposes in the same way after 1945. Nevertheless, despite their technical conservatism, the British and their allies had achieved their aims in Malaysia and Dhofar and their failure in Aden was due primarily to lack of will power on the part of the government in London, rather than to Service failings. Finally it must be said that, vastly different as they were, the highly political approach to defeating insurgents after 1945, encapsulated in Sir Robert Thompson's writings, and the Air Staff's doctrine in the inter-war period had a number of features in common, not least that they were both effective in rural rather than urban conditions and they both tried to minimize civilian casualties.

The War in South Vietnam

Four main factors influence the use of aircraft in unconventional warfare and determine their effectiveness. Public acceptance of the need to use aircraft, the terrain involved, the nature and strength of the guerrilla movement and the suitability of the aircraft and tactics employed. The Vietnam war from 1965 to 1975 reawakened and intensified public hostility to bombing. Violent demonstrations took place in the United States and elsewhere in the West against US involvement in the conflict, and these were evoked in no small part by the intensive use which the American made of air power. The USA had far more aircraft to bring to bear on the conflict than any previous government fighting insurgents had possessed. However, US tactics and strategy in the war were the cause of endless controversy and are still debated heatedly by historians and commentators. On the other side, the National Liberation Front (NLF) and their North Vietnamese allies were much more experienced, clever and battle-hardened than earlier insurgents had been. But the struggle was not a simple one between tenacity and experience on one side and technology on the other. The guerrillas fought alongside regular North Vietnamese divisions equipped with modern Soviet tanks and anti-aircraft weapons. Thus the war became a struggle between rival technologies as well as involving will power, tactics and courage.[1]

Compared with what happened in Vietnam between 1965 and 1975, every earlier use of aircraft in unconventional warfare seems trivial, dwarfed by the thousands of aircraft and billions of dollars expended by the USA in South-East Asia. Before this, aircraft had been used in tens, now they were used in hundreds. By the end of the war the USA had lost 3,221 fixed-wing aircraft and 4,587 helicopters at a time when most European air forces, such as the RAF, had a front line strength of about 600 planes. American airmen flew over 1.24 million fixed-wing sorties and 37 million helicopter sorties during the course of the war.[2] They also dropped 14 million tons of bombs and shells. Of course the bombs were not only intended to hit the guerrillas but also the North Vietnamese, for Vietnam was a double war; a war in South Vietnam with Vietcong and North Vietnamese soldiers, against whom 71 per cent of the high explosives were expended, and a campaign both against North Vietnam to force it to stop supporting the war in the South and against the guerrillas' supply lines through Laos and Cambodia. *(See next section.)*

Following the defeat of the French and the partition of Vietnam at the Geneva conference in 1954, there were a few years of uneasy peace in South-East Asia. Ngo Dinh Diem's anti-Communist government attempted to consolidate its position in the South and Ho Chi Minh set up his government in the North. Hundreds of thousands of Catholics fled from the Communists, thereby bolstering Diem's government which also had the support of the United States. By 1957, when it became obvious that the South was not going to collapse of its own accord, insurgency began again to threaten the government in Saigon. Some 10,000 village headmen and others loyal to the government were killed by the insurgents. At the same time the government persecuted

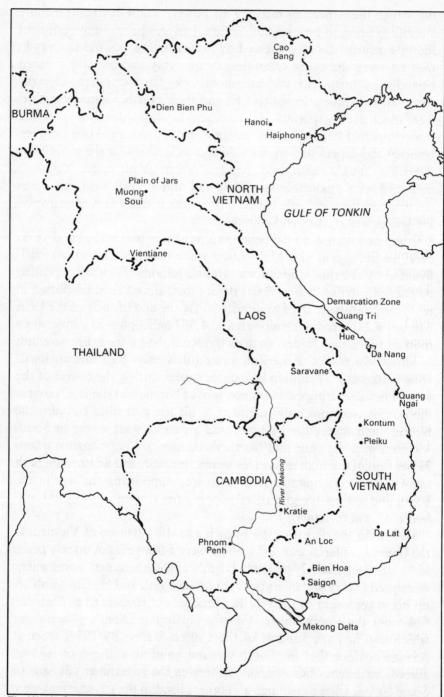

The War in South Vietnam 1964 - 1975

former Vietminh supporters, even though many were simply nationalists rather than Communists. The Southern armed forces were torn
between preparing for an invasion from the North and meeting insurgency in the South. On the whole, they chose the first alternative,
leaving the NLF (or Vietcong—VC) to dominate much of the countryside.[3] This choice in turn increased the pressure on Washington to give
more support to Diem.

President Kennedy allowed US Army Special Forces and USAF Air
Commandos to operate covertly in Vietnam from 1961 onwards—an
operation codenamed 'Farm Gate'. The USA also supplied B-26
bombers and T-28, successors to the Harvard, to the embryonic South
Vietnamese air force but, since few Vietnamese could fly, many of these
planes had to be piloted by Americans. A South Vietnamese officer
was taken on board to maintain the illusion that these were primarily
'training missions', even though they carried out attacks on the insurgents. They made a considerable difference to the military situation.
The government found, for example, as the French had before, that
air cover was the best answer to ambushes. In the first eight months of
1962, 462 convoys were ambushed; in the following twelve months
none of those with air cover were attacked.[4]

Both the US government and the Vietnamese military leaders
became disillusioned with Diem's dictatorial methods and on 1
November 1963 he was overthrown by the South Vietnamese army,
and killed. This made the Saigon government more responsive to
groups such as the South Vietnamese Buddhists, who had opposed
Diem, but it also led to a period of great political instability in Saigon
and of military immobility. In the meantime the NLF further strengthened its hold on the countryside.[5] By 1964 the insurgents were moving
from the guerrilla to the mobile phase of warfare and whole battalions of Vietcong attempted to take over southern towns. Thus Washington gradually and reluctantly concluded that only the use of further
American power could prevent the collapse of the South. On 2 August
the USS *Maddox* off the coast of Vietnam reported that it was under
attack from North Vietnamese torpedo boats and the response was
airborne—the first US bombing raid was made against torpedo boat
bases and oil storage depots in North Vietnam.[6] In December the USA
began openly to attack the Ho Chi Minh Trail through Laos. On 7
February 1965 a US base was attacked in the South and in reprisal
further bombing raids were carried out against targets in the North.
On 8 March 1965 US Marines landed to protect Da Nang airfield and
so the first US ground units had been formally committed to the war.

At about the same time regular units from the North Vietnamese armed forces began to appear in the South. By the end of 1965 the Americans believed that the North had some 53,000 regular forces supporting 100,000 guerrillas, against 570,000 South Vietnamese troops and 184,000 Americans.

The presence of the Americans prevented the fall of Saigon and of other large towns in 1965. However there remained the problem of maintaining communications between the cities and of regaining control of the countryside. The NLF dominated not only the jungle north of Saigon but also most of the villages and hamlets. Road, rail and canal links between the towns were cut by ambushes. The Americans introduced heavy tanks which, with the help of air cover, made it far more difficult for the NLF to stage ambushes and thus kept many of the roads open. It is interesting, for example, to compare the destruction of the French *Force Mobile 100* in 1954 with the experiences of the US 11th Armoured Cavalry which was tasked with keeping open part of Highway One. When the Vietcong attempted to ambush a large convoy on the road in November 1966, US armoured vehicles proved much better able to withstand the guerrillas' weapons than the French had been. More importantly, the Americans had better communications and thus the convoy was rescued by no less than four helicopter gunships, three F-100s dropping napalm and other weapons and two F-5 Freedom Fighters. Not surprisingly the insurgents broke off the attacks and fled. The French had very often failed not only in their efforts at winning over the villages but also in battles against the insurgents after 1950. The Americans had more troops and far more firepower in a smaller area. Consequently the United States was able to win conventional battles whenever it determined to do so.[7]

Re-establishing control of the countryside remained a far more intractable problem. Forays could be made into the jungle and sweeps undertaken through populated areas but the South Vietnamese forces were generally in the habit of returning to the towns at nightfall and leaving the NLF in control. The Americans, for the most part, were committed to the mobile strategy of finding and destroying enemy forces rather than securing the villages. Moreover the insurgents could do more than carry out small ambushes, as they proved decisively at the beginning of 1968. They and their North Vietnamese allies staged a massive offensive attacking 36 of the 45 provincial capitals, 64 of the 242 district capitals and 50 hamlets during the Têt Festival. Anti-government forces may have lost tens of thousands of men but in the process they succeeded in demoralizing many Americans. President

Johnson announced on 31 March 1968 that he would not run for office again and that the USA would cease to bomb most of North Vietnam. Many inside the government and outside became convinced that the war could not be won. We now know that many North Vietnamese and NLF supporters in the South felt the same. But Hanoi was aware of the state of public opinion in the United States, while Washington found it much harder to gauge the morale of its enemies and the American public was far more confused than its government.[8]

After Nixon replaced Johnson as President, American forces in Vietnam were gradually reduced from over half a million until, by the end of 1971, only some 158,000 remained. The Southern forces were now supposed to take the strain. However they had not been able to destroy the guerrillas when the Americans were attacking the North Vietnamese and mobile Vietcong units and it was thus unlikely that they would succeed. They were nearly overrun in 1972 by North Vietnamese tanks and infantry and only the massive use of US air power saved the situation. Nevertheless on 27 January 1973 the USA, the North Vietnamese, NLF and the South Vietnamese signed the Paris Peace Agreement promising the ending of the fighting and the withdrawal of US and other foreign forces. On 28 March the last US troops left the South. Two years later North Vietnamese forces attacked again but the US Congress would not permit the use of American air power as it had done in 1972 and on 30 April 1975 Saigon fell to Northern troops.

The North Vietnamese leadership had a profound understanding of the West's strengths and weaknesses. Ho Chi Minh had lived in Britain and France.[9] He knew that Washington's endurance was limited and that the American people would tire quickly, as the French had done. On the strategic level, he hoped that battles, such as Dien Bien Phu in 1954 or the 1968 Têt offensive, would give the impression that the wars could not be won by the government's forces or might be won only after many punishing years. On the tactical level, ambushes were specifically designed to catch soldiers trained in the tactics of Western military establishments.[10] Northern methods were particularly effective against an open society of the American type. The Vietnam war was the most extensively reported conflict in history. The press could very largely report only on the Southern side. Inherently it would provide negative news and concentrate on what was going wrong rather than what was going right. The way the media treated the conflict undoubtedly had a profound influence on American opinion, making many despair of victory and loathe the bloodshed. The USA also had to co-operate with a regime in Saigon which was unstable, corrupt and habitually used torture on a very large scale. The political difficulties involved were under-lined by the Western media.[11]

In the South, government forces had to respond both to conventional warfare with North Vietnamese and mobile Vietcong units and to the actions of the guerrillas. This two-sided conflict vastly complicated the situation since different skills are called for in the two operations. Commentators, such as Sir Robert Thompson, who have written about operations against guerrillas, have frequently stressed the policing rather than the military aspect of operations. They have argued that the government's first problem is to secure the towns, to win over the citizens and to prevent infiltration by the insurgents. Government forces can then move into the countryside, securing village after village and separating the civilians from the insurgents, thereby depriving the guerrillas of their sources of food. Only in the final stage need the government be concerned about searching out and destroying the guer-rillas.[12] But, by the time American forces landed in the country, the war in the South had many of the elements of a conventional struggle. The US and South Vietnamese forces had to fight full-scale battles with armour and aircraft in the countryside in order to keep the roads open and to protect the cities and US bases. For example, in one of the fiercest battles of the war, some 20,000 Communist troops attacked the US base at Khe San for sixty-six days early in 1968. The Americans made about 850 aircraft sorties each day in defence of the base and the B-52 strategic bombers alone made 2,548 sorties and dropped 53,000 tons of bombs. Battles of this dimension often interfered with the need to win over the Southern population, many of whom were killed or had to flee the fighting by living in the towns. On the other hand US victories in such struggles did not deprive the insurgents of food sup-plies or of recruits from amongst the villagers.

Thus the Pentagon has been bitterly criticized for fighting guerrillas with conventional methods. Critics argued at the time that 'the very availability of an advanced technology tends to inhibit the imagination'. Even ex-President Nixon wrote later:

> our armed forces were experts at mobilizing huge resources, orchestrating logistic support and deploying enormous fire-power. In Vietnam these skills led them to fight the war their way, rather than developing new skills required to defeat the new kind of enemy they faced. They made the mistake of fighting an uncon-ventional war with conventional tactics.[13]

This was to some extent because the conventional military threat seemed the most immediate one in 1965, partly because the Americans expected the South Vietnamese to be better at counter-insurgency amongst their own people and thus often left that part of the struggle to them, and partly because of the nature of American society. It was the most technologically advanced nation in the world and thus it naturally preferred to fight a technological war. Its military tradition pointed in the same direction. It had contributed vast quantities of men, machinery and money to the allied victories in 1918 and 1944–45 and its armed forces were built up to fight a war with the most modern weapons against the USSR. Thus their advanced weapons were the ones most immediately available when they were drawn into the conflict in 1964 and 1965. The navy could launch aircraft attacks against the enemy from carriers off the coast. The US Air Force could use all types of aircraft from the humble Cessna to the B-52 strategic bomber, from the most advanced F.111 fighter-bomber to the lumbering Hercules C-130 transport.

In the event these exertions were never satisfactorily complemented by efforts to win over the countryside. Thus, when Robert McNamara, the US Defence Secretary, visited Vietnam in 1966, he concluded that the mobile war against the NLF was going well but that 'pacification has if anything gone backward'. South Vietnamese officials were often corrupt and incompetent. The South Vietnamese army, like the American, preferred regular warfare to policing; as one senior US official put it, 'its commitment to pacification is negligible'.[14] Of course one should not exaggerate US indifference to pacification, which some units carried out very ably; James McDonough has, for example, described his very typical struggle as a Platoon Leader to protect and pacify the village of Truong Lam near Highway One. In the end, when the Vietcong could not drive the Americans from the village, they decided to destroy it. We also now know that NLF morale was declining rapidly in 1966; as one of their supporters recalled later, 'the truth was that we were losing more than we were winning. The villagers supported the VC, but there wasn't anything like the high morale I remembered. Instead there was an unspoken feeling that we couldn't win now that the Americans were there. They were just too strong—helicopters, jets, B-52s. How could you beat them?'[15]

Moreover one should acknowledge the extent of US technical achievements. They demonstrated for the first time that armour could be used effectively in jungle, freeing mechanized units from being totally dependent upon roads.[16] They introduced laser-guided weapons for great accuracy. Thus they were able to destroy North Vietnamese tanks with Pave Nail weapons, even when the tanks were on top of bunkers occupied by Americans, without killing US troops. One strike by a Phantom armed with laser-guided bombs destroyed the Than Hoa bridge in 1972 when dozens of strikes with conventional bombs had previously failed.[17] They showed how decisively strategic bombers could be used in the tactical role. They employed fixed-wing gunships for the first time in warfare. Dakotas with lines of guns firing 'broad-side' to the aircraft changed the balance of power in the mobile warfare taking place in 1966. By the end of that year the Dakotas had defended 500 forts successfully, expended fourteen million rounds of ammunition and dropped 81,700 flares to protect Southern forces which were being attacked under cover of darkness. Subsequently the Dakotas were replaced by the even more powerful AC-130 Hercules gunships.[18] If the Phantom was the most effective fighter bomber of the war, then the Hercules not only proved an immensely powerful gunship but also dominated the transport effort, carrying supplies right into the battle zone, evacuating refugees and surviving extensive battle damage. In the area of supply, as in so much else, the Americans demonstrated great technical ingenuity.[19]

Above all the Americans made massive use of helicopters and perfected the helicopter gunships pioneered by the French. Armed Huey helicopters were operating in Vietnam from 1962 onwards but the experiment was greatly expanded when the United States became openly involved. At the beginning of 1964 the Americans had some 388 aircraft in Vietnam including 248 helicopters by the end of September the US Army alone had 406 aircraft. The First Cavalry Division (Airmobile) was activated in July 1965 and began to arrive in Vietnam the following month. The first helicopters involved in Vietnam were UH-34s. Some of these were more heavily armed to act as escorts to those transporting troops. However this caused problems because the 'gunships' could not then keep up with the transports. It was not until the AH-1G Cobra came into service in September 1967 that the problem was rectified, because the Cobra had been designed from the beginning as a gunship and was thus much faster and more powerful.

The helicopters transformed the war. They rescued columns which had been ambushed, evacuated casualties and 'downed' airmen, carried out reconnaissance and protected outposts. It was not, therefore, surprising that the Americans made thirty times more helicopter than fixed-wing sorties or that helicopter pilots themselves concluded that 'the major reason our leaders felt we could win when the French hadn't was our helicopters'.[20] Of course many helicopters were lost but they were often used in very difficult circumstances, particularly when they landed troops or evacuated casualties under extremely heavy enemy fire.

The disadvantage was that the Americans sometimes succumbed to the insidious temptation to use helicopters and so avoid struggling through the jungle even when only ground observation and contact could achieve the desired military results. One Vietcong recalled later that his men knew the ground so well that 'usually we could escape . . . even when they used helicopters to surround us. . . . That happened at Soi Cut where they destroyed three villages while they were trying to catch us.' Finally the helicopters vastly increased mobility, leading the British expert on counter-insurgency, Sir Robert Thompson, to conclude that, 'without the helicopter "search and destroy" would not have been possible and, in this sense, the helicopter was one of the main contributors to the failure of strategy'.[21] The point really was that search and destroy operations had to be accompanied by efforts to protect or win over the villagers, as in Malaya and Dhofar, if the government's forces were to succeed.

When they were operating in the South, the Vietcong and their Northern allies responded to the superiority of American firepower by hiding amongst civilians and by building vast complexes of underground tunnels in the countryside. These networks hid them from observation and gave them some protection against bombs and shells. Even in the Mekong Delta, where water was very close to the surface, the guerrillas still went underground. As one explained, 'we had to build surface shelters, hidden in various mounds or tunnels between rice fields. Despite the nightly firing there was surprisingly little loss of life.' Frequently the Americans found that the Vietcong hid in holes in the ground ventilated by hollowed-out bamboo sticks. The guerrillas knew where the South Vietnamese and Americans were; however, with all their technology, the Americans frequently could not find the insurgents, despite the efforts expended.

Many of these efforts involved the use of reconnaissance aircraft such as the OV-1 Mohawk and OV-10 Bronco. These propeller-driven aircraft could carry infra-red surveillance equipment, flares for night photography and side-looking radar. One of the Mohawk's army pilots wrote later:

we flew daily coastal patrols looking for evidence of infiltration by VC from the sea. There were airborne radar missions looking for movement by boat along rivers and canals at night, with helicopter fire teams on call to attack any target located. There were infra-red missions looking for underground bunkers and tunnels and visual photographic reconnaissance as well. All this effort was by the US army. In addition the USAF and US Navy conducted reconnaissance . . . At the height of the US involvement the US Army had an aviation brigade in Vietnam, in addition to the organic aviation assets each infantry division possessed.

One of the results was that there was often more information than the intelligence organizations could process. Sometimes also the tech-nology did not work in practice: 'the "people-sniffer" missions were a case in point. Human sweat leaves trace elements in the air. Design a sensor which is mounted in an aircraft (usually a helicopter). Find same and attack with gunships.' In fact, despite hours of effort, the system never worked in the jungle.[22]

But, whatever the difficulties of finding the insurgents, if their general whereabouts could be discovered, the psychological effects on them of the heavy bombing raids cannot be exaggerated. The Amer-icans knew that the effect on their morale was often more important than the physical impact because, on at least one occasion, the B-52s had dropped their bombs on government forces. But the terror produced seemed to them to justify the $30,000 cost of the sorties which began in 1965. As one NLF leader put it, 'nothing the guerrillas had to endure compared with the stark terrorization of the B-52 bom-bardments . . . It was as if an enormous scythe has swept through the jungle, felling the giant teak trees like grass in its way . . . You would come back to where your lean-to and bunker had been, your home, and there would simply be nothing there, just an unrecognizable landscape gouged by immense craters.' Another insurgent recalled:

> one of the things that demoralized a lot of guerrillas were the B-52 attacks. The fear these attacks caused was terrible. People pissed and shat in their pants. You would see them coming out of the bunkers shaking so badly it looked as though they had gone crazy . . . Even when there weren't direct hits, the pressure from the explosions would kill people in their bunkers.

Accordingly some were modified to give two entrances and allow the pressure to escape. The effect was still horrific:

It was like a giant earthquake. The whole area was filled with fire and smoke. Trees were falling all around. My shelter collapsed on me although it hadn't been hit. I felt as if I were sitting in a metal case which someone was pounding with a hammer. I was sure I was dying. [23]

Many accounts suggest that the guerrillas had warning of impending attacks and were able to flee or hide in their bunkers. They claim that B-52s flying from Guam would be identified by Soviet intelligence vessels in the South China Sea. The heading and air speed of the aircraft would be relayed to the NLF. Flights from Thailand would also be monitored and warning given. Such claims imply that the precise target of the aircraft was known before the bombs fell. This would be surprising, since the heading and speed of the aircraft might well be changed in flight to avoid storms or for other reasons. An alternative possibility was that the anti-government forces were listening in to the 'combat skyspot' system under which those on the ground in Vietnam directed the B-52s to their targets. But perhaps the main point was that the guerrillas knew that B-52s were on their way and took whatever means they could to mitigate the effects. [24]

Even without the bombing raids, life for the anti-government forces in the jungle was very hard. Snakes and disease killed more guerrillas than the government's attacks. Malaria was rampant and although the guerrillas had hospitals in Cambodia, they could often reach these only with difficulty. Thus the death rate amongst them was very high. Sir Robert Thompson calculated that they suffered 50,000 casualties in 1966 alone and the figure was higher the following year. The struggle called for great courage and determination. Yet the anti-government forces kept recruiting from the North or from the villages and thus the rate of attrition was not enough to defeat them.

In some ways the war came to resemble the struggle in the trenches in the First World War. Just as in that war, enough enemy survived artillery barrages to prevent infantry attacks from succeeding; so in Vietnam the great bombing raids could never destroy enough Vietcong and North Vietnamese to give the government permanent control of the countryside. The Americans were, however, able to break up large concentrations of Vietcong and to clear the insurgents out of some areas by the use of armour, aircraft and defoliants. American technology could always prevent the insurgents winning a mobile war, despite the guerrillas' skill in arranging ambushes and building fortifications. But the South Vietnamese forces, whose primary responsibility it was, were never effective at preventing guerrillas from creeping back and re-establishing their influence amongst the population in the country.

Defoliation was a technological solution to the problems faced by the Americans and their allies in the jungle. Aerial crop sprays had been used in the USA since the early 1920s to deal with agricultural pests. The British had experimented with defoliation in Malaya and the Americans had also tested the idea in the USA, using fixed-wing aircraft such as B-29s. From 1961 onwards they were under increasing pressure from Diem to provide his troops with defoliants and some experiments were carried out along Route 13 during that year. The Americans were more sceptical than the South Vietnamese of their military efficacy of defoliants and they rightly worried about the effects on civilians in the area where sprays were used. There were to be frequent complaints from farmers about the results of the sprays on their crops and trees.[25] Gradually, however, the practice spread. Defoliants were used to clear the sides of roads and rivers and thus to reduce the chance of ambushes. They also destroyed crops grown by the Vietcong. Many Americans were critical. Dean Rusk warned in August 1962, 'the way to win the war basically is to win the people. Crop destruction runs counter to this basic rule' since Vietcong and civilian crops could not be distinguished.[26] The South Vietnamese claimed that they would compensate any farmer whose crops were damaged though this proved a slow or non-existent process. The US pilots also genuinely tried to avoid damaging civilian crops and the problems arose from mistakes, drifting sprays and other factors.

The peak year for defoliation missions was 1967 with 1.7 million acres sprayed by US and South Vietnamese forces. By then public and scientific hostility was mounting. The Vietcong had always claimed that the sprays were poisonous. US officials had believed that this was not the case and the South Vietnamese even had officials going round the country eating bread soaked in defoliants in front of the villagers to prove they were not toxic.[27] However there were increasing fears that the Vietcong might be right and there is evidence that Agent Orange in particular caused birth defects and other problems. Since the end of the war, US courts have awarded $200 million to a quarter of a million veterans who might have been damaged by defoliants. At the time less was known about such dangers but defoliation increased the general feeling that the conflict was causing too much damage and suffering to civilians.[28]

The air war in the South in general demonstrated once again the difficulty of using aircraft to attack guerrillas in populated areas without hurting innocent bystanders. For this reason, according to some accounts, Diem had frowned on air strikes and threatened severe punishment for any pilots carrying out attacks which killed civilians.[29] Even then, Western journalists reported cases of casual South Vietnamese attacks on innocent villages. Later the US armed forces usually took far greater precautions than the South Vietnamese to try to avoid civilian casualties.[30] As one typical American Standard Operating procedure put it, 'maximum effort will be made to minimize non-combatant casualties during operations'.[31] Thus President Nixon claimed 'civilians accounted for about the same proportion of casualties as in the Second World War and a far smaller one than in the Korean war'.[32] On the other hand, many civilians were driven out of their homes by bombing even if they were not killed and, because of the political nature of guerrilla warfare, civilian casualties probably had a greater impact on the outcome of the war than they had had in earlier conflicts.

To try to minimize attacks on civilians, the peasants were moved out of some areas which were then declared 'free fire' zones where anything that moved was assumed to be hostile. Thus journalists reported that around Saigon, 'the area is pockmarked with bombs. Villages stand abandoned and half-destroyed amongst waterlogged and derelict ricefields. And the same picture can be seen around all of the inhabited areas of the country.' In the province of Quang Ngai 70 per cent of villages had been destroyed by the end of 1967. Even so the insurgents remained in their tunnels in these areas, from which they emerged to send rockets into the cities. They were also able to infiltrate the cities to arouse fear and confusion by planting bombs and threatening those who associated with the Americans.

Where civilians were allowed to remain in the countryside, great care was needed to avoid killing or wounding them. Thus forward air controllers (FACs) played a vital role, working either with ground troops or in Mohawks and Broncos. They would spend six months as pilots with fighter units then operate spotter aircraft or join US, Korean or South Vietnamese ground forces. When the situation was too dangerous for propeller aircraft to operate, they were replaced by fast jets, such as the TA-4F. But, despite these efforts, the system did not always work. Failures occurred because the FAC made mistakes and incorrectly identified civilians as insurgents. Alternatively those giving the orders (particularly if they were Vietnamese) were prepared to risk civilian lives in order to kill Vietcong, or else some technical problem undermined the system. For example, two fighter-bombers destroyed the villages of Lang Vei on 2 March 1967, killing 100 people and wounding a further 200. The Pentagon attributed the disaster to malfunction of the weapons.[33]

In any case, while pilots were sometimes frustrated by what they regarded as the stupid and dangerous restrictions under which they had to operate, the world's press, watching the conflict with a sceptical eye, was unimpressed by the efforts made to avoid civilian casualties. Too often it seemed to them that the decision was taken to obliterate villages completely because Vietcong were in possession, even when all of the civilians had not necessarily departed. Aircrew also dropped leaflets to warn of their intentions though many of the people could not read. The Vietcong no doubt hoped that the government's forces would alienate the people in this way. For example a 'model' Catholic village, named Thai Hiep, was built to house 1,000 people just outside the large US air base at Bien Hoa. In February 1969 it was infiltrated by Vietcong. When the South Vietnamese Rangers failed to fight their way in and to eject or destroy the intruders 'the decision was taken to bomb Thai Hiep out of existence. The military reasoning was that Bien Hoa base and Long Binh camp were endangered by their presence.'[34] A US spokesman also argued that more casualties would result if the government forces had continued to fight their way back into the village. Furthermore, fifteen minutes before the bombing by F-100s and Skyraiders, loudspeakers warned any civilians left to flee and leaflets were dropped from the air. But could civilians flee in such circumstances or would they be too frightened to move? Where the bodies displayed afterwards all Vietcong? The journalists were unconvinced.

Similar problems occurred in the key battle of the war—the Tết offensive in 1968. Saigon itself was infiltrated by some nine battalions of guerrillas who came into the city in twos and threes disguised as civilians. After hiding for some days they seized part of the US Embassy, the presidential palace and several other American billets. They attacked the Vietnam navy's headquarters, the joint general staff headquarters on the Tan Son air base and they left the Vietnam radio station in flames. Gradually, however, they were forced backwards or destroyed.

Other Vietcong units fought street battles in the crowded suburbs of Cholon in the west, and Phu Nhuan in the north. With permission from the Vietnam army commanders, American helicopters strafed and rocketed the streets. Civilian casualties soared into the hundreds but any more accurate assessment would be guesswork. The Skyraiders also rocketed and left in charred rubble the poor quarter behind the An Quang Pagoda, the headquarters of the anti-government faction of Buddhist monks led by the Venerable Tri Quang.[35]

In the countryside many of the 'model' villages were destroyed after the Vietcong had established themselves there. Another reporter commented, 'the impact of the Vietcong attack is perhaps best underscored by what occurred around Qui Nhon. "What they did was occupy the hamlets we pacified, just for the purpose of having the allies move in and bomb them out" said one American official, "By their presence the hamlets were destroyed".'[36] The former capital, Hué, was also very badly damaged. After three weeks fighting *The Times* reported on 19 February, 'the American Marine battalion engaged in reducing the fanatical Communist resistance in Hué citadel had by this evening lost about half its combat strength in what has become a hellish battle'.[37] Inevitably the struggle caused high civilian casualties and the ruin of much of the ancient town.

Nevertheless, two years after Têt many felt that the government was winning the war in the South. Intelligence reports suggested that shortage of manpower was forcing the Vietcong to recruit more women. Sir Robert Thompson wrote in December 1969, 'in this last year there has been a race back into the countryside which has been won by the South Vietnamese, helped by the Americans'.[38] Thompson believed that South Vietnamese units were now up to strength but that the Vietcong were running short of recruits and that they had lost the 'cream of their army'. Two months previously another journalist had suggested that the Saigon government controlled 85 per cent of the population and 35 per cent of the country.[39] Later accounts by NLF supporters confirm the demoralization both in the North and the South caused by the casualties in the Têt and other offensives. But, if the insurgents' morale was hit, US morale was sinking and far more obviously.

The Americans were indeed becoming even more determined to withdraw their ground troops and to leave most of the fighting to the South Vietnamese. Such a resolution was strengthened in November 1969 when revelations about a massacre of up to 600 men, women and children by US troops at My Lai in Quang Ngai Province received banner headlines.[40] The massacre, by part of General Koster's American Division, had taken place in March 1968 and had been accompanied by unspeakable brutalities. But these had been hidden by members of the Division. Although US spokesmen argued that the incident was atypical and pointed out that far more people had been killed in cold blood by the Vietcong when they captured Hué during the Têt offensive, the reports confirmed all the critics of the war in their opinions. Many argued that the massacre reflected American racism and brutality towards the civilian population. Some believed that they showed that the American army was badly trained, demoralized and incompetent. Such criticisms were not surprising but they were particularly galling to those who had risked their lives in order to minimize civilian casualties or who saw that the problem was partly caused by US troops behaving like the Vietnamese themselves. In any case the incident confirmed public support for Nixon's plan to leave most of the fighting to the Vietnamese. Two-thirds of those polled in July 1969 were in favour of some withdrawals.[41]

In April 1972 most of the American troops had thus left and only the massive use of US air power saved the South, the North Vietnamese forces attacked with some 200,000 men and 600 tanks[42] and twelve South Vietnamese fire bases were quickly overrun. By the beginning of May the Southern army had decided to withdraw from Quang Tri. Panic followed and the USA had to send in helicopters to rescue the Southern regulars. One US officer reported, 'it was an appalling sight. From Fire Base Nancy to the May Canh river along Highway One there was just a complete litter of US built armoured personnel carriers, tanks and trucks.'[43] Hué itself was threatened but US air power gradually wore down the attackers; An Loc, 60 miles north of Saigon, was defended by 5,000 South Vietnamese though it was US B-52s and fighter bombers which broke the attack and saved the defenders. By the end of May the South Vietnamese lines had hardened after the South Vietnamese and Americans had increased their sortie rate to 15,000 a month. The disaster was temporarily averted but the Americans could not intervene in the same way three years later, partly because of Congressional opposition, and thus South Vietnam collapsed.

Looked at in one way, Vietnam was the climax of the use of air power in inconventional warfare. Far more aircraft were used more innovatively than ever before, bombing caused much greater and more widespread protests and demonstrations than ever before and the insurgents were much more capable. Thus, on the face of it, air power proved ineffective. On the other hand, this was partly because it was not just confronted with an insurgency but also by conventional attacks. Had the Americans been faced with an insurgency of the scope and type that the British had to deal with in Malaya or Dhofar, then they might have developed the same means to defeat it, using military power in general merely to supplement pacification measures. As it was, the combination of regular and irregular warfare proved highly effective against them because pacification and all-out conventional warfare co-exist extremely uneasily together.

Before the Americans openly committed ground forces in March 1965 some parts of their armed forces had given much thought to unconventional warfare and to the use of air power in such conflicts. The Rand Corporation, in particular, had produced a series of excellent reports on Malaya, Algeria and other insurgencies.[44] The Americans were also the first power since 1945 to develop an air force comprising cheap, slow and accurate aircraft dedicated to fighting guerrillas. One expert journalist, who was allowed to examine the equipment at Eglin in Florida in 1963, was evidently greatly impressed by the efforts expended. The Americans were already equipping B-26, C-46 and T-28 aircraft specifically for defeating guerrillas.[45] The T-28 had been replaced by the T-7 as the standard US trainer and thus very large numbers were available for modification by the addition of two 0.50 machine-guns and bomb racks. The B-26 was already a veteran of French anti-guerrilla operations in which it had proved highly effective.[46] It had also achieved fame, or notoriety, in April 1961 as the aircraft which was to back up the American invasion of Cuba at the Bay of Pigs. Some writers still maintain that the invasion might have been successful if President Kennedy had allowed the B-26s to be used more widely.[47] Certainly if the air force established at Eglin had been carefully used to back up pacification measures against guerrillas it might have been very effective indeed.

But by the time Washington agreed to become openly involved, the war had become a mobile as well as a guerrilla operation and, from that time onwards, the US had to fight North Vietnamese regulars as well as guerrillas. Thus all types of US forces were committed and, not surprisingly, they proved capable of defeating the North Vietnamese and their Southern supporters whenever they were openly challenged. The North could never have moved from the mobile to the final phase of an insurgency while the US was fully involved. But US staying power was limited and the US also could never be victorious because, as pointed out earlier, the South Vietnamese government proved incapable of winning over the villagers and the Americans were never fully dedicated to this task. Thus it was US willpower which broke first and aircraft helped in this process by raising the costs to the American taxpayer and by making the war appear more bloody and destructive.

The Problem of Sanctuaries

Most, if not all, successful guerrilla movements in recent history have received supplies and support from a friendly neighbouring country.[1] Sympathizers in Syria were immensely helpful in providing help for the Palestinian insurgents between 1936 and 1939; the withdrawal of support by the regimes in Albania, Yugoslavia and Bulgaria was the crucial factor in determining that the insurgents would fail in Greece after 1948; the fact that the guerrilla movements in Kenya and Malaya were not assisted by governments in Africa and South-East Asia respectively played no small part in enabling the British to defeat them; French success in interdicting supplies and reinforcements flowing from Tunisia into Algeria greatly aided their forces there. Conversely the establishment of a Communist government in China in 1949 radically changed the balance of power in Indochina and enabled the Vietminh to expel the French in 1954.

The presence or absence of a sanctuary in a neighbouring country is thus often the key factor in determining whether a government will defeat the insurgents, as Bernard Fall and others have pointed out. Governments faced with an insurgency theoretically have a number of options in meeting the problem but in practice many of these are often not realistic; they can ignore the source of the supplies reaching the guerillas, they can build physical barriers along their frontier, they can bring political and economic pressure to bear on the state providing sanctuary to persuade it to change its policy, they can launch attacks exclusively against the insurgents within the neighbouring country or they can assail the 'sanctuary state' itself.

The final military options have rarely been chosen. The Greeks and their Anglo-American advisers were too afraid of causing a Third World War to contemplate attacks on Bulgaria or Yugoslavia. Similarly the French clearly had to avoid a war with China in 1950, however much assistance Peking provided for Ho Chi Minh's forces. But they were not afraid of Tunisia and Morocco and were limited in their attacks on bases in their territory more by opinion amongst their allies than by other factors. They were also enthusiastic about the Suez operation in 1956 partly at least because they believed that Colonel Nasser was supporting the FLN in Algeria. On the other hand all such attacks brought international protests [and it was the line of obstacles which the French built between Algeria and Tunisia that handicapped the insurgents, not such retaliation]. The British were restricted from taking reprisals against Yemeni territory during the insurgency in Aden not by Yemen's strength but by the storm of protests in Britain which followed one airborne operation. The Soviets and their Afghan allies launched attacks on refugee camps in Pakistan but did not make a full-scale ground and air attack on Pakistani territory presumably for fear of drawing in increasing quantities of US arms, if not American armed forces. One writer has thus argued that 'compared with almost every Western nation faced with externally-supplied insurgency [Soviet] behaviour has been the model of restraint'.[2] This is an exaggeration; the Americans, the South Africans and the Israelis are the only nations which have responded to the problem of sanctuaries by making deep and prolonged conventional attacks on guerrillas or their supporters in a 'sanctuary state'. The USA confined its response largely to air attacks against North Vietnam but, in co-operation with its South Vietnamese allies, it invaded Laos and Cambodia. Similarly South Africa has occupied parts of Angola since 1975 in order to prevent the government there supporting the SWAPO guerillas in South-West Africa. Israel took over part of the Lebanon in June 1982 to try to drive out the Palestian Liberation Organization (PLO).

From the point of view of the use of air power, the US attacks on North Vietnam are more illuminating than the other attacks on sanctuaries. The war in Vietnam presented the USA with a series of acute dilemmas. According to US figures, the North sent the Vietcong about 30 per cent of their supplies and the rest they acquired in the South. Hanoi transmitted these provisions together with its own troops down the Ho Chi Minh trail through Laos and Cambodia and into the South. Faced with this situation officials in Washington considered the possibilities to be: (i) invading the North and breaking up its forces; (ii) persuading Hanoi to stop interfering in the South by bombing its territory; (iii) bombing or attacking the Ho Chi Minh trail through the neutral states of Laos and Cambodia; (iv) ignoring the problem and concentrating on defeating the guerrillas and North Vietnamese troops in the South. All courses had serious disadvantages. An invasion of the North would have been a very large military enterprise. The North's conventional forces would presumably have been quickly defeated but the struggle would still have continued in the jungles and the outcome would simply have been a guerrilla war spread over both parts of Vietnam. More importantly, officials in Washington assumed that it would bring the Chinese into the war as the invasion of North Korea had done a decade and a half earlier.[3] General Wheeler, the Chairman of the Joint Chiefs of Staff was nevertheless in favour of invading the North, though his views were rejected.[4]

But, if an invasion of the North was dismissed, so was the possibility of simply ignoring the problem of sanctuary and concentrating on operations in the South, since many US military officers argued that the Vietcong could never be defeated while North Vietnam, Laos and Cambodia provided it with a sanctuary.[5] As far as the North was concerned, the United States chose to attack it from the air but not to invade. Apart from the fear of bringing in China if they sent in ground forces, one of the reasons the Americans selected this option was that the bombing was not only intended to coerce Hanoi. General Maxwell Taylor, the US Ambassador in Saigon, argued in November 1964 that the continuation of the bombing would (i) bolster morale in the South; (ii) encourage political stability in Saigon; (iii) help the campaign against the insurgency; (iv) persuade the North to give up trying to overthrow the Southern government.[6] It is impossible to prove that Southern morale or political stability was improved by the raids. No doubt many were pleased that the fighting and suffering was not confined to the South but how large a proportion of the Southern people knew what was going on or could imagine the raids? Successful operations in the South would seem likely to have been more important to most Southerners, although it is true that the Saigon government protested when US presidents from time to time halted the bombing. As far as the anti-insurgency campaign was concerned it could only have been assisted if the bombing helped the interdiction of supplies from the North and, as we shall see, the interdiction campaign did not prove very successful.

Knocking out the North or forcing it to abandon the war in the South by heavy air strikes was much the most ambitious and important of General Taylor's projected aims. It also proved very difficult to achieve, partly because of the dearth of suitable targets, partly because of the totalitarian nature of Northern society and partly because Northern defences became stronger as time went on. The situation was not helped by the US decision to 'escalate' gradually, which gave Hanoi time to prepare and also allowed public opinion to become more and more hostile to the enterprise both in the USA and in the rest of the world. Memories of Guernica, Coventry and Dresden still remained and hostility to bombing attacks against cities was fierce. Accordingly, the Americans tried to limit their attacks to military targets but this proved difficult because SAM sites and military transport were often deliberately placed in residential locations. Furthermore, aiming errors inevitably occurred and women and children were killed, thus reinforcing the worldwide hostility to the operation.

Against this background the US Air Force gradually extended its bombing raids. In August 1964 there were strikes against ports, naval bases and petroleum stocks as a retaliation for alleged attacks on US destroyers in the Gulf of Tonkin.[7] These were followed in February and March 1965 by attacks on communications in North Vietnam below the 19th Parallel and thus well away from Hanoi. In July 1965 the first US fighter was shot down over the North and Johnson and McNamara allowed attacks on SAM sites which were firing at US aircraft below the 20th Parallel. The war was further expanded with attacks on the Hanoi area and the port of Haiphong in June 1966. By the end of 1966 the USA was flying 12,000 sorties a month against the North and in the following year the number of permitted targets was increased to include power stations, airfields, industrial sites and the railway between North Vietnam and China. Meanwhile between 1965 and 1968 Johnson halted the bombing of the North sixteen times in the hope that the policy of 'carrots and sticks' would push the government in Hanoi towards a compromise peace.[8]

Then in 1968 Johnson abandoned the 'Rolling Thunder' attacks on the North after the US had made 304,000 fighter-bomber sorties and 2,380 B-52 raids and dropped 643,000 tons of bombs. However, Nixon restarted the raids again later, not least in the massive Linebacker 1 offensive in May 1972. This involved carpet bombing attacks much closer to Hanoi and Haiphong and the blocking of all North Vietnam's harbours, including Haiphong, by mines. US air power halted the North Vietnamese offensive which was threatening to overrun Saigon, although it is unclear how much this was due to the tactical offensive against North Vietnamese forces in the South and how much to the strategic offensive against the North. The even more massive Linebacker II offensive was launched on 18 December 1972, when the peace negotiations were at a standstill and the US administration hoped to force Hanoi to make concessions.[9]

The effects of the gradual build-up of US bombing before 1968 were ambiguous. As far as Northern morale went, one of the more experienced correspondents argued, 'the bombing of the North was aimed not only at hindering the movement of men and materials to the South but weakening the spirits of the civilians in Hanoi and Haiphong. Instead, the constant pounding built up a "Battle of Britain" type of resistance amongst the people.' Similarly Sir Robert Thompson believed that the attacks rallied the North Vietnamese people round their government. In fact it was difficult at the time to be sure how the North Vietnamese people responded. Western correspondents going to the North were often sympathetic to the Vietcong and, in any case, were only shown what the Northern authorities wanted them to see.[10] We now have a great deal more evidence and know that the response was complex. There are plenty of authenticated cases of Northerners volunteering to fight because their friends and relatives had been killed by the bombing; as one recalled later, 'during one of the air strikes on Haiphong my fiancé was killed by an American bomb. Immediately afterwards I decided that I had to go south to fight . . . If I didn't join up straight away I'd miss my chance for revenge.' We also know that the bombing greatly increased hatred for the Americans and thus strengthened the Northern government: 'during the bombings everyone suffered. Hatred for the Saigon side and the Americans grew even stronger than it had been before. A lot of young people volunteered for the army at that time.'[11]

However we also now know that the privations of the war accentuated by the bombing wore down the Northern people. Many became demoralized and more and more tried to avoid being conscripted into the war. People noticed that the anti-aircraft weapons were being placed in civilian zones thus increasing the casualties.They also saw that many of the sons of government officials were avoiding being sent southwards and that none of those who did go returned. Many deliberately maimed themselves in order to avoid service or bribed the officials involved. A Vietcong member who visited the city at the end of the war, and thus saw more than Westerners were allowed to do, was certainly struck by Hanoi's dreariness, the bomb damage, the neglected buildings, the look of grim preoccupation amongst the people and the 'air of melancholy given off by people who seemed to have aged prematurely'.[12] What is certain is that the bombing did not effect the determination of the government in Hanoi to win the war and that the number of soldiers infiltrating southwards actually increased from perhaps 7,000 to 24,000 a month—a fact which the US authorities recognized.[13] The point was that the early hatred caused by the bombing had an actual impact because it increased the odium of the Americans and encouraged Northerners to go South and fight more ferociously. The subsequent demoralization was invisible to the USA and thus it did not encourage Washington to continue the war; nor because of the closed nature of Northern society, did it cause Hanoi to sue for peace.

Equally certain is the way that the bombing dominated press comments and much of the diplomacy of the war. The extent of the opposition was reflected in the anti-American demonstrations across the Western world. Even Alastair Buchan, the first Director of the Institute for Strategic Studies, could write in December 1970 of the 'anger and contempt which . . . area bombing in North Vietnam arouses in this country, most particularly among those of us who admire the achievements and respect the values of American society'. Ironically, considering France's own campaigns against guerrillas, General de Gaulle commented 'we find it totally detestable that a small country should be bombed by a very big one'.[14] One of the leading US experts on guerrilla warfare, Edward Lansdale, argued later that opposition to bombing would have been reduced if each raid had been a reprisal for a specific insurgent action in the South.[15] Many raids were explicitly made for such reasons but there seems little cause to believe that the opposition was any the less. The original US attacks were in response to the Gulf of Tonkin incident. On 5 February, 3 May and 20 November 1970, US aircraft bombed North Vietnamese SAM sites in response to attacks on unarmed reconnaissance aircraft. Finally, as we have seen, the US B-52 raids in April 1972 were designed to try to halt the Northern invasion of the South. All attacks north of the 20th Parallel were stopped once again on 23 October 1972 then resumed on a massive scale on 18 December when the Paris talks were deadlocked.[16]

None of this 'fine tuning' appeased those opposed to the bombing. Many objected to any sort of bombing, particularly if civilians were killed. Others felt that Washington's explanations were simply excuses, and inadequate ones at that. Had Northern warships really attacked US warships in the Gulf of Tonkin? If reconnaissance aircraft had been fired at in 1970 then they should not have been flying over North Vietnam. If the Northern invasion of the South in 1972 could only be repelled by bombing Hanoi, did this not show that the Southern regime was doomed? Finally and most importantly, the whole trend of world opinion was increasingly hostile to Western military actions in the Third World. Of all types of military action, bombing is perhaps the most difficult to justify, particularly when carried out by a superpower against a small nation. Presentationally, there was very little that Presidents Johnson and Nixon could do to make it palatable.

Technically, the bombing of the North was a considerable achievement, requiring immense courage from those who participated and suffered high losses. Many were killed, others were badly treated if they fell into Northern hands.[17] At the beginning of the bomber offensive in 1964 Northern defences were primitive but they were rapidly improved with Chinese and particularly Soviet assistance. Within a year nearly 200 radars and 7,000 anti-aircraft guns were deployed.[18] There were probably some thirty MiGs in North Vietnam in 1964 but this total had more than doubled by the following year and in September 1966 they made a major attempt to disrupt the offensive. The highly manoeuvrable MiG 21 was most effective against American aircraft but older MiG 17s and 19s were also involved; Phantoms, Thunderchiefs, B-52s, F-111s and various naval aircraft were used by the Americans.[19] Older US aircraft, such as the Super Sabre, Starfighter and Canberra, quickly proved too vulnerable. At the other extreme, the F-111s had only just entered service and their radars were affected by tropical conditions. The Thunderchiefs were fast aircraft which could take considerable punishment but they suffered heavy losses and had to be escorted by Phantoms when the MiG threat increased. It was the Phantoms and B-52s, therefore, which bore the later burden of the offensive.

In the early part of the war the Americans relied upon Sparrow and Sidewinder missiles for air defence of their aircraft but the F-4Es had an internal cannon which proved quite effective for aerial combat. The accuracy of air-to-air missiles improved although the Americans found that ten Sparrows or five Sidewinders had to be fired for the loss of one enemy aircraft.[20] Approximately two-thirds of the air force's losses during the war were attributed to AA fire rather than enemy fighters or to ground-to-air missiles. Nevertheless aircraft still had to take vigorous action to evade the SAMs. ECM pods were fitted in 1966 and, though these were not always effective, 'many SAMs went ballistic because of jamming and missed their targets'.[21] The fighter pilots learned how to evade the missiles by executing a 'hard-diving turn, then [making] an abrupt four-g rolling pull-out, keeping the speed up throughout the manoeuvre. If this manoeuvre were followed at the correct time, the SAM would not be able to follow.' The Americans also used chaff to confuse missiles and radar and specialized fighter units called 'wild weasels' were trained for attacking SAM sites. The North Vietnamese countered this tactic both by placing the SAMs in densely-populated areas, where the US aircraft were not allowed to bomb, and by attacking the US formations with MiGs to break them up before unleashing the SAMs. Nevertheless, we now know that such attacks had a considerable impact making Northern batteries reluctant to be the first to open fire for fear that they would be the one attacked.[22]

Even B-52s were vulnerable to the long-range SAMs when operating over North Vietnam. On the first night of the massive raids on Hanoi in December 1972, three were shot down and two damaged. On the third night, four were shot down and two were crippled and crashed later. Subsequently the loss rate fell as the North Vietnamese used up their SAMs and US tactics improved.[23] But 15 B-52s had been destroyed by SAMs and three badly damaged during the 740 sorties. The ageing B-52s carried their twenty-eight tons of bombs from Guam in the Marianas and from Thailand; the first group had thus to make a gruelling 5,200 mile round trip to and from the battlefield. Reports suggested that the overworked bomber force was under considerable strain and that 'only half [were] serviceable at any one time. Crews complain that a breakdown is expected on every mission. Engine "flame-outs" are common . . . the fuel systems give problems, with leaks, crossfeed failures and pump breakdowns the most dangerous. And the aircraft are vulnerable to the monsoon and typhoon conditions in the area.'[24]

Had US air attacks on North Vietnam forced Hanoi out of the war and had the Vietcong collapsed as a result, then all this effort would have been worthwhile for the American administration. Washington would also have found an immensely important way of dealing with the problem of 'sanctuaries'. Such a solution would not have been applicable in every case since the Second World War; France could not, for example, have forced China to cease supporting the Vietminh in 1950 but in some cases such coercion could have been replicated. Many military writers still argue that bombing might have ended the Vietnam war and that the only mistake was not to use air power more massively and at an earlier stage.[25] Hanoi would then have sued for peace and the NLF would have collapsed. In support of this thesis, they cite the great bombing attacks in December 1972 which some believe forced Hanoi to make the concessions which brought about the Paris ceasefire agreement on 27 January 1973.[26] But, although Hanoi did not obtain the coalition government in the south that it had demanded, signature of the ceasefire agreement was much less of a concession by Hanoi than this argument implies. President Thieu's government had announced on 12 December 1972 that it would never sign the agreement whilst the regular Northern forces, which had invaded South Vietnam in April, remained there. It was Saigon which dropped this crucial demand and made the major concession which led to the 'peace' agreement.[27]

The fact was that in one crucial respect North Vietnam was much less vulnerable to air attack than Germany or Japan had been in the

Second World War—it was a far more primitive society. Those who believe that air attacks could have won the war suggest that these should have been directed at the 'heart' of the country and that 'only an obvious indication that the destruction of their society was imminent could have dissuaded' the North Vietnamese government from continuing the war. Similarly General Keegan believed that 'a bombing campaign like Linebacker II . . . could have brought the war to a close as early as 1965'.[28] But there was no way in which North Vietnam's 'heart' could have been destroyed except with nuclear weapons. Even if the major towns of Hanoi and Haiphong had been reduced to dust, their inhabitants could have been dispersed throughout the countryside. The dykes, which protected the plains from the waters of the Red River, might have been smashed. Hundreds of thousands might have drowned yet others would have survived in the hills, however demoralized many of them had become. General hostility to the war effort in the USA and elsewhere would have been immeasurably increased. The one primary resource that the North had was its people and these the USA could not destroy, even it if had wanted to.

But the arguments against the bombing campaign are more far-reaching still. Even if the North's regular forces had been withdrawn from the South, air attacks were inherently unlikely to produce the results suggested. At any stage Hanoi could have ceased temporarily to support the Vietcong. The insurgents in the South were not, however, entirely the creatures of the North and low level insurgency would have continued. The total failure of the Southern government to understand the problem of pacification would not have changed. Indeed if it had apparently been freed from the Northern threat, the Southern government might have grown even more indifferent to rural opinion and villages in the South would have remained in guerrilla hands. Faced with this situation would Washington have announced that Hanoi was not playing the game and resumed bombing? Alternatively would it have been prepared to go on bombing Hanoi into the indefinite future whenever the rebellion seemed to threaten the government in Saigon? Colonel Gropman, one of the enthusiastic supporters of the victory by air power thesis, criticizes McNamara for wanting to use aircraft mainly for close air support of the ground forces in the South. This assumed a protracted war and 'in such a war, there was no way that Hanoi was likely to become convinced that they could not outlast the United States, a country fighting halfway round the world with its major national interests elsewhere'.[29] Yet the Vietnam war was bound to be protracted because Hanoi could increase or decrease the intensity of the conflict to suit its interests. Air power could not provide a miraculous short cut to victory. By investing enormous amounts in the bomber offensive and greatly increasing the unpopularity of the war, Washington itself was making it more, not less, likely that the NLF and its Northern backers would be able to outlast its own efforts.

Some might argue that the Greek example shows that such a long-term commitment by outside governments to the insurgents was not inevitable. Once the support of the Communist Balkan states disappeared, the Greek rebellion withered and collapsed. But a much closer analogy is with the Israeli problem vis-à-vis the Palestinians. The Israelis can carry out reprisals whenever the Palestinians stage some coup. For example, Israeli troops attacked Beirut airport on 28 December 1968 and destroyed thirteen airliners in retaliation for a Palestinian attack on an Israeli airliner in Athens. Again the Israeli invasion of the Lebanon in 1982 was triggered by an Arab attack on the Israeli Ambassador in London. But Palestinian attacks on airliners and diplomats have continued and the Palestinian problem has not been solved by such tactics since the guerrilla movement is too deeply entrenched amongst the Palestinian people. Similarly, in Vietnam the hostility to the Saigon regime was too widespread and too deeply entrenched for it to collapse with the temporary and perhaps partial withdrawal of Northern support.

The US attempt to halt Communist supplies passing through Laos and Cambodia also failed, despite the effort and ingenuity involved. Sensing devices were, for example, dropped along the trail. These relayed information via aircraft or drones to a central post which decided how to respond to traffic levels. Tribesmen were also employed to watch the trail and relay reports. The Americans and South Vietnamese bombed the Ho Chi Minh trail from 1965 onwards with growing intensity. At first they were able to attack almost unimpeded but, as the North Vietnamese increased their anti-aircraft cover, the Americans had to use more advanced aircraft and tactics. Furthermore the Communists steadily improved the trail until, by the end of the war, it was not a trail but a complex series of roads leading southwards. Teams of coolies were constantly ready to move forward and repair bomb damage. Conditions for those on the trail were dreadful and the bombing certainly increased their fears but it did not stop them; as one recalled later, 'at places along the trail were the hulks of military vehicles and graves, graves of NVA soldiers . . . There were graves all over in some areas. Inside I was sure that everyone was frightened but nobody said a word about it.'

Thus, whilst losses of trucks were high and drivers were sometimes chained to their vehicles to prevent them escaping, the Americans were never able to do more than handicap the insurgents' supply efforts. The US Air Force General George Keegan said later: 'Interdiction worked about as we expected. I know of no responsible airman who has ever judged publicly that the Air Force could do more than impede maybe 10–15 per cent of the flow of the enemy's logistics.' The insurgents wanted only twelve tons of outside supplies each day and, even if all supplies from the North had been cut off, the insurgency would have continued in the South because 70 per cent of the guerrillas' food came from there and many of their weapons were captured or bought from government forces.[31]

Prince Sihanouk, the Cambodian ruler, strove for many years to keep his country neutral. However by the end of the 1960s he was afraid that its use as a conduit for NLF supplies was drawing Cambodia inexorably into the fighting. As a result he started to hinder the passage of Vietcong supplies through the port of Sihanoukville and secretly agreed to US air raids on the Ho Chi Minh trail and Communist camps in his country.[32] The Marxist Khmer Rouge insurgency had already begun inside Cambodia and this intensified towards the end of the 1960s. In response to Sihanouk's move against their supply lines the Vietcong co-operated with Cambodian guerrillas to attack the government from the Left, whilst senior officers in the armed forces criticized it from the Right. Caught between the opposing forces, Sihanouk was overthrown when he was on a visit to Paris on 18 March 1970.[33] The new leader Marshal Lon Nol was willing to co-operate openly with the Americans to cut Communist supply routes. However he only managed to dominate a part of the country. Many of the peasants remained loyal to Prince Sihanouk or moved away from the Vietnamese frontier to avoid the fighting and into areas dominated by Khmer Rouge guerrillas. William Shawcross and others have also argued that US bombing attacks on the Ho Chi Minh trail, which continued until August 1973, radicalized much of the peasantry, pushing them into the arms of the insurgents.[34]

At the end of April and beginning of May 1970, following B-52 attacks, American and South Vietnamese troops crossed the frontier into Cambodia to try to destroy Vietcong headquarters and to cut off their supplies—in itself an admission that air interdiction alone was ineffective. Although the Communists had long expected the incursion, many of their leaders were nearly cut off and the Vietcong 7th Division had to fight bitterly to enable them to escape. Although they were pursued in their flight by aerial attacks they eventually reached the safety of the northern Cambodian province of Kratie. The Americans were unaware 'how close they were to annihilating or capturing the core of the Southern resistance—élite units or our frontline fighters along with the civilian and much of the military leadership'.[35] However the Vietcong concluded that the long-term results were beneficial to them, Nixon and Kissinger 'had traded a few immediate and short-term military gains for the unpredictable consequences of intruding into an already volatile Cambodia and for severe, long-term political debits at home'.[36]

To keep Lon Nol in power after its own troops left the country on 29 June 1970, the USA had to use air power on an increasing scale. By March 1973 'the windows of the capital shudder[ed] every night from the B-52 raids'. The reputation of the Cambodian army, never high, sank gradually lower as the months passed and as the guerrillas closed in on Phnom Penh. During the last few months of the war, the capital was kept supplied entirely by US transport aircraft.[37]

In Laos the USA supported anti-Communist forces from the late 1950s onwards. It encouraged the formation of armies amongst the Meo tribes to combat the Left-wing Pathet Lao. Much of the support for the Meo took the form of food, arms and ammunition supplied by air. The main carrier was 'Air America', an ostensibly independent air line which was employed by the CIA and eventually grew to be the largest in the world because of its activities in South-East Asia. The main tactical transport involved in the early years was the Helio-Courier which needed only 120 ft of airstrip to land and could fly as slowly as thirty-five miles per hour. Later this was partly replaced by the Pilatus Porter, Dornier DO-28 and de Havilland Beaver. As the chronicler of the operation puts it:

> Dozens of crude landing strips were hacked out of the jungle and mountain ridges were plained to enable Air America to land . . . Air America . . . provided the air transport for the CIA's recruitment drive as it built up the clandestine army . . . Operators and Meo officers flew to isolated mountain villages, leapfrogging from peak to peak in helicopter and Helio-Courier aircraft. They offered the villagers grain, rice and money in exchange for recruits.[38]

Air America also operated in Vietnam and elsewhere but Laos was its most important and dangerous field of operations. Few of the airfields which it used there were defended effectively from the Pathet Lao and air traffic control was minimal.

To weaken the Pathet Lao, Air America pilots occasionally dropped crudely-made napalm on their entrenchments. More frequently they supplied the bombs for the T-28s of the Royal Laotian Air Force and dropped counterfeit money to disrupt the Pathet Lao economy. They also supplied the Nung tribesmen who watched the trails leading to South Vietnam and reported on enemy movements. The fighting, and perhaps particularly the bombing operations, turned tens of thousands of Laotians into refugees. By 1968 there may have been 600,000 out of a total population of some three million. Many of these had to be moved by Air America to safer areas, others were kept alive by the air line's relief operations. Some of the Meo economy, and particularly the activities of its most charismatic leader, Vang Peo, depended upon the production of drugs and Air America aircraft were, knowingly or unwittingly, used to move these.[39]

Despite these efforts, the war gradually undermined the weak non-Communist government. In June 1969 Communist Pathet Lao guerrillas captured the strategic town of Muong Soui and the following month the US lost two fighter bombers and two helicopters in abortive efforts to retake the town. The Laotian Prime Minister, Prince Souvanna Phouma, claimed that some 60,000 North Vietnamese troops were operating in the country. In August the government stronghold of Xieng Dat fell and in September US, Thai and Lao troops made an unsuccessful attempt to stage an offensive in the Plain of Jars, which fell to the Pathet Lao forces five months later. On 9 June 1970 Saravane, the last main town in government hands in Southern Laos, fell to the Communists. With most of the country under North Vietnamese control, South Vietnamese forces, backed by massive US air suport, made a foray into Laos on 8 February 1971 to cut the Ho Chi Minh trail. The attack had long been expected and the north Vietnamese were fully prepared. Critics of the operation argue that the US army alone lost 107 helicopters supporting South Vietnamese ground forces which, in turn, suffered 1,519 killed and 5,423 wounded. Its defenders maintain that the proportion of aircraft lost was not very high considering the tens of thousands of sorties flown. They also maintain that the South Vietnamese captured vast quantities of Northern stores and disrupted their operations.[40]

Traffic down the Ho Chi Minh trail was nevertheless unaffected by the incursion in the long run. Bombing was somewhat more effective, though also immensely costly. The US and South Vietnamese dropped almost one ton of bombs on Laos for each of its citizens[41] and this inevitably increased the cost of supplying the South. According to General Keegan, for every ten pounds of supplies that entered the panhandle of Laos in 1968, only one pound reached the South. The rest went into food, anti-aircraft ammunition, medical evacuation and road repair.[42] But the flow of supplies to the South did not stop and bombing did not 'prop up' the neutralist Laotian government—quite the contrary. In February 1973 government and guerrilla forces signed a ceasefire calling for the withdrawal of all foreign forces within sixty days and in April 1974 the Pathet Lao joined a coalition government. Two months later the last US advisers left the country. Like Cambodia and South Vietnam, Laos became a fully Marxist state. On 3 December 1975 the monarchy was abolished and a People's Democratic Republic set up in its place, with Souphanouvong, the Pathet Lao leader, as President.[43]

In retrospect the use of US air power outside South Vietnam was based on a series of miscalculations. North Vietnam was less vulnerable than many thought and some still believe. Hanoi could not be forced out of the war and, even if had temporarily pulled its own units out of South Vietnam, the war would not have ended—any more than it ended after the so-called 'ceasefire' of 27 January 1973. The other aims of the bombing, such as the improvement of morale and stability in the South, were too nebulous to be sensible bases for strategy. The interdiction campaign was equally mistaken. If only 30 per cent of Vietcong supplies came down the Ho Chi Minh trail and if only 10–15 per cent of this could be interdicted the cost of the campaign to halt some three per cent of Vietcong supplies ludicrously outweighed any advantages. Some argue that Laos and Cambodia fell to the Communists because the US widened the war in their territories and that Sihanouk and the Laotian government would have been able to preserve a degree of neutrality if the war had not embroiled them. Others contend that they would in any case have fallen—domino fashion—once Saigon had collapsed. We can never know what the alternatives would have been; on the one hand China would have been anxious to support Laotian and Cambodian independence from North Vietnam; on the other hand, Vietnam had for centuries been pushing gradually into Khmer territory and this historic movement had only been temporarily halted by the French occupation in the nineteenth century. Thus Hanoi would eventually have wanted to assert its domination over the area. What we can be certain about is that the human cost of bombing of the Ho Chi Minh trail and other parts of Laos and Cambodia was very high.

The costs to the Americans of the decision to widen the war were also considerable. There were the losses of the aircrew and their planes. Those who were captured also gave the North Vietnamese a bargaining-counter against Washington which they used in the negotiations with some effect.[44] Moreover, because the American government knew that bombing was unpopular, it kept halting the attacks in order to negotiate with the North Vietnamese. These offers were eventually accepted in April 1968 and the talks began on 13 May, though it was not until 18 January 1969 that the South Vietnamese and NLF began to participate. But what in the end was there to negotiate about? Either South Vietnam was to be a separate plural state or it was to be part of Communist Vietnam. The Southern government knew this but Washington seemed unwilling to see it. Of course the Southern government should have tried to broaden its support in the South and to separate some of the radicals from the Vietcong but that was not the same as negotiating with the North.[45]

Finally, no other issue (except possibly the My Lai massacre) compared with the bombing in the polarizing effect it had on opinion in the USA and the hostility which it evoked elsewhere. As a high US official commented presciently in May 1966.

> The air campaign against heavily defended areas costs us one pilot in every forty sorties. In addition, an important but hard-to-measure cost is domestic and world opinion . . . The picture of the world's greatest superpower killing or seriously injuring 1,000 non-combatants a week, while trying to pound a tiny, backward nation into submission on an issue whose merits are hotly disputed, is not a pretty one. It could conceivably produce a costly distortion in . . . the world image of the United States.[46]

Many Americans felt that 'the legal case for American bombing in the rest of Indochina is untenable'. The loss of public support for the war also left the US armed forces with a dangerous 'stab in the back' explanation for their defeat only too similar to the German army's excuse for its defeat in 1918.

What seems strange is that US leaders evidently did not expect the tide of domestic and international criticism of their bombing policies in South-East Asia. The British had, after all, watched public reaction to bombing with the greatest care ever since the 1920s and yet their government system was much less open, democratic and susceptible to criticism than the American. Moreover, the Americans had themselves criticized the French for bombing Tunisia during the Algerian war and the British for their actions in Aden and elsewhere. Why then were they so taken aback by the public response? The answer comes from the experience of the Korean war. At that time virtually all the criticism of the Truman administration was from the Right, from General MacArthur and his supporters. When China began to send troops across the Yalu river to support North Korea at the end of 1950, MacArthur, the Commander of the UN forces in the Peninsula, wanted the USA to bomb China and Manchuria, even if this evidently risked starting a Third World War. Truman was determined to keep the war limited. In Congress the China lobby accused the administration of 'losing' China to the Communists and then handicapping MacArthur, thus threatening American lives. On several occasions MacArthur was warned not to voice his criticisms of the policy of limited war in public. However on 24 March 1951 he complained again about 'the inhibitions which now restrict the activity of the UN forces and the corresponding military advantages which accrue to Red China'. Truman promptly sacked the insubordinate General but he returned home to a hero's welcome. Millions turned out to cheer him in his triumphal tour across America.[47] It was the policy of limiting war that seemed unpopular, not the excesses of bombing and thus at the start of the Vietnam war it was this experience which the Johnson administration remembered, not the protests from Britain and America's other allies about MacArthur's threats to expand the Korean war.

In the event, the torrent of criticism of US policy had a major impact whilst the problem of sanctuary was not solved by US air power during the Vietnam war, as the US government's own 'Jason' studies and CIA reports made clear in 1967. Of course one cannot say that air attacks will never be sufficient to force a country to cease supporting guerrillas. During the Afghan war there were suggestions that 'Teheran has tried to stop [Afghan guerrillas operating in Iran] for fear of Soviet retribution following a particularly deep and heavy "hot pursuit" strike in 1982'.[48] However these claims have to be treated with some caution and, even if they are true, the Iranian government was in a specially weak position because it was involved in a prolonged campaign against Iraq. Any Western state fighting an insurgent movement would hesitate before ignoring the political, economic and human costs of making air attacks on a sanctuary. There are a number of alternatives which may be more attractive. First of all the French showed in Algeria that a frontier can sometimes be largely sealed by mines and barbed wire. They believed that the Morice and other lines virtually halted the flow

of insurgents and armaments from Tunisia and Morocco.[49] Such
methods will not always be possible and the length of Vietnam's frontiers, together with the nature of the terrain, meant that they were not
generally applicable to the conflict in South-East Asia.

Counterattacks on guerrilla sanctuaries can often be both covert and
effective. Public outcries greeted British air attacks into the Yemen
during the war in Aden and, as we have seen, there were suggestions
that this undermined the consensus in favour of continuing to fight and
thus lost the war.[50] Yet, at the very same time, British troops made
covert raids—codenamed 'Claret'—into Indonesian territory which
were far more effective and caused no opposition whatsoever, in
Britain. SAS units and Gurkhas crossed the frontier and staged devastating raids on the camps from which Indonesian soldiers were infiltrating Malaysia. Such raids were kept so secret that the main history
of the war, published in 1974, treated Indonesian claims that British
forces had crossed the border with a great deal of scepticism.[51] The
Americans had initially followed the same strategy on the Ho Chi Minh
trail and the Soviets used covert methods against the guerrillas in Pakistan during the Afghan war.[52] In retrospect we can see that the use of
secret operations with special forces was the correct strategy for the
USA to continue to follow in order to inhibit Vietcong supplies. The
frontiers were too long to be sealed, but such methods would have
delayed the guerrillas and North Vietnamese, avoided the civilian casualties caused by bombing and thus evaded the bitter opposition in the
USA and elsewhere in the West which forced the Americans to abandon
the struggle in South-East Asia.

The Afghan War

During the war in Afghanistan commentators and politicians often
drew parallels between the Soviet involvement there and US involvement in Vietnam in the 1960s. Certainly there were many similarities,
not least the way in which both the USA and the USSR made widespread use of aircraft, and particularly helicopters, in their attacks on
guerrillas. Yet the main factors which have influenced the balance of
power between aircraft and insurgents all operated in different ways in
Afghanistan from the way they operated in Vietnam.

Although a poll published in November 1987 suggested that 53 per
cent of Muscovites were in favour of withdrawal from Afghanistan and
only 27 per cent in favour of fighting on, the Soviet public could not
object to the widespread use of bombing in the same way that the

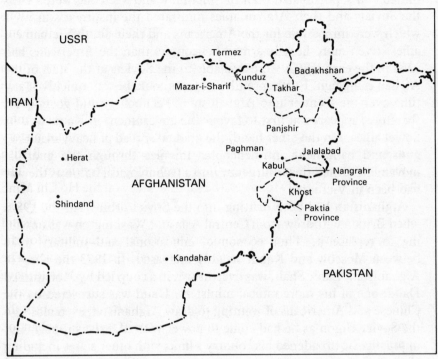

The Afghan War 1979-89

American public objected to the bombing campaigns in Vietnam. Even if people outside the Soviet Union voiced their opposition, this was unlikely to have a decisive influence upon the Kremlin. Nor did the Soviet press report such operations as the world media did in the Vietnamese case. The Mujahadeen guerrillas were also incomparably less united and sophisticated than the Vietminh and Vietcong were. Thus the Soviets and their Afghan allies infiltrated the insurgents in ways which were impossible for the Americans and their South Vietnamese allies. Even more heavily armed helicopters than the Americans had used in the early 1960s were available to the Soviets at the start of the Afghan campaign. Further reinforcements could be sent quickly at any time over the frontier into Afghanistan. Technology and geography, therefore, appeared at first to favour the government in Kabul and its Soviet allies. On the other hand, the gradual spread of heavy machine-guns and hand-held anti-helicopter missiles through the guerrilla movement turned this insurgency into a technological battle as the war had been in Vietnam.

Afghanistan had been drifting into the Soviet orbit from the 1950s when Britain withdrew from Central Asia and Washington was unwilling to replace it. Thus economic, educational and military links between Moscow and Kabul steadily increased. In 1973 the King of Afghanistan, Zahir Shah, was overthrown in a coup led by Mohammed Daud, one of his more radical ministers. Daud was suspected by the Chinese and Americans of wanting to draw Afghanistan even closer to the Soviet Union as he had come to power with Marxist support. But in practice he broadened his country's links with other states including China.[1] For this and other reasons the Afghan Communists regarded Daud as too cautious and in April 1978 he was himself overthrown by a Marxist-inspired coup led by the Afghan armed forces. Subsequently the rapid changes imposed by the new rulers evoked violent resistance amongst conservative Moslems. Quarrels also broke out between the various factions in the Communist People's Democratic Party of Afghanistan (PDPA). In September 1979 President Taraki resigned and was replaced by Hafizullah Amin, who took an even stronger line. To maintain the Marxist regime in power the number of Soviet military advisers in the country had reportedly grown to some 20,000 but the Soviets found Amin too intractable and too unwilling to moderate the ideology of his regime in order to win over the Afghan people. Thus in December 1979 they overthrew and killed Amin and installed another Afghan Marxist, Barbrak Karmal, in power. They expected Karmal to be more effective and amenable to their wishes. To maintain their dominance they sent large numbers of troops into Kabul using some medium and heavy transport aircraft and deploying a further 15,000 troops along the roads from the Soviet frontier.

Violent resistance to the regime increased rather than diminished after Soviet intervention. As one Soviet writer put it,

> a struggle is being waged amidst the marketplaces, bazaars, mosques, pomegranate orchards and country roads gashed by steel. Fierce extreme clashes of passions and ideals have drawn in many lives. They clash in the ravines, on the paths, in meetings and in attacks, in mosques and universities, at funerals and festivals.[2]

Soviet forces had control of Kabul, Kandahar, Herat and the other large towns for most of the time, though both Herat and Kandahar occasionally fell into rebel hands and the guerrillas were able to operate even in the capital, Kabul. However government control over the countryside was minimal and the Afghan army itself melted away, falling from some 100,000 men to about a third of this figure. As one observer noted, 'in some ten years of war reporting, I have rarely seen such unimpressive-looking fighting men or a bunch whose loyalty— both to their own commanders . . . and to their Soviet overlords—was more obviously in doubt'.[3] Yet, like the Americans in Vietnam, the Soviets had counted on the indigenous army to give them control of the countryside and had built up the Afghan air force until it had some 180 aircraft including MiG 17s, 19s and 21s.

Initially the Soviet army appeared to have been both wooden and over-confident. It had clearly given little thought to counterinsurgency and had not studied Western experience. When it did venture out into the rural areas of Afghanistan it pushed its tanks and armoured personnel-carriers along the bottom of the valleys. There the ill-trained reserve forces became easy targets for the insurgents' mines and rockets. Soviet NCOs proved inadequately trained and the army followed the American pattern in Vietnam and rotated troops so quickly that they never became fully experienced. Officers moved after only six months; men stayed for longer.[4] Night operations were rarely used although the guerrillas normally moved at night in order to avoid Soviet aircraft.[5] It was only after several years that the Soviets experimented with smaller units and more flexible tactics and began using special forces such as the *Raydoviki* and *Vysotniki*. They experimented with mixed brigades combining helicopters, parachutists, riflemen and armour. There were also reports that Cubans and Vietnamese had been asked to go to Afghanistan to advise the Soviets on counter-guerrilla operations.[6] Gradually their tactics improved and they responded more quickly to attacks. For example in April 1984 guerrillas destroyed the Mattok bridge, south of the vital Salang tunnel through which Soviet supplies to Kabul had to pass. However, when they tried to repeat this exercise, the Soviets were reported to have driven them into a 'killing zone' and used enhanched-blast bombs to wipe out between, 1,500 and 2,000 insurgents.[7]

On their side the insurgents remained disunited, sometimes even fighting each other, though a few able guerrilla leaders emerged. Amongst the most famous in the West was Ahmed Shah Masud who survived nine major Russian offensives against him and several assassination attempts whilst he led the resistance in the Panjshir valley.[8] In 1986 he organized the resistance in the northern provinces of Baghlan, Kunduz, Badakhshan and Mazar-i-Sharif. Without effective leadership of Masud's type, the insurgents tended to attack the Soviet forces when they felt like it and without any strategic plan. Some of the insurgents also tired of the conflict and accepted the Afghan government's peace terms at the beginning of 1987. *Tass* claimed that refugees were also returning to Afghanistan as a result of the government's moves.[10] But the majority of insurgents continued to fight.

In November 1985 Western sources estimated that the Soviet forces had suffered 10,000 killed, 20,000 wounded and many more seriously affected by disease. The war had cost some $12 billion, and against this the Soviets could only set the growth of imports of raw materials from Afghanistan such as natural gas, chrome, bauxite and iron.[11] Some Russians were also captured though there was a tendency on both sides to kill captives and few Soviet prisoners were handed over to the Red Cross.[12] Roads were blocked, power stations and electricity lines destroyed and 1,700 schools were obliterated in the fighting; the economy stagnated and sympathizers with Kabul fled from the villages.[13] The insurgents in turn moved their families into Pakistan and then returned to attack the Soviets more effectively.

As the Americans discovered in Vietnam, the Soviets found that the quickest and easiest way to bring force to bear on rural guerrilla groups was by the use of air power. Thus they built or enlarged air bases in Afghanistan at Bagram, Kabul, Mazar-i-Sharif, Jalalabad, Herat, Shindand, Farah, Lashkar Gah, Serden Band, Askargh and (two) at Kandahar.[14] Bagram, north of Kandahar, was best equipped and was the base for operations by more advanced aircraft such as Frogfoot,

MiG 23, 25 and 29. The Soviets had been preparing for the same sort of technically-advanced warfare as the Americans and had, no doubt, the same institutional reasons for using aircraft on a very wide scale. They even took into Afghanistan chemical protective equipment and other weapons which seemed to have no relevance to the conflict. Nevertheless they had had some experience of using helicopters to attack guerrillas in Angola and, more importantly, in the Ogaden War in Ethiopia where they played a major part in the capture of the key town of Jijiga in 1978.[15]

Since 1973 the Soviets had been producing large numbers of helicopters to move troops and to counter NATO armoured forces in Europe. By 1988 the IISS listed Soviet ground forces as having some 1,560 armed and 2,138 transport helicopters. With an unloaded weight of 14,300 lb, a speed of 170 miles an hour and heavy firepower, the Hinds proved the most feared and effective of Soviet weapons in Afghanistan.[16] The Soviets used Hind D and E helicopter gunships in the close air support role, whilst the Afghan air force employed its older Hind-A helicopters mainly for convoy protection.[17] The Hind-D had a 'chin' turret, which gave its 12.7 mm or 14.5 mm machine-guns a very wide range of fire, and the Hind-E carried 23 mm cannons. Some Hinds carried up to 192 rockets on their wings. Different sources emphasized various aspects of the Hind which gave the guerrillas some hope at least of destroying it. Some stressed the vulnerability of the turbine intakes, the tail rotor assembly and the oil tank in the fuselage. Others suggested that the main rotor was itself vulnerable to heavy machine-gun fire and that the cockpit glass could be penetrated by 14.5 mm bullets.[18] Perhaps, as a result of these problems, the Hind-Ds had thicker windscreens and titanium protection on the underside of the fuselage.

At the start of the campaign, many Hinds hovered at low altitude and engaged the guerrillas at close range but this proved too dangerous, as the French had found in helicopter operations in Algeria. Later they dived on the guerrillas firing 57 mm rockets and dropping bombs. When this also proved unsatisfactory, the Hinds began low level attacks 10–30 metres above the ground and fired their weapons from the maximum range, as the French had done. The aircraft were not, however, designed for operation at this altitude and there were reports of rotors striking the main fuselage.[19] The aircraft were also too large to make an ideal gunship and the ability of some versions to carry troops and others to transport supplies was irrelevant to gunship operations. The Hinds were also difficult to manoeuvre. To offset all these problems the aircraft attacked in groups and so gave each other cover; sometimes one aircraft advanced alone to draw enemy fire while others waited behind the hills to engage any guerrillas who 'took the bait'.

Apart from the Hinds, the Soviets had the Mi-2 Hoplite, a light general-purpose helicopter capable of carrying up to eight people and used by senior officers in Afghanistan to observe battles from above. The Mi-4 Hound could carry fourteen passengers but was used in Afghanistan for leading helicopter assaults by strafing guerrilla positions, then flying to higher altitudes where it tried to decoy Sam-7 missiles away from the Hinds by using flares.[20] To transport troops, the Russians also used the Mi-8 Hip helicopter which usually carried up to thirty-two passengers and, more rarely, the Mi-6 Hook which was capable of carrying sixty-five men or a load of 26,450 lb. The Hip was used to lay mines; it could be armed with six UB-32 pods containing 192 rockets and the Hook with a machine-gun mounted in the nose.[21] The Hips and Hooks tended to keep further away from the Chinese-manufactured heavy machine-guns used by the guerrillas and to leave the close support role to the Hinds; one Hip shot down in November 1983 was reported to be carrying the General commanding the Second Afghan Army. An advanced version of the Hip, designated Mi-17, also appeared in Afghanistan as did the Mi-26 heavy-lift helicopter.[22] All these vastly increased the mobility of Soviet forces.

The Soviet armed forces had been accustomed since 1945 to carrying out all their maintenance at their main airfields and they had to learn in Afghanistan to carry out some work in more primitive conditions. Technicians learnt to put patches over holes in aircraft caused by machine-gun fire, although they would normally have regarded this as the job of specialists. Much Soviet equipment proved hard to maintain in the field. The Hip had been previously regarded as particularly easy to service but it was apparently difficult to change its engine quickly. Low flying by the Hinds increased their maintenance problems—important components had a life of 2,000 hours but major overhauls had to be carried out at Termez in the Soviet Union after every 200 hours. The Soviets also abandoned equipment much more readily than the Americans had in Vietnam and appeared to make little attempt to recover downed helicopters by using their Mi-26s. Nevertheless the whole campaign did provide the Soviets with very useful experience of active operations and the maintenance problems which went with them.

There were perhaps 15–20 Soviet helicopters in Afghanistan in January 1980 and 175–200 by July of the same year. In 1981, 240 helicopter gunships were in operation and some 500–700 helicopters of all types were alleged to be in service there by 1982.[23] This enabled the Soviets to mount very large numbers of sorties and to 'saturate' guerrilla-held areas. During the offensive in the Paghman area near Kabul in October 1985, for example, diplomats claimed that the Soviets had mounted 300 sorties in one day, including 86 in one two-hour period;

> Diplomats reported witnessing an engagement in which 32 Mi-8 and Mi-24 helicopters bombed and strafed the lower ridges of the Paghman range south-west of Sharkahardarn. Mi-8 were seen landing briefly while pairs of Mi-24s gave covering fire. Overhead an Antonov 26 circled, presumably acting as a mobile command post.[24]

To combat ambushes, which were one of the favourite guerrilla tactics, as convoys advanced along the roads the Hips dropped commandos on the high points alongside, returning to pick them up once the convoys had passed. Thus aircraft proved, as they had done in Palestine, Algeria and Indochina, one of the most effective ways of preventing ambushes.

The Soviet air force also used MiG 21, 23 and 27 fixed-wing fighter aircraft against the insurgents but these proved as inaccurate as their Western equivalents had often done elsewhere. One reporter with the guerrillas noted afterwards:

> We were bombed by three or four jets every day. They would dive at our positions with such speed that hardly anyone had time to run for cover. However, they were usually hopelessly off target . . . In one raid they hit their own positions with rockets killing several Soviet militiamen.[25]

From 1981 they also began to deploy the Su-25 Frogfoot aircraft which were just being introduced into service.[26] Somewhat similar to the US A-10 aircraft, these were designed for the close air support mission and thus could use their 10,000 lb weapons load much more effectively than the MiGs were able to do.

It is notable that the Soviets did not employ slow trainers to achieve greater precision, as all Western air forces had done in guerrilla wars. Part of the explanation may lie in doctrinal conservatism and part in the faith placed in helicopters and Frogfoot in the close air support role. In other cases the Soviets may not have been interested in bombing accurately as they staged attacks on towns such as Herat, and on crops. The high flying Tu-16 Badger bombers from Termez in the Soviet

Union itself were used in this way.[27] Carrying nearly 20,000 lb of
bombs, they devastated Herat and other targets. By the end of 1987
there were still no reported cases of the Soviets using precision-guided
munitions, though they did use area-denial weapons. These combined
incendiary, shrapnel and blast effects and were said to be particularly
effective against guerrillas hiding in villages. When they were not
threatened by Sams, the Mig 21s and Su-25s flew at low level and
dropped cluster bombs to cover a wide area and so hit the elusive
guerrillas.[28] At the same time decoy aircraft sometimes flew overhead
to drop flares if the guerrillas used anti-aircraft missiles.

At the start of the war the guerrillas fired twin-barrelled heavy machine-guns against Soviet aircraft. Later these were supplemented with
Soviet-manufactured Sam-7 missiles, allegedly coming from China and
Egypt or bought from the PLO went it left Beirut.[29] The 4 ft 6 in missile
had a range of about 2.3 miles. It was optically aimed and had a heat-
seeking warhead. The missile had already caused difficulties for the
Americans in Vietnam and for the British in the Dhofar War[30] and in
1983 it was credited with forcing Soviet MiG 21s to fly at higher altitude
and with compelling the Hinds to protect themselves with flares. However, either these measures made the Sam-7 ineffective or the missiles
became more unreliable with age; as one observer commented in 1984,
'of the three attempted firings I witnessed this past summer only one
was successful'. One Sam-7 short-circuited during the firing process,
one failed to lock on to an An-12 transport but the third hit an Mi 6.[31]
Partly as a result of the decreasing efficacy of the Sams and partly
because of improved Soviet tactics, the struggle seemed increasingly to
be swinging in the Soviets' favour in 1986. This remained the case even
after reports began to emerge of 300 British-made Blowpipe missiles
reaching the insurgents. Abdul Haq, one of the guerrilla leaders, was
quoted in June 1987 as saying, 'we have received only very few systems.
Those who are using Blowpipes do not praise them. We cannot even
shoot down slow-moving helicopters.'

The real turning-point was the American decision to supply the
much more effective Stinger missile which had a range of nearly 6,000
metres and was less easy to decoy with flares than the Sam-7. Three
hundred Stingers were sent 'covertly' to Afghanistan in 1986 and twice
as many in 1987. But there was some doubt about how many Stingers
actually reached the rebels and several apparently even fell into Soviet
and Iranian hands. There were also initial worries about whether the
Stinger would prove too complex for the Afghans.[32] According to one
report the missile 'requires its handler to take eighteen steps before

firing at an enemy jet or helicopter. He then has to remember to hold his breath to avoid inhaling high levels of hydrogen chloride.' Nevertheless the rebels found Stinger easier to use than Blowpipe and so effective that at one stage they claimed to be shooting down one aircraft a day and, even in 1988, they maintained that they were successful about once a week. The missiles were also forcing aircraft to fly much higher, or so low that they bombed inaccurately. Even if the success rates were exaggerated, all this had a very important effect on the war, particularly in mid-1987 when the Americans began to supply rebel groups away from the frontier. They also trained the operators in Pakistan and sent Tennessee mules to carry the missiles. Thus the insurgents could stand up to the Soviets in 1987 in ways which had proved impossible the previous year when Zhawar Kili in Paktia province was overrun.[33] Observers reported that helicopters were far less in evidence in the mountains from 1987 onwards because of their vulnerability to Stingers. In the flat areas near Herat they flew very low in flights of four or six. Sometimes they also tried to resupply garrisons at night though the insurgents had some night sights which made their weapons effective during the hours of darkness.

Apart from Afghan opposition, the conditions in Afghanistan obviously made flying much more difficult for the Soviet aircraft than it would have been in Europe. As the Soviets themselves argued:

The extremely rugged topography makes search and observation more difficult, while a lack of continuous radar coverage complicates the monitoring and command and control of aircrews from the ground. Nor is it a simple matter to select a direction of attack in mountainous terrain. In addition, the sudden forming of low cloud-covering areas between mountains, valleys and gorges, abrupt changes in wind direction and velocity, as well as temperature drops, create additional difficulties for flying procedures, navigation and orientation. Mountains are a harsh schoolmaster.[34]

Even without enemy resistance the air currents in the mountains would have caused losses, particularly amongst the helicopters. Western sources suggested that some 500 aircraft had been destroyed by the end of 1986.

In any guerrilla war reconnaissance is vitally important and both helicopters and transport aircraft were used by the Soviets in this role. Their efficacy was variable. Observers reported numerous cases when aircraft flew over guerrilla bands and then disappeared in the distance, either because they could not see them or because they were tasked for some other duty from which they could not deviate.[35] These handicaps were not, however, so obvious to the guerrillas; as one journalist commented.

> Travelling with the guerrillas in Nangrahr province in mid-1980, I found tribesmen panic-stricken by the appearance of gunships on the horizon . . . Not realising they were practically invisible from the air against a backdrop of rocks, trees and bushes, they would scatter screaming and moaning, as the helicopter passed overhead. Fortunately, in most cases, the machine would continue on its course unless it had come specifically to bomb the village.[36]

As in other areas of the war, there was, however, evidence that the Soviets improved their reconnaissance and their operational control techniques as the war progressed. In particular the 'Mainstay' version of the IL-76 transport was seen in Afghanistan. This was the equivalent of the American early-warning aircraft with a large rotordome over the fuselage which should have improved Soviet reconnaissance.[37]

The Soviets seemed to have had the same problems with relations between their army and air force which have worried all other countries in counter-insurgencies. All fixed-wing aircraft belonged to the air force. Consequently reports suggested that requests for help from the army were passed first to the divisional army level and then to the air force. As a result, targets of opportunity were missed and ambushed columns were not given air support. Afghan army commanders were also, in theory, able to summon air support though this was probably even slower than in the Soviet case.[38] Friction between the ground and air forces may have been one of the reasons for the army's reliance upon helicopters which were flown by air force pilots but came under army control.

Soviet and Afghan troops were moved around both by helicopter and by Antonov An-12 and 26 transports. The An-26 was powered by two turboprops and could carry up to forty passengers or a payload of 4,687 lb. Transport aircraft and helicopters played a vital role in supplying beleagured outposts. Barikot was, for instance, said to have been besieged from 1981 to 1985 and to have been supplied entirely by helicopter.[39] Similarly during the siege of Khost in 1983, An-12 transports made 150–180 sorties a day to keep it supplied. It was noteworthy that the Russians decided that they would have to fight their way through to Khost on the ground at the end of 1987, presumably because Stingers made it impossible to resupply the town of 40,000 people from the air. As a result one of the largest winter battles of the war took place. Transport aircraft were also used to drop flares in order to light up night operations. Soviet flares could illuminate up to three kilometres for ten minutes.

The guerrillas concentrated many of their attacks on the transports and airfields. In 1984 guerrillas claimed to have shot down a transport carrying 250 troops near Kabul, while in June 1986 they are said to have brought down a plane carrying 100 Afghan troops from Kabul to Kandahar.[40] In February 1987 they claimed to have destroyed an An-26 with over thirty passengers near Khost and by November 1987 five of these aircraft had been shot down within the year. The guerrillas also staged attacks on Soviet airfields. One observer watched an attack on Bagram airfield on 13–14 July 1984. The guerrillas used 107 mm Chinese rockets and a variety of mortars and succeeded in closing the airport for much of the day. Observers commented on the absence of defensive patrols around airfields and the poverty of efforts to illuminate them, compared with US attempts to protect their airfields in Vietnam.[41] Thus, in December 1982 guerrillas destroyed twelve helicopters at Jalalabad and in July 1985 they claimed twenty jets at Shindand airfield.[42] In 1987 they maintained that they had closed Kandahar airport for a week with the help of Chinese-made artillery.

Such claims were normally impossible to verify. Press coverage of the years of warfare which followed the Soviet invasion in December 1979 was episodic. Western journalists accompanied bands of Mujahadeen guerrillas from time to time but they could only see a small part of the war. Few of the reporters were military experts and most were thus unable to comment with any great knowledge on Soviet techniques. Furthermore, most of the reports on the war were datelined from Kabul, New Delhi and Pakistan and attributed to Western diplomats. The reliability of the reports of losses and gains by the combatants must therefore be suspect, particularly as both sides were only too well aware of the importance of propaganda. The guerrillas had an interest in stressing the indiscriminate nature of Soviet air attacks. They also had an interest in persuading the West of the importance of supplying them with anti-aircraft weapons. For their part, the Soviets and their Afghan allies emphasized the way in which Mujahadeen attacks harmed the civilians and the consequent growth in support for the government.[43]

Apart from the very restricted number of press reports, there were many other differences between Afghanistan and Vietnam. South Vietnam was covered in jungle, which made observation of guerrilla movements from the air even more difficult than it was in Afghanistan. Afghanistan was an arid, mountainous region peopled by deeply conservative Moslems. South Vietnam was bordered by the Communist regime in Hanoi to the north and by weak governments in Laos and Cambodia which could not prevent the flow of supplies to the guerrillas. Afghanistan was bordered by the USSR, China, Iran and Pakistan. All but the USSR had some sympathy for the anti-Soviet guerrillas but Iran was fully occupied with its internal problems and with its prolonged war with Iraq. Soviet air attacks in reprisal for guerrilla incursions from across the Iranian frontier were said to have deterred further actions of this sort.[44] The Chinese frontier with Afghanistan was only some 75 to 100 kilometres long and was quickly blocked by Soviet forces, though the Chinese were still said to be aiding the guerrillas financially and many of the weapons in guerrilla hands, such as their heavy machine-guns, were of Chinese manufacture.[45]

Thus Pakistan was not only the main refuge of the three to five million refugees who had fled the battle zone, but also the main conduit for arms supplies. On the other hand the Pakistani government was naturally keen to hide the extent of its involvement. They had no desire to play 'North Vietnam to Afghanistan's South Vietnam' and to become ever more directly involved in the campaign. As it was, the war constantly threatened Pakistan's neutrality. In April 1985 four Afghan planes bombed Pakistan, killing a civilian. Five months later Afghan planes killed twelve Pakistanis. The previous month two Soviet Hind helicopters piloted by Afghans fled to Pakistan and in January 1986 Pakistani F-16 aircraft, supplied by the USA, shot down an Afghan fighter allegedly flying nine miles inside Pakistan.[46] It is impossible to say definitely whether Afghan incursions into Pakistan airspace were deliberately contrived to deter the Pakistanis from becoming more involved in the war and to persuade them to halt guerrillas crossing the frontier from the refugee camps in Pakistan or simply errors of navigation. *Tass* warned Pakistan in March 1986, 'the Zia ul-Haq regime should recognize into what dangerous ventures Pakistan's overseas patrons are trying to draw the country, with results which could be disastrous for it'. Whatever the effects of such warnings, although US and Moslem support for the Mujahadeen grew steadily, it was dwarfed by the level of Soviet support for the North Vietnamese and Vietcong during the 1960s.

Nor did the Soviets increase their commitment to Afghanistan in the way that the Americans enhanced their military presence in Vietnam. The number of their forces in the country, according to Western sources, remained roughly constant at 100,000–130,000 for most of the war. Possibly they found this the easiest level to maintain economically and militarily. Furthermore they lacked the impatience of the Pentagon and the public pressure either to achieve quick results or to abandon the enterprise. They might have hoped that the Americans and others would become tired of supporting the guerrillas and they knew that the world press would increasingly ignore the conflict. They were obviously aware of the deep divisions within the guerrilla movement— a drastic contrast with the situation in Vietnam in the 1960s—and perhaps they believed that these divisions would increase with time. Finally they found that offensive operations could best be carried out by highly-trained *Spetsnaz* units and that other less highly trained conscripts often became demoralized and were best used in defensive roles in Afghanistan. 'The speciality of these crack troops is in ambushing the ambushers. They work at night, being helicoptered to lie in wait on tracks used by the Mujahadeen.' The *Spetsnaz* were equipped with night sights, silenced pistols, mortar bombs and mines.[47]

Spetsnaz operations were designed to win the war by defeating the guerrillas but it was an open question whether the Soviets deliberately tried to drive huge numbers of Afghans out of the country by air attacks and by reprisals. Some writers claimed that

> deliberate attacks on civilians are . . . part of the Kremlin's policy of 'migratory genocide', designed to rid the countryside of all inhabitants capable of supporting the Mujahadeen . . . As far as the Soviets were concerned, they were not out to fish [for guerrillas] but to drain the lake. Provoking conditions that would force the population exodus to continue so as to deny local support to the resistance movement remained an essential element of this policy.[48]

Short of access to high level documents, the allegations were impossible to prove but certainly the effect of Soviet attacks was to destroy many of the Afghan villages and to drive a higher proportion of the population into exile than fled abroad in any similar post-1945 insurgency.

There were, however, suggestions during 1986 that the Kabul government was placing less weight on aircraft firepower and more on intelligence. In November the Soviets decided to demote Karmal and give power to Dr Najibullah, the former head of the Khad secret police.

Najibullah appeared to have reinforced the move towards more political measures. Kabul infiltrated guerrilla groups to try to cause discord between them.[49] It also sent agents to plant bombs in Peshawar and other guerrilla centres in Pakistan, killing ninety-nine Afghans in one year including six guerrilla commanders.[50] In 1985 the Kabul government began ingratiating itself with the Afridi tribesmen on the Afghan-Pakistan frontier and encouraged them to interdict guerrilla supply routes. The government allegedly gave the tribesmen 300,000 Kalashnikov rifles which, if true, represented a magnificent gift in an area where men place such worth on weaponry.[51] Furthermore Kabul paid local chiefs to come over to its side or to remain neutral rather than attempting to strengthen the Afghan army itself on any scale. The army was indeed plagued by desertions and by the belief that it was being used by the Russians as 'cannon fodder'. In any case, expansion of local forces was exactly the sort of measure which Western anti-guerrilla theorists, such as Sir Robert Thompson, would have recommended. Finally since 1983 Kabul had been pushing ahead with the land reform programme which would give the peasants title to their own plots and which the government still hoped would win them to its side, despite their intense initial hostility to such measures.

Of course the Kabul government and its Soviet allies certainly did not abandon the use of aircraft. Rather the more subtle, political measures were carried out at the same time as air operations against the guerrillas. In April 1986, for example, insurgent groups 'reported heavy fighting in Paktia province and said Soviet and Afghan fighter bombers and helicopter gunships were . . . causing heavy losses'. In December 1986 Soviet jets bombed the centre of Herat and Kandahar, apparently by mistake but allegedly killing seventy civilians in the first case and 100 in the second.[52]

By the spring of 1988 it had become clear that the Soviet leadership, led by Mr Gorbachev, had decided to withdraw from Afghanistan. From the point of view of the Soviet state as a whole, the campaign had achieved little and it was clearly becoming more unpopular amongst the Soviet people. For the Soviet armed forces it had been a new experience in counter-insurgency and it had led to modifications in equipment, tactics and training, all of which could be put to good use if the Soviets became militarily involved elsewhere. From the point of view of guerrilla warfare in general, it had shown that totalitarian states do not necessarily have a 'magic formula' for defeating insurgents. Once again it had demonstrated that bombing civilians can be counter-productive[53] and it had underlined the importance of helicopters, and thus of anti-helicopter weapons. Of course the political aspects of the campaign cannot be ignored. If the Afghan people had not been united at least in their hostility to Soviet interference, no amount of Stingers would have won the war for them. Given the Afghans' determination, it was presumably the impact of the missiles which finally decided Mr Gorbachev and his associates that the war was costing more than it was worth.

Past and Future

The prevalence of guerrilla wars obviously depends upon political conditions. Most of the insurgencies in the immediate post-1945 period involved the colonial powers. This phase is now long past and guerrilla struggles have been waged against Communist governments in Afghanistan and Kampuchea and against other Third World governments from El Salvador to Burma and from East Timor to Peru. Urban guerrilla struggles are also being waged by secessionist groups in parts of the developed world including Northern Ireland and Spain.[1] There seems no reason to believe that the number of such wars will decrease during the last decades of the twentieth century.

The success of the guerrillas involved will depend not only upon political and economic factors but also upon the march of military technology, including the technology of air power. Thus one American commentator in 1986 described the helicopter as the 'queen' of the battles being fought in the Third World. He stressed the importance of the four helicopter gunships and thirty-six general-purpose helicopters in the war in El Salvador and of twenty-four Soviet-built helicopters in the struggle between the Nicaraguan government and the Contra guerrillas.[2] In fact the conflict between helicopters and anti-helicopter missiles is being waged in places as diverse and far apart as Enniskillen and Kabul, San Salvador and Luanda. More and more armed forces in the Third World are equipped with advanced helicopters and nothing but economics constrains this process. Even governments which are subject to arms boycotts, such as South Africa or North Korea, can still acquire helicopters because there is so little difference between civilian and military models or because they buy them through third parties.[3] Fixed-wing trainer aircraft which, as we have seen, are particularly suitable for counter-insurgency, are also widely available.

Thus one of the most significant changes in the composition of the armed forces of Third World countries over the last twenty years has been the increase in the number of aircraft designed for countering insurgency. Obviously this is particularly the case with countries which are currently faced with insurgencies; the International Institute for Strategic Studies believes the Philippines has two squadrons with twenty-six T-28D and one wing with forty-one Bell UH-1H and sixteen S-76 helicopters dedicated to fighting Moslem separatists and Communist guerrillas. Similarly Indonesia, which is crushing the independence movement in East Timor, has one squadron armed with thirteen OV-10F Bronco aircraft for counter-insurgency and Peru, which is threatened by Communist 'Shining Light' guerrillas, has sixteen Mil Mi-25 helicopters. However, even Third World states which are not currently suffering from guerrilla warfare also have a number of aircraft for fighting guerrillas. Argentina has two squadrons equipped with forty Pucara fixed-wing aircraft and two with Hughes and Bell helicopters. Brazil has ninety-eight AT-26 aircraft which the IISS lists as dedicated to counter-insurgency, and Chile has two squadrons equipped with twenty-seven A-37B aircraft.[4]

Technically Third World governments have not yet shown great inventiveness in their struggle against insurgencies. There are, for example, no reports of them making use of fixed-wing gunships, though converting old transports for this role should be relatively easy. Indeed it would seem that the USA is the only country currently producing fixed-wing gunships for use in unconventional warfare. The Rockwell Corporation was awarded a contract to produce Hercules AC130U gunships in July 1987. The first aircraft of six, which will be technically far more advanced than those used in Vietnam, is due to be delivered in 1990.[5] Admittedly there have been suggestions that the Soviets and their allies have resorted to new technologies against insurgents in Afghanistan and South-East Asia by making use of mycotoxins and other lethal chemicals. But these cases have not been fully proven and in any case the technology was undoubtedly Soviet rather than Laotian or Afghan.[6]

Most of the tactical and technical innovations for countering insurgency continue to appear in the West. Faced with more than a decade of unrest in Northern Ireland, the British have made increasing use of helicopters in the area and the Army Air Corps had two squadrons of Lynx and Gazelle helicopters as well as Beaver light aircraft.[7] Reconnaissance along the border by Beaver aircraft came to light in December 1987 when one strayed forty miles into Southern Ireland. The Southern Irish army uses Alouette III helicopters to move bomb disposal squads and to carry out patrols on the border, the British employ their rotary-winged aircraft to move troops securely away from ambushes and mines on roads and to chase wanted cars. On 9 April 1971 helicopters were used to carry troops and police who rounded-up and interned those suspected of supporting the IRA. Technically, though not politically, the operation was a great success. On another occasion, before the British cleared the barricades which the Catholic population of Londonderry had set up, they sent helicopters over the area 'with special equipment which could detect newly turned earth'.[8] This was indeed discovered and the army concluded that the Provisional IRA might have mined the area. Thus specially-equipped tanks were sent in to clear the obstacles.

Intelligence is as essential to successful operations against urban as against rural guerrillas and helicopters have been used increasingly to carry out reconnaissance by means of what are described as 'heletele instant air-to-ground TV reconnaissance surveillance systems'.[9] A Lynx helicopter carrying such a system was loitering over an IRA funeral in March 1988 when two British soldiers were murdered. Reports suggested that the colour cameras had zoom lenses and were 'fixed externally on the Lynx on a non-vibrating gyroscopic mounting [and] would be able to pick out the faces of those involved'.[10] The security forces nevertheless reacted fairly slowly because they were not sure what was going on and what action to take. In other cases reconnaissance by helicopter has circumscribed guerrilla actions. One guerrilla leader complained: 'It is increasingly difficult to operate with impunity. In Belfast there are three helicopters in the air in touch with plain clothes units on the the the streets.'[11]

Not surprisingly, the Provisional IRA has tried to equip itself with hand-held anti-helicopter missiles which are increasingly becoming spread across the world. The Russians have long supplied their allies with Sam-7s; the British have produced over 36,500 Blowpipes and by the spring of 1988 they were in service with fourteen nations. The RSS-78 Rayrider missile made by Bofors has also equipped eight nations and the USA has sold Stingers to some of its more favoured allies and supplied them to the Afghan rebels.[12] It is not, therefore, astonishing that 'seepage' into guerrilla hands is slowly taking place. In November 1987 the French police seized twenty Sam-7s aboard the *Eksud*, a freighter apparently loaded in Libya and bound for Northern Ireland.[13] The arrival of Sam-7s in the province would make less difference than the acquisition by the IRA of Blowpipes or, most threateningly (and least likely) of all, of Stinger missiles. The helicopters have already been modified with infra-red countermeasures against heat-seeking missiles of the Sam-7 type. Nevertheless, the countermeasures might not always work and the Chief of the Royal Ulster constabulary, Sir John Hermon, warned in December 1987 that the IRA was likely to acquire such weapons despite the capture of the *Eksud*. They could be used against transport aircraft approaching airfields if they were ineffective against military helicopters.[14]

One option for any government which finds that anti-aircraft weapons are making its helicopters too vulnerable is to use remotely-piloted vehicles (RPV) for reconnaissance. During the period 1964-75 the US Strategic Air Command flew 3,435 unmanned RPV missions over South-East Asia.[15] Some involved tiny aircraft with only 13 ft wingspans; other RPVs had spans of 82 ft. Many were launched from C-130s to discover the effects of US strategic bombing over North Vietnam and to locate prisoner-of-war camps so that US prisoners would not be killed in American attacks. On average, each RPV flew ten missions before it was shot down and its destruction caused none of the problems with captured or dead pilots that conventional reconnaissance created. Subsequently it was Israel that used such weapons most intensively to fly over Cairo before the Camp David agreement and later to reconnoitre Syrian positions in Lebanon.[16] Technology has also advanced in this area and RPVs can now be linked electronically to the ground so that they can relay photographs of the situation instantly to commanders, instead of having to return with them. More futuristically, it is possible to imagine the development of unmanned transport aircraft capable of dropping their cargo from parachutes over the correct zone. This would be particularly useful for the developed countries which are once again assisting insurgents as they did in the Second World War. The USA has been acutely embarrassed by the capture of American pilots shot down whilst supplying the Contra guerrillas in Nicaragua.[17] The main constraints on RPV development are lack of funds and the unwillingness of air forces to procure unmanned rather than manned aircraft.

Assuming that the United States does not become involved in another massive and prolonged war of the Vietnamese type, most of these new weapons are likely to be introduced very slowly. In the meantime Third World governments may sometimes acquire other highly destructive but more conventional weapons. Modern fragmentation bombs can now cover areas the size of football fields with flying fragments of metal which kill and maim. Drops of petroleum can be spread in a gas over an area and then exploded to form what are called fuel-air explosives which be immensely destructive.[18] The use which would be made of such weapons would depend on factors which have determined the relationship between air power and guerrillas ever since aircraft came to be used in Iraq and elsewhere in the 1920s. It was possible then, and even easy, for the RAF to fly over the homes of Iraqi tribesmen and to kill them in large numbers. The constraints were political not technical, and this has been the case ever since. Modern weapons can easily lead to mass killings in guerrilla war, as in any other type of war. Fortunately, however hard governments now try to insulate guerrilla wars from outside observation, reporters sometimes manage to penetrate into the area and describe what is happening.[19] The danger of receiving adverse publicity may be enough to persuade some governments only to use 'area denial weapons' when there are known to be no civilians in the region.

Certainly one should not assume that all Third World governments are impervious to criticism of their use of air power against insurgents. When the Sri Lankan government was faced with Tamil Tiger guerrillas in the mid-1980s, it fought a constant propaganda battle to prove that its aircraft were not killing civilians indiscriminately. Tamil spokesmen said that large numbers of civilians had been killed early in 1986 by 'two converted trainer type aircraft with rockets and small bombs strapped underneath, and four helicopter gunships'.[20] In May 1986, Jaffa residents claimed that helicopters had killed eight civilians and at one time the Indian Prime Minister, Rajiv Gandhi, even said that hundreds of Tamils had been killed by Sri Lankan carpet bombing attacks.[21] In April 1987 the Tamils maintained that 250 civilians had been killed; the government suggested that it was in fact eighty insurgents. Furthermore, to put a stop to such exaggerations, it pointed out that its offensive air power consisted of ten (later 17) Bell and two Dauphin helicopters and six Sia Marchetti trainers. These had dropped some 50 lb bombs, but usually they relied upon rockets and on handgrenades in bottles, which exploded when the bottle burst on hitting the ground. Sri Lanka, being a democratic and open state, could not exclude reporters. Indonesia has been able to use whatever weapons it has available to attack the independence movement in East Timor. But in some cases public opinion may be an important limiting force even in the Third World.

Hence, some conclusions can be drawn about the impact of air power on unconventional warfare which fit most circumstances. From the government's point of view:

• Air power on its own cannot defeat an insurgency which has the support of the majority of the population. The use of massive firepower against such an insurrection will only cause great bloodshed.

Consequently, if a government is to defeat insurgents without destroying the population or driving it into exile, the first categorical imperative is to separate the rebels, physically or emotionally, from the mass of the population. The use of of air power will only be constructive if it does not go against this axiom.

- The second categorical imperative for a democracy fighting insurgents is that it must convince its own people that it is not using excessive force and not attacking civilians indiscriminately. If air power is to be used it must conform with this axiom.
- It will also inconvenience a government if other countries can claim that it is using excessive force and it is easy to mount a propaganda campaign castigating governments using aircraft against guerrillas.
- If aircraft are available, helicopters will vastly increase the mobility of ground forces, particularly in difficult terrain and when they are not themselves threatened by missiles or aircraft.
- Slow fixed-wing aircraft of the trainer type are often more useful in anti-guerrilla operations than faster and more sophisticated ones because of the difficulty of locating the insurgents. Although precision-guided munitions may make faster aircraft more useful, larger and faster aircraft are usually only really effective if the guerrillas choose to stand and fight as they did in Greece at the end of the civil war and, from time to time, in Vietnam.
- Because war between guerrillas and governments is usually a test of endurance, cheap and obsolete aircraft may be more useful than expensive and modern ones, the loss of which will only make the war more unpopular with those who are paying for it.
- Against guerrillas who do expose themselves to air attack, fixed-wing and helicopter gunships can bring immense firepower to bear and can thus be very useful, provided they do not undermine the first two proportions listed above. Aircraft may be particularly effective in protecting convoys as the British found in Palestine and Cyprus, the French and Americans found in Indochina and the Soviets in Afghanistan.
- Aircraft can be immensely useful to the government's forces for reconnaissance and intelligence-gathering, particularly against guerrillas operating in open country, but they can be important even in jungles and in urban insurgencies such as Northern Ireland.
- In areas where no civilians are living and where guerrillas are operating, attacks by heavy bombers can have a considerable impact on rebels' morale, even when they do not actually kill or wound many of them. In the future, smaller ground attack aircraft may be able

to use fuel-air explosives and similar ground attack aircraft may be able to use fuel-air explosives and similar weapons with the same effect but all such operations are difficult to justify to public opinion. The operational advantages have to be very considerable to outweigh the presentational disadvantages.

- Even if the danger of widening the war can be ignored, most Western governments will find the odium attached to air attacks on sanctuaries in other states outweigh the operational advantages.
- Where there is no enemy air threat, it may be more efficient to give the ground forces commander control over all aircraft operating against guerrillas. If this is not possible the closest liaison between ground and air forces is essential.
- Precisely because aircraft can be so effective in some circumstances, anti-aircraft weapons can sometimes undermine this effectiveness and have a decisive effect on conflicts as was the case in Afghanistan.

From the insurgents' point of view the strategy must be the opposite of the goverment's.

- If the government uses air power offensively the insurgents must try to present such attacks as indiscriminate and to use them to weld the people together behind their activities.
- They must also try to mobilize international opinion against governmental atrocities and so encourage the supply of weapons. It may, therefore, be wise to invite correspondents, particularly from the government side or from neutral states, to accompany guerrilla forces; houses damaged by bombs make good photographs. Governments find it generally more difficult to provide evidence of guerrilla atrocities.
- The insurgents must therefore operate amongst the civilian population in the towns and villages, to tempt the government to bomb them.
- If the government's forces dominate the skies in the daytime the insurgents may have to operate primarily at night.
- Careful preparation of hiding places and bunkers, as in Cyprus and, far more comprehensively, in Vietnam, can mitigate the impact of bombing. Such preparations also make airborne reconnaissance less effective and provide some protection against sweeps by government ground forces.
- The establishment of sanctuaries in a neighbouring state can enable the guerrillas to re-form and recuperate from battle. If the

government's forces attack the sanctuaries yet more states will be encouraged to support the guerrillas; if they do not, they will concede a great operational advantage to the rebels.

• Guerrillas must try to wear down the government by a strategy of attrition; anything which makes the war expensive is to their advantage. Attacks on air bases and the destruction of costly aircraft and the killing of highly-trained pilots can be particularly effective.

• Guerrillas should not usually stand and fight but hand-held anti-aircraft missiles may enable them to make the war very expensive for the government and may even drive the government's aircraft from the skies.

NOTES

Introduction

1. For a history of guerrilla warfare see Walter Laqueur, *Guerrilla, A Historical and Critical Study* (Weidenfeld and Nicolson, London, 1977). See also Robert B. Asprey, *War in the Shadows, The Guerrilla in History* (Macdonald and Jane's, London, 1976); Peter Paret and John Shy, *Guerrillas in the 1960s* (Pall Mall Press, London and Dunmow, 1962) and Peter Paret, *French Revolutionary Warfare* (Pall Mall Press, London and Dunmow, 1964).
2. Joseph C. Harsch, 'Queen of battle; the helicopter gunship', *Christian Science Monitor* 15–21 September 1986.
3. Tony Geraghty, *Who Dares Wins* (Fontana/Collins, London, 1981), p. 139. William Shawcross, *Sideshow; Kissinger, Nixon and the Destruction of Cambodia* (Andre Deutsch, London, 1979), p. 209. Major General J. D. Lunt, 'Air control; another myth?' *RUSI Journal* December 1981.
4. Lieutenant General Sir John Glubb, *War in the Desert, An RAF Frontier Campaign* (Hodder and Stoughton, London, 1969), p. 30. See also P. S. Allfree, *Hawks of the Hadhramaut* (Robert Hall, London, 1967), p. 160.
5. William Morwood, *Duel for the Middle Kingdom* (Everest House Publishers, New York, 1980), p. 188.
6. Morwood pp. 196 and 201. See also Dick Wilson, *Mac: The People's Emperor* (Futura Publications, London, 1978), pp. 163 and 169.
7. Morwood, *op. cit.* p. 211.
8. Asprey, *op. cit.* p. 728.
9. Truong Nhu Tang, *Journal of a Vietcong* (Jonathan Cape, London, 1986), p. 145.
10. For comments on dissociation see Ralph Littauer and Norman Uphoff, *The Air War in Indochina* (Beacon Press, Boston, 1971), p. 28. For Mussolini's comments see Bertrand Russell, *Power* (Unwin Books, London, 1962), p. 21. For comments on the dissociation produced by combat in the air see W. A. Bishop, *Winged Warfare* (Penguin, Harmondsworth, 1938), p. 214; 'As I said before it was not like killing a man so much as bringing down a bird in sport.'
11. Lieutenant General W. R. Peers, *The My Lai Inquiry* (Norton, New York, 1979), pp. 67–74 and 158.
12. David Wragg, *Helicopters at War* (Robert Hall, London, 1983). For the use of air power against guerrillas see also Otto Heilbrunn, 'Guerrillas in the 19th Century', *RUSI Journal* May 1963.
13. General George Grivas-Dighenes, *Guerrilla Warfare and EOKA's Struggle* (Longmans, London, 1964), p. 76.
14. See for example, Joseph Koster, *The Struggle for South Yemen* (Croom Helm, London, 1984), p. 72. But there was plenty of information from the guerrilla side in the war in Cyprus, see Charles Foley (ed.), *The Memoirs of General Grivas* (Longmans, London, 1964). For the war in Kenya see Donald L. Barnett and Karari Njama, *Mau Mau From Within* (Macgibbon and Kee, London, 1966).
15. David Chanoff and Doan Van Toai, *Portrait of the Enemy; The Other Side of the War in Vietnam* (I. B. Tauris and Co., London, 1987).

213

Chapter 1: Biplanes and Nomads 1918–39

Iraq and Jordan

Recent histories of Iraq during this period include Peter Slugett, *Britain in Iraq 1914–1932* (Ithaca Press, London, 1976), Stephen H. Longrigg, *Iraq 1900 to 1950* (OUP, London, 1953), and Abbas Kelidar (ed.), *The Integration of Modern Iraq* (Croom Helm, London, 1979). The best recent histories of the use of force to maintain the British Empire are Anthony Clayton, *The British Empire as a Superpower 1919–1939* (Macmillan, London, 1986) and Brian Bond, *British Military Policy Between the Two World Wars* (Clarendon Press, Oxford, 1980). Memoirs and biographies of those who served with the RAF there include Air Chief Marshal Sir Basil Embry, *Mission Completed* (Methuen, London, 1957); Sir Gerald Gibbs, *Survivor's Story* (Hutchinson, London, 1956); Albert E. Cowton, *With the First in the Field* (Cowton, Norwich, 1963); Air Chief Marshall Sir Arthur Longmore, *From Sea To Sky 1910–1945* (Geoffrey Bles, London, 1946) and Sir John Maitland Salmond, *Swifter than Eagles* (William Blackwood, London, 1964).

1. See for example, M. Cooper, *The Birth of Independent Air Power* (Allen and Unwin, London, 1986) and B. D. Powers, *Strategy Without Slide Rule* (Croom Helm, London, 1976).
2. Lieutenant General Sir John Glubb, *War in the Desert: An RAF Frontier Campaign* (Hodder and Stoughton, London, 1969), p. 69.
3. D. S. Woolman, *Rebels in the Rif: Abd el Krim and the Rif Rebellion* (OUP, Oxford, 1969), p. 97 *passim.*
4. *Loc. cit.* p. 161.
5. Jean du Chaffal, 'Avec l'Aviation au Maroc au Temps Heroique de la Pacification', *Forces Aeriennes Françaises* December 1959.
6. John Wright, *Libya* (Earnest Benn, London, 1969), pp. 151 and 155 *passim.*
7. K. Holomboe, *Desert Encounter* (Harrap, London, 1936).
8. For operations in Egypt see Clayton, *op. cit.*, p. 116. For General Hoskins' report see WO/32/5828. For the meeting between Trenchard and Milner see A. Boyle, *Trenchard* (Collins, London, 1962), p. 366.
9. See 'Air Vice Marshal John Gray, Dauntless Airman who beat the Mad Mullah', *The Times* 10 June 1987 and *The Memoirs of General the Lord Ismay* (Heinemann, London, 1960), p. 35 *passim.* L. S. Amery, *My Political Life, Vol. 2* (Hutchinson, London, 1953), p. 201. Bond, *op. cit.* p. 85.
10. AIR/9/12, Under Secretary of State's report on Somaliland, 17 February 1920 and Air/9/11, Minuted by CGS India, 16 May 1926.
11. AIR/9/14, Minute of 19 February 1920. Viscount Templewood gave Trenchard credit for suggesting the scheme to Churchill, see *Empire of the Air* (Collins, London, 1957), p. 48. See also Sir John Maitland Salmon, *op. cit.* p. 150.
12. AIR/5/224, Note to the Chief of Air Staff by W. Churchill, 29 February 1920.
13. *Loc. cit.*
14. General Sir Aylmer Haldane, *The Insurrection in Mesopotamia, 1920* (Blackwoods, Edinburgh, 1922). See also Clayton, *op. cit.* p. 120 *passim.* For the political causes see S. H. Longrigg, *op cit.* p. 112 *passim.* See also a 'Selection of lectures and essays from the work of the officers attending the third course at the Staff College', Air Ministry, July 1924, copy in RAF Staff College Library.
15. Boyle, *op. cit.* p. 376.
16. AIR/5/553, 'Notes on the work of the RAF in Mesopotamia'. Cox later became a convert to air policing, see L. Hart, *op. cit.*, p. 153 *passim.* For Churchill's role at the Cairo conference see Martin Gilbert, *Winston Churchill Vol. IV, 1916–1922* (Heinemann, London, 1975). See also Lady Bell (ed.), *The Letters of Gertrude Bell* Vol. 2 (Ernest Benn, London, 1927), p. 539 and Boyle, *op. cit.* p. 382 *passim.*
17. AIR/5/553, First meeting of the military committee, 12 March 1921.
18. Air papers, *loc. cit.* See also Churchill's summary of the situation in AIR/9/14, 'Mesopotamia 1922–1923', 4 August 1921. According to Slugett the cost of policing Iraq fell from £32 million to £4 million by 1926–7. For the views of the Air Staff see AIR/5/168, 'the power of the Air Force and the operation of this power to hold and police Mesopotamia'.
19. AIR/5/168, *loc. cit.*
20. AIR/9/14, Memorandum of 23 January 1922 and AIR/5/189, 'transition of control in Iraq

and withdrawal of troops' and letter to the Air Ministry from the officer commanding troops in Iraq, 7 March 1922. For an example of typical military hostility to air policing see J. F. C. Fuller, *On Future Warfare* (Sefton Praed and Co., London, 1928), p. 260. Sir B. H. Liddell Hart was much more open-minded; see *The British Way in Warfare* (Faber and Faber, London, 1922), p. 140.

21. AIR/5/189, GOC Iraq, 7 March 1922.
22. AIR/9/12, Haldane letter of 25 June 1921.
23. AIR/8/57, High Commissioner in Iraq to Secretary of State for the Colonies, 9 December 1922.
24. AIR/8/55, Trenchard Minute to the Secretary of State. For RAF life in Iraq see Longmore, *op. cit.* p. 101 *passim* and Embry, *op. cit.* p. 37. See also AIR/5/1260, Cox to the Colonial Office, 28 October 1922 and AIR/5/189 Group Captain Borton telegram of 22 January 1922.
25. AIR/5/256 part 1, Cox telegram of 22 October 1922.
26. Embry, *op. cit.* p. 39.
27. *Loc. cit.* See also AIR/5/256 part 1, report of 6 September 1922.
28. AIR/5/544, Ludlow Hewitt to Sir John Salmond.
29. Lieutenant General Sir John Glubb, *War in the Desert, An RAF Frontier Campaign* (Hodder and Stoughton, London, 1969). For the Balaibel incident see 'A Selection of lectures and essays from the work of officers attending the second course of the RAF Staff College, 1923–4', Air Ministry, August 1924.
30. Glubb, *op. cit.* p. 336. See also AIR/5/544.
31. Glubb, *op. cit.* p. 147.
32. Gibbs, *op. cit.* p. 39. Number One Squadron flew Snipes in Iraq until 1926, Number Six had Bristol Fighters until 1932, Numbers 8, 55 and 84 had DH 9as, see O. Thetford, *Aircraft of the Royal Air Force since 1918* (Putnam, London, 1979).
33. Longmore, *op. cit.* p. 134.
34. AIR/5/338, letter from Iraq to Trenchard, 6 August 1924. See also Bell, *op. cit.* p. 710.
35. For a summary of the flying difficulties see note 29 *supra.*
36. Trenchard was originally against giving such rewards. See Boyle, *op. cit.* p. 388.
37. AIR/9/12, 'Notes on the conduct of air operations against tribes on the North-West Frontier of India'. The ransoms sometimes worked, see Cowton, *op. cit.* p. 318.
38. AIR/9/14, War Office letter of 17 August 1921.
39. Slugett, *op. cit.* p. 122.
40. AIR/5/338, Secretary of State to High Commissioner, 31 January 1924 and High Commissioner Dobb to Secretary of State, 1 March 1924. Lansbury is quoted in Legett, *op. cit.* p. 264 *passim.* For War Office attacks on air policing see note of 17 August 1921, AIR/9/14 and for the size of the garrison see Clayton, *op. cit.* p. 125.
41. AIR/8/57.
42. AIR/5/256 part 2, letter of 3 November 1924.
43. AIR/5/338.
44. AIR/5/338, Salmond letter from Iraq to Trenchard, 29 November 1923. See also Salmond, *op. cit.* p. 161 and Air Commodore Portal, 'Air Force co-operation in policing the Empire', *RUSI Journal* May 1937.
45. AIR/5/544.
46. AIR/5/256 part 1, W. F. MacNeece, report 30 September 1921.
47. Woolman, *op. cit.* p. 198 *passim.*
48. AIR/9/12, 'Italian Operations in Libya'.
49. See also the papers in AIR/9/14. Portal, *loc. cit.* p. 354.
50. Glubb, *op. cit.* p. 30.
51. Peter Slugett, *op. cit.* p. 269. Slugett argues that Iraqi governments survived only because of RAF support. See also Dobb's report of 10 January 1924 in AIR/5/544, part 2.
52. AIR/5/1260, part 2, 'The situation in Iraq', printed 7 February 1924 and AIR/9/12, 'Some fallacies and misconceptions in regard to air control.'
53. Glubb, *op. cit.*
54. Kelidar, *op. cit.* p. 88 *passim.* See also AIR/5/1260, part 3, 'Notes on the internal situation in Iraq.'
55. *Loc. cit.* p. 105. AIR/5/440, Discussion of 5 July 1927.
56. AIR/5/1260, the posts closed down were at Samawah and Sulman. See also AIR/9/14.
57. Godfrey Lias, *Glubb's Legion* (Evans Brothers, London, 1956), p. 124 *passim.*

58. Among the relevant studies of Trans-Jordan in the 1920s are Uriel Dann, *Studies in the History of Transjordan, 1920–1949* (Westview, Boulder and London, 1984); Godfrey Lias, *Glubb's Legion* (Evans Brothers, London, 1956); John Bagot Glubb, *The Story of the Arab Legion* (Hodder and Stoughton, London, 1948). There are fewer accounts of RAF life there than of life in Iraq but the subject is covered in Sir Arthur Longmore, *From Sea to Sky* (Geoffrey Bles, London, 1946), especially p. 112 and Sir Gerald Gibbs, *Survivor's Story* (Hutchinson, London, 1956), p. 46.

59. Dann, *op. cit.* p. 3. G. E. Kirk, *A Short History of the Middle East* (University Paperback, London, 1966), p. 159 *passim*.

60. AIR/9/19, M. Adams (ed.), *The Middle East, A Handbook* (Anthony Blond, London, 1971), p. 229.

61. Lias, *op. cit.* p. 63 *passim*.

62. AIR/5/1234, Air Operations Palestine 1920–1930. Clayton, *op. cit.* p. 138.

63. *Loc. cit.* demonstration over Kerak, January 1922.

64. AIR/9/19, folio 3.

65. AIR/5/203 part 2. Glubb, *op. cit.* p. 61.

66. AIR/5/203 part 1. Note of 16 September 1923.

67. Lias, *op. cit.* p. 70 *passim*. Glubb, *op. cit.* p. 62.

68. *Loc. cit.*, p. 70. See also AIR/5/1243, report on operations, 15 August 1922.

69. Lias, *op. cit.* p. 72.

70. Glubb, *op. cit.* p. 63.

71. *Loc. cit.*

72. AIR/5/1243, report from McEwen, 16 August 1924.

73. Glubb, *loc. cit.*

74. AIR/23/8492. See also AIR/5/203, part 4, letter to Chief Secretary, Jerusalem, 29 February 1928.

75. AIR/23/8492.

76. Lias, *op. cit.* p. 103.

77. Glubb, *op. cit.* p. 206 *passim*.

78. AIR/5/293, note of 15 January 1923.

79. AIR/5/203 part 2, particularly Peake's letter of 24 August 1924.

Aden

There are a number of excellent histories of the Yemen and accounts by political officers who served there. See particularly R. Bidwell, *The Two Yemens* (Longmans and Westview Press, Boulder and London, 1983); R. J. Gavin, *Aden under British Rule 1839–1967* (C. Hurst and Company, London, 1975); Harold Ingrams, *The Yemen, Imams, Rulers and Revolutions* (John Murray, London, 1963). See also P. S. Allfree, *Hawks of the Hadhramaut* (Robert Hall, London, 1967); J. Kostiner, *The Struggle for South Yemen* (Croom Helm, London, 1984); Sir Kennedy Trevaskis *Shades of Amber, A South Arabian Episode* (Hutchinson, London, 1968).

1. CO/846/1 Aden Administration report, see also AIR/5/377, Air Intelligence Report on Aden Protectorate.

2. CO/846/1.

3. See Ingrams, *op. cit.* especially chapters 5 and 6.

4. Bidwell, *op. cit.* p. 70.

5. AIR/5/1300, Aden Operations Summary. See also AIR/9/12.

6. AIR/9/12, Memorandum of 9 April 1929.

7. AIR/5/1300, Aden Operations Summary. For mapping operations see Air Marshal Sir Robert Saundby, 'Aden revisited', *Air Power* Spring 1959.

8. See also AIR/6/9110. For later operations see AIR/24/1 RAF Record Book Headquarters British Forces in Aden.

9. See note 5 *supra*.

10. AIR/8/45, Speech to the Parliamentary Army and Air Committee, 21 June 1932.

11. AIR/24/1 Report of December 1931. See also Bidwell, *op. cit.* pp. 87 and 90. Bidwell gives the figure of 40 airfields. See also Flight Lieutenant F. M. V. May, 'The Arabian Survey Flight', *RUSI Journal* November 1935 and, for operations against the Quteibis, Air Commo-

dore C. F. A. Portal, 'Air Force Co-operation in Policing the Empire', *RUSI Journal* May 1937.
13. Bidwell *op. cit.* p. 88.
14. On the question of the transfer from India to the Colonial Office see CO/935/8 and Bidwell *op. cit.* p. 75. The Air Ministry was in favour of the move, many of the local people were not.
15. CO/935/14. Resident to the Secretary of State 29 April 1935. See also *loc. cit.* CID subcommittee on questions arising in the Middle East.
16. For Ingrams see David Ledger, *Shifting Sands, The British in South Arabia* (Passover Peninsula, London, 1983), p. 18 and Trevaskis, *op. cit.* p. 13. Bidwell, *op. cit.* p. 90.
17. CO/935/23, Future Policy in Aden Protectorate and Hall to the Secretary of State, 23 December 1941. Gavin, *op. cit.* p. 306.
18. AIR/23/8460. See also the article by Air Vice Marshall H. T. Lydford, 'The Aden Command', *RUSI Journal* February 1950.
19. AIR/20/7357, Inspector General visit to Aden, October 1950 and letter from Watts in Aden.
20. Squadron Leader P. Barker DFC, 'Aden and the RAF', *Air Clues* June 1955.
21. See note 18 *supra*. For operations against the Ahl Billeil see AIR/23/8364.
22. AIR/23/8365, Report of Operations against the Quteibi tribe, November–December 1947.
23. AIR/23/8367. Report of ground and air operations against Nogi bin Nogi.
24. AIR/23/8369.
25. AIR/23/8373.
26. Bidwell, *op. cit.* p. 97. For operations in 1950 see AIR/23/8368 and for 1951 see AIR/29/1991.
27. Bidwell, *op. cit.* p. 92. For the 1955 operation see K. Diacre 'Aden 1955', *Army Quarterly* January 1956.
28. Stephen Harper, *Last Sunset* (Collins, London, 1978), p. 36. Ingrams, *op. cit.* p. 117.
29. Bidwell, *op. cit.* p. 101. Trevaskis, *op. cit.* p. 207.
30. Allfree, *op. cit.* p. 160.
31. Bidwell, *op. cit.* p. 87.
32. Letter to the author, 9 September 1987.
33. Interviews.

The RAF and the North-West Frontier of India

Recent studies covering British relations with Afghanistan include, Leon B. Poullada, *Reform and Rebellion in Afghanistan, 1919–1929* (Cornell University Press, Ithaca and London, 1973); C. Millar, *Khyber, The Story of the North West Frontier* (Macdonald and Jane's, London, 1983) and R. T. Stewart, *Fire in Afghanistan* (Doubleday, New York, 1973). For an account of RAF activities in the area see A. J. Young, 'Royal Air Force North-West Frontier, 1915–1939', *RUSI Journal* March 1982.
1. Lord Roberts, *Forty-One Years in India* (Macmillan, London, 1897), Vol. 2, p. 102 *passim*. See also WO/208/3, 'Military Geography of Afghanistan', September 1941.
2. Millar and Poullada, *loc. cit.*
3. A. Draper, *The Amritsar Massacre* (Buchan and Enright, London, 1985). For an account sympathetic to Dyer see Lieutenant-Colonel A. A. Irvine, *Land of No Regrets* (Collins, London, 1938), p. 240 *passim*.
4. AIR/8/45. 'Notes on the army in small wars'. For the RAF's part in the campaign see Clayton, *op. cit.* pp. 167 and 170.
5. Amanullah is quoted by Stewart, *op. cit.* p. 71. Nevertheless Stewart accepts the RAF's view of the efficacy of the air attack, p. 59 *passim*. See also WO/287/22, 'History of Afghanistan' and B. H. Liddell-Hart, *The British Way in Warfare* (Faber and Faber, London, 1932), p. 141.
6. AIR/5/177, vol. 2, CAS Memorandum on the Afghan War. The account of the effects of the attack on Jalalabad is taken from the War Office's history.
7. AIR/8/45, Memorandum by Wing Commander Hodsoll, November 1929.
8. AIR/9/11, comments by Denys Bray, 24 August 1922.
9. AIR/5/558, CAS Minute of 10 June 1921. See also AIR/9/25, Minute of 23 March 1925.
10. WO/208/7.

11. AIR/9/11, 'Rearmament and Preparedness for War', July 1927.
12. AIR/5/177, Note by CAS for CID sub-committee on Indian military requirements.
13. AIR/9/11, 'Note on Frontier Operations from November 1919 to February 1920.'
14. AIR/5/183, 'Effects of defective equipment on efficiency and morale of RAF in India.'
15. For CGS' views see AIR/5/183; for lectures at Quetta see Papers of Sir T. W. Corbett, Churchill College Archives, CORB/2/1, 'Frontier Tour Discussion 1932'. For the condition of the RAF in India see E. Cowton, *With the First in the Field* (published by Mrs E. Cowton, Norwich, 1963), p. 190 and Sir John Maitland Salmon, *Swifter than Eagles* (William Blackwood, London, 1964), p. 153.
16. See note 14 *supra*. See also Dudley Saward, *Bomber Harris* (Cassell, Buchan and Enright, London, 1984). For RAF use of radar see Clayton, *op. cit.* p. 175.
17. Sir Philip Joubert de la Ferte, *The Fated Sky* (White Lion Publishers, London, 1952), p. 133.
18. AIR/19/11, Memorandum on Sir John Salmond's report, 23 August 1922. See also Memorandum by CGS, 16 May 1926.
19. AIR/9/12, CAS memorandum, 26 April 1920. For the Moplah and Akali rebellions see Clayton *op. cit.* p. 180 *passim*.
20. Chelmsford's views are quoted in Stewart *op. cit.* p. 104. See also *loc. cit.* pp. 214 and 420. For Bray see note 8 *supra*.
21. *Loc. cit.* Trenchard's complaints about the India Office are in AIR/5/312.
22. AIR/9/12, letter from CAS to Maconachie, 10 January 1933. For Embry's account see Air Chief Marshal Sir Basil Embry, *Mission Completed* (Methuen, London, 1957), p. 77.
23. *The Times* also argued that it was illogical to reject a ban on bombing at the Geneva disarmament conference.
24. 'Guarding the Frontier', *The Times* 30 May and 2 June 1933.
25. Harold Binns, letters to the *Manchester Guardian* 25 and 29 March 1933; See also J. A. Chalmier's letter in the same paper, 1 April 1933. All this correspondence was carefully collected in the Air Ministry files.
26. AIR/9/12, 'Aircraft in frontier warfare'.
27. Copies of debates are in AIR/9/12.
28. *Loc. cit.*
29. AIR/9/11, Chief Commissioner on the North West Frontier, 3 September 1923. Complaints from the tribesmen are quoted in R. T. Stewart, p. 214. Stewart accepts the existence of a link between the murders and RAF policy (see pp. 215 and 235 *passim*) but does not explain why political officers and the murderers themselves denied such a link.
30. *Loc. cit.*
31. AIR/8/122, Air staff note on 'the situation on the North-West Frontier', 13 May 1930.
32. Air papers, *loc. cit.* 'India, the North-West Frontier, measures proposed by the government of India for dealing with Afghanistan', 30 September 1930.
33. *Ibid.* Liddell-Hart *loc. cit.* p. 150.
34. Corbett papers, CORB/2/5.
35. *Loc. cit.* lecture by Lieutenant-Colonel C. E. Bruce.
36. Papers of Sir P. J. Grigg, Churchill College Archives, PJGC/2/21–25, letter from the Viceregal House, 13 March 1935.
37. Embry, *op. cit.* p. 80. De la Ferte, *op. cit.* p. 140.

The Revolt in Palestine

1. For a good early history of the revolt see John Marlowe, *Rebellion in Palestine* (Cresset Press, London, 1946). For official views see particularly WO/275/111, 'Notes on the Arab Rebellion in Palestine 1936–9.'
2. AIR/9/19, folio nine.
3. A. Boyle, *Trenchard* (Collins, London, 1962), p. 370.
4. But note Marlowe's scepticism about the patriotic motives involved, Marlowe, *op. cit.* p. 177. See also Clayton, *op. cit.* p. 487 *passim*.
5. Marlowe, *op. cit.* p. 156.
6. WO/282/6, draft 'Report on the military lessons of the Arab rebellion in Palestine', 1936.
7. *Loc cit.* Clayton, p. 491.

8. Marlowe, *op cit.* p. 166.
9. *Loc. cit.* p. 167.
10. CO/935/21, Narrative despatches from the High Commissioner for Palestine to the Secretary of State for the Colonies, 26 September 1937 to 31 December 1938.
11. Marlowe believed that the Mufti was allowed to escape, p. 186.
12. *Loc. cit.* p. 200.
13. Noel-Baker papers, Churchill College Library, NBKR/4/551, Arab Centre report quoting a paper from the Mukhtar of Kafr Masr Village and Arab Centre report of 17 June 1939 dealing with alleged events in Beit Runah.
14. Marlowe, *op. cit.* p. 214.
15. AIR/5/1244, Report on operations carried out by British forces in Palestine and Trans-Jordan, 7 April 1938 by Wavell.
16. Marlowe, *op. cit.* p. 206. MacMichael remained Governor of Palestine until 1944 when he was attacked by Jewish assassins.
17. CO/935/21, note of 23 November 1937.
18. *Loc. cit.* note of 14 July 1938.
19. *Loc. cit.* notes of 13 September 1938 and 24 October 1938.
20. CO/935/22.
21. WO/282/4, Dill to Air Vice Marshal Courtney, 28 September 1936.
22. *Loc. cit.*
23. SO/282/6, Peirse letter to General R. H. Haining on the War Office's history of the operations, 22 June 1938.
24. WO/282/4, Brooke-Popham's reply to Dill's letter of 28 September 1936.
25. D. Saward, *Bomber Harris* (Cassell/Buchan and Enright, London, 1984), p. 64. For Montgomery see also 'Field Marshal Montgomery', *The Times* 25 March 1976.
26. CO/935/21, report of 29 December 1938.
27. On the general efficacy of aircraft in dealing with disturbances, see AIR/9/19, folio 14, note by Plans, 9 October 1929.
28. See note 6 *supra*.
29. *Loc. cit.*
30. *Loc. cit.* comments on events of 20 July 1936.
31. *Loc. cit.* For radar communications see Donald Portway, *Military Science To-day* (Oxford 1940), p. 78 *passim*.
32. Saward *op. cit. loc. cit.*
33. WO/282/4, Dill to Air Vice Marshall Courtney, 28 September 1936. See also Air Commodore C. F. A. Portal, 'Air Force co-operation in policing the Empire', *RUSI Journal* May 1933, p. 346.
34. See note 6 *supra*.
35. *Loc. cit.*
36. The Hardy stayed in service until 1941, see O. Thetford, *Aircraft of the RAF* (Putnam, London, 1979), p. 330.
37. Air Chief Marshal Sir Basil Embry, *Mission Completed* (Methuen, London, 1957), p. 45.

Conclusion

1. AIR/9/19 Folio nine. See also Portal, *loc. cit.*
2. 'Aircraft in small wars', *RUSI Journal* August 1928.
3. *The Army and Navy Gazette* 5 June 1933.
4. AIR/9/12.
5. Donald L. Barnett and Karari Njama, *Mau Mau from Within* (Macgibbon and Kee, London, 1966), p. 238.
6. AIR/9/11, 'India 1919–1937'.
7. J. F. C. Fuller, *The Reformation of War* (Hutchinson, London, 1923), p. 208.
8. A. E. Cowton, *With the First in the Field* (Cowton, Norwich, 1963), p. 216.
9. Sir Gerard Gibbs, *Survivor's Story* (Hutchinson, London, 1956), p. 47.
10. Malcolm Smith, *British Air Strategy Between the Wars* (Clarendon Press, Oxford, 1984), pp. 116–20; A. J. P. Taylor, *English History 1914–1945* Clarendon Press, Oxford, 1965), pp. 364–5.

11. For attitudes towards war and bombing, see *What would be the Character of a New War?* (Victor Gollancz, London, 1933); Major K. A. Bratt, *That Next War* (George Allen and Unwin, London, 1930); N. Shute, *What Happened to the Corbetts?* (Heinemann, London, 1939) and Uri Bialer, *The Shadow of the Bomber* (Royal Historical Society, London, 1980).
12. AIR/8/166, Chief of the Air Staff to Vansittart, 5 January 1934.
13. *Loc. cit.* Admiralty to Vansittart, copied to the Air Ministry, 10 January 1934 and Vansittart to Chatfield of the same date.
14. *Loc. cit.* Vansittart to Ellington, 6 January 1934. See also AIR/8/31, AIR/8/92 and AIR/8/171. See also Sir Arthur Longmore, *From Sea to Sky 1910–1945* (Geoffrey Bles, London, 1946), pp. 151–4.

Chapter 2: Lysanders, Liberators and the Resistance 1939–45

Introduction

1. For guerrilla operations in the Second World War see particularly W. Laqueur, *Guerrilla* (Weidenfeld and Nicolson, London, 1977), pp. 152–202; R. B. Asprey, *War in the Shadows* (Macdonald and Jane's, London 1975), Chapters 45–51; M. R. D. Foot, *Resistance: An Analysis of European resistance to Nazism 1940–45* (Eyre Methuen, London, 1976), Henri Michel, *The Shadow War, Resistance in Europe* (André Deutsch, London, 1972), J. G. Beevor, *SOE Recollections and Reflections* (Bodley Head, London, 1981); Otto Heilbrunn, *Partisan Warfare* (George Allen and Unwin, 1962), Chapter eight; *Chindit Operations in Burma* (Rand Memorandum 3654–PR) and *Allied Resistance to the Japanese on Luzon, World War II* (Rand Memorandum, 3655 PR).
2. Gibb McCall, *Flight Most Secret, Air Missions for SOE and SIS* (William Kimber, London, 1981), especially pp. 26–31.
3. Michel, *op. cit.* p. 125.
4. McCall, *op. cit.* p. 48 *passim*. O. Thetford, *Aircraft of the Royal Air Force* (Putnam, London), p. 551 has higher figures for Lysander sorties but these may include operations into Burma. See also Michel, *op. cit.* p. 128, and Air Commodore L. M. Hodges, 'Flying secret agents to and from enemy territory', *RAF Quarterly* Spring 1962.
5. McCall, *loc. cit.*

France

1. F. O. Miksche, *Secret Forces—The Technique of Underground Movements* (Faber and Faber, London, 1950).
2. Beevor, *op. cit.* p. 153 *passim*.
3. Asprey, *op. cit.* p. 474. McCall, *op. cit.* pp. 29–31.

Yugoslavia

1. Martin van Creveld, *Hitler's Strategy 1940–41, The Balkan Clue* (Cambridge University Press, Cambridge, 1973), p. 139 *passim*.
2. H. Seton-Watson, *The East European Revolution* (Methuen, London, 1961); p. 120, *passim*; Beevor, *op. cit.* p. 110; Asprey, *op. cit.* p. 513.
3. Fitzroy Maclean, *Eastern Approaches* (Four Square, London, 1967), p. 294 *passim* and Maclean's lecture at the RUSI, 'The setting for guerrilla warfare', *RUSI Journal* August 1963.
4. F. S. Deakin, *The Embattled Mountain* (OUP, London, 1971).
5. Deakin, *op. cit.* p. 18.
6. Deakin, *op. cit.* p. 25. Maclean in the *RUSI Journal* p. 210.
7. Deakin, *op. cit.* p. 51.
8. Deakin, *op. cit.* p. 54.
9. Deakin, *op. cit.* p. 58.
10. Maclean, *op. cit.* p. 262.
11. Maclean, *op. cit.* pp. 282 and 315. Milovan Djilas, *Wartime With Tito and The Partisans* (Secker and Warburg, London, 1980), p. 217. Heilbrunn, *op. cit.* p. 127.
12. Maclean, *op. cit.* p. 329.
13. Maclean, *op. cit.* p. 333.
14. Maclean, *op. cit.* p. 345.
15. Maclean, *op. cit.* p. 382.

16. Beevor, *op. cit.* p. 121. Maclean, *op. cit.* p. 383.
17. Maclean, *op. cit.* p. 388.
18. Maclean, *op. cit.* pp. 364 and 381, Foot, *op. cit.* p. 121 *passim.*
19. Maclean, *op. cit.* p. 362.
20. Maclean, *op. cit.* p. 413.
21. Maclean, *op. cit.* p. 413.
22. Maclean, *op. cit.* p. 410.
23. Maclean, *op. cit.* p. 420.
24. Djilas, *op. cit.* p. 403. For the impact of aircraft on guerrilla warfare see Albania in David Smiley, *Albanian Assignment* (Sphere Books, London, 1985), pp. 15, 50, 84–5, 133 and 145.

Greece

1. C. M. Woodhouse, *The Struggle for Greece, 1941–49* (Hart Davis MacGibbon, London, 1976), Chapter Two. See also John O. Iatrides, *Greece in the 1940s, A Nation in Crisis* (University Press of New England, Hanover and London, 1981), p. 36 *passim.*
2. Beevor, *op. cit.* p. 94 *passim.*
3. Michel, *op. cit.* p. 123.
4. Asprey, *op. cit.* p. 547.

Norway and Poland

1. *Loc. cit.* p. 464.
2. Michel, *op. cit.* p. 130.
3. *Loc. cit.*
4. H. Seton-Watson, *op. cit.* p. 116.

Malaya

1. F. Spencer Chapman, *The Jungle is Neutral* (Chatto and Windus, London, 1949). For Japanese atrocities see especially pp. 215, 217 and 305 and see also John Cross, *Red Jungle* (Robert Hale, London, 1975), p. 79 and Beevor, *op. cit.* p. 217.
2. Chapman, p. 332. Note that Cross mainly ascribes the guerrillas' unwillingness to grow food to lack of initiative and to conservatism.
3. *Loc. cit.* p. 287 and Cross, *op. cit.* p. 80.
4. Asprey, *op. cit.* p. 639. C. Cruickshank, *SOE in the Far East* (OUP, Oxford, 1983), Chapter Eight. Cruickshank's excellent history also covers Burma and other Far Eastern theatres.

Conclusion

1. Taylor, *op. cit.* p. 516. Laqueur, *op. cit.* p. 237.
2. Foot, *loc. cit.*
3. K'Tut Tantri, *Revolt in Paradise* (Heinemann, London, 1966); Raymond Westerling, *Challenge to Terror* (William Kimber, London, 1952).
4. Mao Tse-tung, *Selected Works* (Foreign Languages Press, Peking, 1965).
5. For the weakening of European colonialism see Bernard Porter, *The Lion's Share* (Longman, Harlow, 1984), p. 303 *passim*; R. F. Holland, *European Decolonisation* (Macmillan, London); R. Jeffrey (ed.), *Asia the Winning of Independence* (Macmillan, London, 1981).

Chapter 3: Harvards, Marxists and Nationalists 1945–54

The Greek Civil War

For the impact of aircraft on the insurgency in Greece I have drawn mainly on the Air Ministry papers in the Public Record Office. The standard account of the war is C. M. Woodhouse, *The Struggle for Greece 1941–1949* (Hart Davis MacGibbon, London, 1976). See also K. Matthews, *Memories of a Mountain War, Greece 1944–1949* (Longman, London, 1972); H. Maule, *Scobie, Hero of Greece, the British Campaign 1944–5* (Arthur Baker, London, 1975); Colonel J. C. Murray, 'The anti-bandit war', in Colonel T. N. Greene (ed.), *The Guerrilla and How to Fight Him*

(Frederick A. Praeger, New York, 1962), pp. 65–111; John O. Iatrides, *Greece in the 1940s; A Nation in Crisis* (University Press of New England, Hanover and London, 1981); Robert Asprey, *War in the Shadows* (Macdonald and Jane's, London, 1976), pp. 786–800.

1. AIR/24/753, Operations Record Books, Appendices, Air HQ Greece, 1944–5, 26 August 1944. See also Maule, *op. cit.* p. 50.
2. *Loc. cit.* Annex, see also Woodhouse, *op. cit.* p. 56 and Matthews, *op. cit.* p. 74.
3. AIR/24/756, Report of British Mission Meeting, 26 June 1945. Asprey argues that the British greatly underestimated Communist power, p. 786.
4. Woodruff, *op. cit.* Chapter Five, Maule, *op cit.* p. 87.
5. AIR/24/753, Report of Squadron Leader Wynne on the Peleponnese. For the general chaos see Noel Baker papers, Churchill College, Cambridge, NBK/4/43, letter of June 1944.
6. Woodhouse, *op. cit.* p. 121.
7. Woodhouse, *op. cit.* p. 128, Matthews, p. 87.
8 AIR/24/753, report of the capture of Air HQ Greece by Air Commodore W. Tuttle.
9. *Loc. cit.* see also AIR/24/752, Operations Red Book, Report on Air Operations, 5 December 1944 to 27 January 1945.
10. AIR/24/753, 'Air support in Greece'.
11. Woodhouse, *op. cit.* p. 133.
12. Woodhouse, *loc. cit.* Matthews, *op. cit.* p. 94.
13. AIR/24/754, Minutes of the meeting of 24 April 1945.
14. AIR/24/753, report of the week ending 27 May 1945.
15. Woodhouse, *op. cit.* Chapter seven.
16. AIR/24/753, the aims of training were laid down by Slessor in November 1944.
17. Woodhouse, *op. cit.* p. 173.
18. *Loc. cit.* p. 184.
19. AIR/46/62, Operational efficiency of the RHAF, 8 March 1947.
20. Woodhouse, *op cit.* Chapter ten.
21. *Loc. cit.* p. 185.
22. AIR/46/35, reconnaissance requirements in a tactical air force, Air Commodore John Gray to Air Commodore Atcherley, 10 September 1947.
23. *Loc. cit.* see also Owen Thetford, *Aircraft of the RAF Since 1918* (Putnam, London, 1979), pp. 39–42, 411 and 415.
24. AIR/46/35, Group Captain Rainsford's letter to Gray on 22 October 1947 and Gray's reply on 30 October.
25. Major J. B. Dicksee AAC(ret.) 'Independent air observation flight Eritrea 1950–1952', *Army Air Corps Journal* 1985, No. 11. For criticisms of the British advisers see Asprey, *op. cit.*
26. AIR/46/62, report of anti-bandit operations up to 15 May 1947. Murray, *op. cit.* p. 106 points out that the RAF made mistakes sometimes and attacked army units.
27. See note 22 *supra.*
28. Murray, *op. cit.* pp. 83–4 and 107.
29. AIR/46/62, Wing Commander W. P. Kemp, 'an independent air assessment of the revolution in Greece'.
30. AIR/46/62, report by Wing Commander Broad, 5 September 1947.
31. AIR/24/754, minutes of meeting of 24 April 1945.
32. *Loc. cit.*
33. AIR/46/62, report by Wing Commander Broad, 10 July 1947.
34. Air papers, *loc. cit.*
35. *Loc. cit.* report of anti-bandit operations up to 15 May 1947 by Air Commodore Gray. Murray *op. cit.* p. 70.
36. AIR/46/62, Operations of the RHAF, 3 May 1947.
37. *Loc. cit.* report of 5 September 1947.
38. *Loc. cit.* report of June 1947.
39. *Loc. cit.*
40. *Loc. cit.* report of anti-bandit operations up to 15 May 1947 by Air Commodore Gray.
41. Murray, *op. cit.* p. 69, Asprey, p. 798.
42. Murray, *op. cit.* p. 89. Woodhouse, *op. cit.* p. 236 *passim* is very critical of the slow arrival of US arms.
43. For Gray see 'Air Vice Marshal John Gray', *The Times* 10 June 1987 AIR/46/62, letter from Air Commodore Gray, 6 September 1947.

44. Air papers, *loc. cit.* report by Wing Commander Broad, 5 September 1947.
45. Air papers, *loc. cit.* review of anti-bandit operations by Major General Rawlins, October 1947.
46. See note 29 *supra*.
47. Murray, *op. cit.*, p. 95; Woodhouse, *op. cit.* p. 242.
48. AIR/46/62, report by Wing Commander Broad, 25 July 1947.
49. 'The Greek Army today', *The Times* 21 October 1950.
50. Matthews, *op. cit.* p. 268.
51. Murray, *op. cit.* p. 107.

The Malayan Insurgency

The standard history of the war is Anthony Short, *The Communist Insurrection in Malaya 1948–1960* (Frederick Muller, London 1975). See also R. Clutterbuck, *The Long Long War; The Emergency in Malaya 1948–1960* (Cassell, London, 1966); Air Vice Marshal Sir Francis Mellersh, 'The campaign against the terrorists in Malaya', *RUSI Journal* August 1951; Brigadier K. R. Brazier-Creagh, 'Malaya', *RUSI Journal* May 1954; Group Captain K. R. C. Slater, 'Air Operations in Malaya', *RUSI Journal* August 1957.

1. A. H. Peterson, G. C. Reinhardt and E. E. Conger, *Symposium on the Role of Airpower in Counterinsurgency and Unconventional Warfare: The Malayan Emergency* RM-3652 PR, Rand Corporation, Santa Monica, July 1963, p. 9.
2. AIR/24/1917, Operations Record Book, Air Headquarters Malaya, January 1947–December 1948.
3. Short, *op. cit.* p. 36. For wartime relations with the MPAJA see Charles Cruickshank, *SOE in the Far East* (OUP, Oxford, 1983); F. Spencer Chapman, *The Jungle is Neutral* (Chatto and Windus, London, 1949) and John Cross, *Red Jungle* (Robert Hall, London, 1975). See also AIR/23/8437, Memorandum on the value of air strikes, 8 December 1950.
4. WO/268/709, Quarterly Historical Report, 31 March 1947.
5. Short, *op. cit.* p. 114.
6. AIR/24/1917, 3 July 1947.
7. *Loc. cit.* report of 21 December 1948.
8. AIR/23/8443, report of 29 April 1949.
9. *Loc. cit.* report of 4 May 1949.
10. *Loc. cit.* report on air strike of 27 May 1949.
11. AIR/23/8437, Air Marshal F. J. Foggarty to Air Vice Marshal Mellersh, 27 January 1950.
12. *Loc. cit.* extracts from bandit statements.
13. *Loc. cit.*
14. AIR/23/8444, report on anti-bandit operations 4–8 June 1950. Peterson p. 60.
15. AIR/23/8443, interrogation of surrendered bandits, 30 September 1949.
16. *Loc. cit.* See also AIR/34/8443, report on Abdullah bin Arsad.
17. AIR/23/8443, lessons of operations by Squadron Leader J. C. Dent.
18. *Loc. cit.* report by Lieutenant Colonel Pine-Coffin, 28 February 1949.
19. Peterson, *op. cit.* p. 56.
20. AIR/23/8444.
21. Group Captain Gordon Gilbert, 'Sunderland operations in the Malayan emergency', March 1988 (unpublished).
22. Slater, *op. cit.* p. 379. See also Mellersh, *op. cit.* p. 414 for comments on the Brigand aircraft and jets.
23. AIR/23/8437.
24. AIR/23/8437, Briggs's paper of 22 December 1950.
25. AIR/23/8437, draft letter to Briggs, 28 December 1950.
26. AIR/23/8437, letter to Briggs, 13 February 1951 and meeting at Air Headquarters Malaya to discuss Air-Army co-operation in the anti-bandit campaign, 9 August 1950.
27. Short, *op. cit.* p. 451 *passim*. See also AIR/23/8421, Minute by Wing Commander A. G. Dudgeon, 9 November 1949; AIR/23/8592; the jungle was often strafed before spraying began in order to frighten any aborigines away. The government also considered using non-lethal gases against insurgents and experimented with some types on Pulau Tenggol island,

off the coast of Malaya. However the experiments were not very successful, the Foreign Office was worried about international protests and insufficient aircraft were available. See AIR/23/8593.
28. AIR/23/8558 and AIR/27/8553, report of 15 July 1952; also Brazier-Creagh, *op. cit.* p. 180.
29. AIR/23/8558.
30. AIR/27/8553, reports for July–September 1952.
31. Tony Geraghty, *Who Dares Wins; The Story of the SAS 1950–1980* (Fontana/Collins, London, 1981), p. 42. Slater, *op. cit.* p. 383.
32. AIR/23/8443, report on Operation Lemon.
33. AIR/23/8421, report on Operation Watershed and summary of air operations 1950.
34. Short, *op. cit.* p. 371 *passim.* Mellersh, *op. cit.* p. 408.
35. Peterson, *op. cit.* p. 31.
36. O. Thetford, *Aircraft of the Royal Air Force since 1918* (Putnam & Co., London, 1979), p. 554. WO/216/542, Helicopters in Malaya; for the evacuation of the Cameronians see AIR/23/8553, report of 11 March 1952; for comments on flying the Sycamore see Wing Commander L. Eley, 'Helicopters in Malaya', *RAF Quarterly* Spring 1966.
37. AIR/26/7357. See also 'Westland Prize Essay', *RUSI Journal* August 1953.
38. *Loc. cit.*
39. *Loc. cit.* and Thetfield, *op. cit.* p. 558.
40. WO/216/542, Templer letter of 8 May 1952.
41. Peterson, *op. cit.* p. 72. See also WO/216/542, director of plans, Malaya, 29 April 1952. See also Douglas W. Nelms, 'HC Mk 1, the new Chinook helicopter for the RAF', *RUSI Journal* June 1980.
42. Mellersh, *op. cit.* p. 409.
43. Slater, *op. cit.* p. 380. See also Sergeant J. Woodrow, 'Army Austers in Malaya'. *Air Power* Spring 1959.
44. Short, *op. cit.* p. 483.
45. *Loc. cit.* p. 495.
46. *Loc. cit.* p. 502. Astonishingly, just as the British were abandoning air policing, the British experience in colonial wars became the basis of a US proposal to put pressure on the Soviet Union by threats from the air. See Tami Davis Biddle, 'Handling the Soviet air threat; Project Control and the debate on American strategy in the early cold war period', Conference of the Society for Historians of American Foreign Relations, 9–11 June 1988.
47. M. J. Armitage and R. A. Mason, *Air Power in the Nuclear Age, 1945–1984* (Macmillan, Basingstoke, 1985), p. 68.
48. *Loc. cit.* See also Clutterbuck's comments in the Rand Symposium.
49. Slater, *op. cit.* p. 380.

The Mau Mau Insurgency

The most interesting account of the impact of air attacks from the insurgents' side is Donald L. Barnett and Karari Njama, *Mau Mau From Within* (Macgibbon and Kee, London 1966), (hereafter Njama. The Kenyan point of view is also expressed in Josiah Mwangi Kariuki, *Mau Mau Detainee* (OUP, Nairobi, 1963) and the settlers' in Ione Leigh, *In The Shadow of Mau Mau* (W. H. Allen, London, 1954). For the background to the revolt see E. A. Ayandele, *The Growth of African Civilization* Vol. 2 (Longmans, London, 1971), p. 352 *passim.* See also Robert Asprey, *War in the Shadows* (Macdonald and Jane's, London), p. 931 *passim.*
1. WO/216/863, 'Appreciation of future military policy in Kenya'.
2. CO/822/437, letter from the Member for Law and Order, Nairobi, 2 September 1952.
3. WO/27/106, Kenya Emergency Scheme, 1 March 1950.
4. WO/216/861, letter from General Erskine of 3 October 1954.
5. CO/822/471, letter from Canon Bewes to the governor, 28 January 1953.
6. See the 'Appreciation of Crime and Subversion' in CO/822/447.
7. *Loc. cit.* Police Commissioner's report of 27 November 1952.
8. CO/822/499, 'Ill treatment of Mau Mau suspects by screening teams'.
9. Njama, *op. cit.* p. 405.
10. WO/216/863, 'Appreciation of future military policy in Kenya'.

11. Njama, *op. cit.* p. 460.
12. CO/822/437, paper of 13 September 1952 and telegram to Kenyan government 16 September 1952. See also CO/822/468.
13. CO/822/468, General Brian Robertson to GIGS, 12 January 1953.
14. WO/216/811, War Office to East African Command, 3 November 1952.
15. *Loc. cit.*
16. Njama, *op. cit.* p. 125 *passim.*
17. CO/822/481, 'Notes on planning and housing aspects of resettlement and development of new villages', 14. See note 8 *supra.*
18. WO/236/16, draft despatch by General Erskine.
19. *Loc. cit.* This phrase was repeated by Erskine in a lecture at the RUSI. See General Sir George Erskine, 'Kany-Mau Mau', *RUSI Journal* February 1956.
20. Njama, *op. cit.* p. 291.
21. See note 9 *supra.*
22. Asprey, *op. cit.* p. 955.
23. See note 15 *supra.*
24. *Loc. cit.*
25. Njama, *op. cit.* p. 238.
26. A. J. Blackburn, 'Aircraft versus Mau Mau', *Flight* 12 November 1954.
27. Njama, *op. cit.* p. 267.
28. *Ibid.* p. 292.
29. *Ibid.* p. 293.
30. WO/32/13525, note by Air Vice Marshal Dawson, November 1952, letter of 22 January 1954.
31. *Loc. cit.* See also John Fricker, 'High level helicopter operations in Kenya', *The Aeroplane* 11 March 1955. For Churchill's views see 'Churchill plan to scare Mau Mau', *The Times* 4 January 1984.
32. See note 15 *supra.* See also John Fricker, 'Flying Against the Mau Mau', *Flight* 25 March and 1 April 1955 and Squadron Leader E. Newitt DFC, 'Mau Mau,' *Air Clues* October 1954. For settlers' complaints about the cost of the Lincolns see Leigh, *op. cit.* p. 197.
33. Njama, *op. cit.* p. 310.
34. *Ibid.* p. 315.
35. Leigh, *op. cit.* p. 188.
36. AIR/8/1886, message from HQ Middle East Land Forces, 15 October 1954.
37. *Loc. cit.* note by ACAS (ops), L. F. Sinclair, 16 November 1954.
38. WO/236/18, Report by General Erskine, 25 April 1955.
39. WO/236/18, Report by General Erskine, 25 April 1955.
40. *Loc. cit.* On the use of torture see also CO/822/503.
41. CO/822/471, comments by Canon Bewes.
42. WO/216/879, Erskine letter to the CIGS, 7 January 1955.
43. AIR/8/1886, Minute of 19 May 1955.
44. *Loc. cit.* Minute of 4 June 1955.
45. AIR/8/1886, Minute of 10 June 1955. Note also WO/216/879, 'forecast of security operations in 1955', Erskine himself suggests that by April 1955 medium bombers would no longer be necessary.
46. Njama, *op. cit.* pp. 330, 334 and 430.
47. WO/236/19, see particularly the attack by Elspeth Huxley.
48. Frank Kitson, *Gangs and Counter-gangs* (Barrie and Rockliff, London, 1960).

The French Experience in Indochina

1. 'Ho Chi Minh; A Leader of Lenin's Stature', *The Times* 5 September 1969.
2. E. O'Ballance, *The Indochina War 1945–1954* (Faber and Faber, London, 1964), p. 58. See also Robert Asprey, *War in the Shadows* (Macdonald and Jane's, London, 1976, p. 717 *passim.*
3. Lucien Bodard, *The Quicksand War: Prelude to Vietnam* (Faber and Faber, London, 1967), part iv.
4. Asprey, *op. cit.* p. 767.
5. For Navarre see 'General Henri Navarre', *The Times* 25 June 1983. For Dien Bien Phu see

Asprey, *op. cit.* p. 869 *passim* and Bernard Fall, *Hell in a Very Small Place* (Pall Mall, London, 1967).

6. R. F. Futrell and M. Blumenson, *The Advisory Years to 1965* (Office of Air Force History, Washington, 1967).
7. B. Fall, *Street Without Joy: Insurgency in Indochina 1946–1963* (Pall Mall Press, London, 1963), p. 257. (Hereafter Fall).
8. Futrell and Blumenson *loc. cit.* see also 'Indochina War', *Air Clues* February 1952.
9. *Loc. cit.*
10. Lieutenant Colonel Jacquard, 'A war devoid of air opposition', *Air Clues* February 1952.
11. For the conventional view of napalm see Jacquard *loc. cit.* and Capitaine A. Lemaire, 'Air transport indispensible instrument against Vietminh', *Air Clues* February, 1953.
12. Lemaire *loc. cit.*
13. Fall, *op. cit.* p. 67. See also *Air Clues* February, 1953.
14. Phillipe de Pirey, *Operation Waste* (Arco Publishing, London, 1954), p. 161.
15. General G. J. M. Chassin, 'Lessons of the War in Indochina', *Interavia* No. 12, 1952. (Hereafter Chassin).
16. Truong Nhu Tang, *Journal of a Vietcong* (Jonathan Cape, London, 1986), p. 29.
17. Fall, *op. cit.* p. 33.
18. Henry Ainlie, *In Order to Die* (Burke, London, 1955), p. 106.
19. De Pirey, *op. cit.* p. 109.
20. Fall, *op. cit.* p. 187 *passim*.
21. S. E. Nguyen De, 'Le Viet Nam dans le Monde aerien', *Forces Aeriennes Français* January 1953.
22. See also General Chassin 'Un an d'operations Aeriennes', *Forces Aeriennes Françaises* 1953.
23. Lemaire, *loc. cit.*
24. Fall, *op. cit.* p. 36.
25. R. Riesen, *Jungle Mission* (Hutchinson, London, 1957).
26. Fall, *op. cit.* p. 141 *passim*.
27. Futrell, and Blumenson, *op. cit.* pp. 17–19.
28. Fall, *op. cit.* p. 315 *passim*.
29. Futrell, and Blumenson, *op. cit.* pp. 17–19.
30. Asprey, *op. cit.* p. 872 *passim*.
31. William Courtney OBE, 'Air Power in Indochina', *The Aeroplane* 4 December 1953.
32. Chassin, *loc. cit.*
33. Asprey, *op. cit.* p. 874.
34. William Courtney, *loc. cit.*
35. *Ibid.* Jacquard, *loc. cit.*
36. Chassin, *loc. cit.* For Nghialo see Lemaire, *loc. cit.* Fall, *op. cit.* pp. 111 and 319.
37. Lieutenant Delalouche, 'Helicopters prove their worth in Indochina', *The Aeroplane* 4 December 1953.
38. *Loc. cit.* Fall, *op. cit.* p. 260 *passim*.
39. Fall, *op. cit.* p. 256.
40. *Loc. cit.* p. 260.
41. Chassin, *loc, cit.*
42. *Ibid.*
43. Bodard, *op. cit.* p. 294.
44. Fall, *op. cit.* pp. 108 and 279.
45. David Chanoff and Doan Van Tai, *Portrait of the Enemy* (I. B. Tauris and Co., London, 1987), pp. 13 and 14.
46. Chassin, *loc. cit.*
47. Jacquard, *loc. cit.*
48. A. H. Peterson, G. C. Reinhardt and E. E. Conger, (eds), *Symposium on the Role of Airpower in Counterinsurgency and Unconventional Warfare: The Malayan Emergency* (Rand, Santa Monica, 1963).
49. Ainley, *op. cit.* p. 221.
50. De Pirey, *op. cit.* pp. 56, 63, 151 and 253.

Chapter 4: Helicopters and Insurgents 1954–88

The Algerian War

1. The standard secondary sources on the Algerian war is A. Horne, *A Savage War of Peace, Algeria 1954–1962* (Macmillan, London, 1977); Peter Paret, *French Revolutionary Warfare from Indochina to Algeria* (Pall Mall Press, London and Dunmow, 1964). There are also accounts by Michael K. Clark, *Algeria in Turmoil* (Thames and Hudson, London, 1960); Edward Behr, *The Algerian Problem* (Penguin, Harmondsworth, 1961); Edgar O'Ballance, *The Algerian Insurrection, 1952–1962* (Faber and Faber, London, 1967). Pierre Leulliette, *St Michael and the Dragon, A Paratroop in the Algerian War* (Heinemann, London, 1961) gives a vivid personal account but by far the most important account of airborne operations in English is A. H. Paterson, G. C. Reinhardt and E. E. Conger, *Symposium on the Role of Airpower in Counterinsurgency; The Algerian War* (Rand Corporation, Santa Monica, July 1963).
2. Pierre-Etienne Flandin, 'Debates sur l'Algeria', *Revue des deux Mondes* October, 1957.
3. Paterson, *op. cit.* p. 7.
4. This is the French air force's figures in Paterson; O'Ballance, *op. cit.* gives 8,500 guerrillas and 21,000 auxiliaries in 1956 (p. 49).
5. Paterson, *op. cit.* p. 10.
6. Leulliette, *op. cit.* p. 115, Clarke, *op. cit.* p. 177.
7. Paterson, *op. cit.* p. 7. See also John Talbott, *The War without a Name, France in Algeria 1954–1962* (Faber and Faber, London, 1981), p. 73.
8. Paterson, *op. cit.* p. 6.
9. Paret, *op. cit.* p. 45 *passim*. Yvonne Pagniez, 'a SAS instrument de pacification', *Revue des Deux Mondes* October 1955.
10. Paterson, *op. cit.* p. 51.
11. *Loc. cit.* p. 58 *passim*. O'Ballance, *op. cit.* p. 92.
12. *Loc. cit.*
13. *Loc. cit.*
14. Leulliette, *op. cit.* p. 231; Talbott, *op. cit.* p. 91.
15. *The War without a Name*, p. 38.
16. Colonel Victor J. Croizat, 'Helicopter warfare in Algeria', *Marine Corps Gazette* August 1987. Leulliette, *op. cit.* pp. 247–9.
17. Paterson, *op. cit.* p. 21. For statistics on French operations see 'L'Arme de l'air en Algerie en 1959', *Forces Aeriennes Françaises* March 1960 and for the importance of aircraft for liaison and casualty evacuation see Capitaine Tricaud, 'Aviation de liaison en Algerie', *Forces Aeriennes Francaises* July 1959.
18. Paterson, *op. cit.* p. 16 *passim*.
19. *Loc. cit.* p. 34; Behr, *op. cit.* p. 106, O'Ballance, *op. cit.* p. 81.
20. Paterson, *op. cit.* p. 20. For French euphoria over the advent of helicopters see 'L'helicoptre lourd dans les operations . . . en Algeria', 'La grande Kabylie fiel de la rebellion' and Lieutenant Colonel Arupurt, 'Aspects des operations helicoptres en Algeria', *Forces Aeriennes Françaises* July 1959 and April 1960.
21. *Loc. cit.* p. 55.
22. Leulliette, *op. cit.* p. 65.
23. Paterson, *op. cit.* p. 37. For French appreciation of the B26 see Capitaine Menanteau, 'Le bombardment en AFN', *Forces Aeriennes Françaises* July 1959.
24. *The War without a Name* p. 64. See also 'Commandos Parachutistes', *Forces Aeriennes Françaises* January 1959.
25. Paterson, *op. cit.* p. 42.
26. *Loc. cit.* p. 24.
27. B. Fall, *Street without Joy* (Pall Mall Press, London and Dunmow, 1963), pp. 261 and 350.
28. Paterson, *op. cit.* pp. 35–44.
29. Leulliette, *op. cit.* p. 88.
30. Paret, *op. cit.* p. 34.

The British in Four Wars

1. Robert Thompson, *No Exit from Vietnam* (Chatto and Windus, London, 1969), p. 136. For a good summary of the position of helicopters in the 1950s see the Westland Prize Essay in the *RUSI Journal* August 1953 by Colonel P. A. Tobin.
2. WO/32/13525, 'A study of the potential roles of helicopters', 11 August 1945. For operations in Burma see A. H. Peterson, *The Role of Air Power in Providing Tactical Mobility in Past COIN Operations* (Rand P-2968), p. 6.
3. War Office papers, *loc. cit.* 'Review of British, American and Russian helicopters', 29 April 1947.
4. War Office papers, *loc. cit.* letter from Colonel J. S. Barnetson in the War Office to Brigadier Young in Malaya, 'a final objection by the Air Ministry botched the whole project'. See also Young to Barneston, 4 May 1949.
5. WO/32/15177, Minute to VCIGS, 12 December 1952, 'Modern transport helicopters'.
6. See also War Office papers, *loc. cit.* Minute to CIGS, 2 February 1953.
7. War Office papers, *loc. cit.* DCIGS Minute of 16 February 1953.
8. War Office papers, *loc. cit.* comments by Group Captain M. C. Collins and by the Commandant of the School of Land/Air Warfare, 29 July 1953.
9. War Office papers, *loc. cit.* Minute of 2 January 1954. See also Major General N. Crookenden, 'Aviation in the British Army today', *RUSI Journal* August 1956 and Lieutenant Colonel J. F. Scott, 'Joint Experimental Helicopter Unit', *Air Power* Spring 1959.
10. WO/32/13525, 'Light support helicopters', paper prepared for ECAC, 26 August 1953. For comments on helicopters in 1959 see Major T. M. P. Stevens, 'Helicopters', *RUSI Journal* February 1959 and Brigadier P. W. Mead, 'Army aviation', *RAF Quarterly* Summer 1962. The figures for defence expenditure in 1927 are taken from the *League of Nations Armaments Yearbook 1932* Geneva, p. 342.
11. AIR/2/11377, Minute of 15 October 1952.
12. Air Papers, *loc. cit.* 'construction of a joint headquarters for the Middle East', 25 February 1953.
13. R. F. Holland, *European Decolonisation 1918–1981* (Macmillan, London, 1985), p. 250. Robert Asprey, *War in the Shadows* (Macdonald and Jane's, London, 1975), p. 962. On the Cyprus War see also W. Byford-Jones, *Grivas and the Story of Eoka* (Robert Hall, London, 1959); C. Foley (ed.). *The Memoirs of General Grivas* (Longmans, London, 1964) and N. Crawshaw, *The Cyprus Revolt* (George Allen and Unwin, London, 1978).
14. Byford-Jones, *op. cit.* p. 40. Iatrides, *op. cit.* p. 49. 'General George Grivas: Guerrilla leader who fought for the union of Greece and Cyprus', *The Times* 29 January 1974.
15. CO/69/60, Cyprus Administration Reports, 1956, Cyprus Broadcasting Service; the record library was also bombed there on 31 August 1955 but neither bomb stopped the service broadcasting.
16. Holland, *loc. cit.* Crawshaw, *op. cit.* pp. 167–73.
17. AIR/8/1921; Owen Thetford, *Aircraft of the RAF Since 1918* (Putnam, London), pp. 556–560.
18. Air papers, *loc. cit.* Minute by ACAS (P), 20 July 1956.
19. Thetford, *op. cit.* p. 156, Foley (ed.), *op. cit.* p. 111. See also David Wragg, *Helicopters at War* (Robert Hale, London, 1983), p. 113, and Richard Gardner and Reginald Longstaff, *British Service Helicopters* (Robert Hale, London, 1985), p. 58.
20. General Grivas, *Guerrilla Warfare and EOKA's Struggle* (Longmans, London, 1964), pp. 61 and 75.
21. Grivas, *op. cit.* p. 46. For British views of the ability of aircraft to locate caves etc, *loc. cit.* p. 108.
22. Grivas, *op. cit.* p. 76.
23. *Ibid.* p. 106 *passim.*
24. *Ibid.* pp. 52–54.
25. *Ibid.* p. 74.
26. AIR/8/1921, telegram of 18 June for CAS.
27. Air papers, *loc. cit.* Minute by R. J. Penney, 19 June 1956 and telegram from Middle East Air Force, 21 June 1956.
28. W. Laqueur, *Guerrilla, A History and Critical Study* (Weidenfeld and Nicolson, London,

1977), pp. 309–310 and 368–9. See also Kenneth Diacre, 'Cyprus 1956', *Army Quarterly* July 1956, Foley (ed.), *op. cit.* pp. 82–3 and Asprey, *op. cit.* p. 968.

29. Foley (ed.), *op. cit.* p. 136. Crawshaw, *op. cit.* pp. 293–4, Grivas, *op. cit.* p. 44 *passim.*
30. Foley (ed.), *op. cit.* pp. 125 and 129.
31. *Loc. cit.* p. 127.
32. *Loc. cit.* p. 135.
33. *Loc. cit.* p. 179 *passim.* For aircraft transport of troops see *The Aeroplane* 1958, p. 880.
34. Laqueur, *op. cit.*
35. For the situation in 1987 see P. Savigear, 'The elusive Cyprus settlement', *Contemporary Review* May 1987.
36. Bruce Grant, *Indonesia* (Penguin, Harmondsworth, 1967), p. 186 *passim.* See also Guy Wint, *Asia, A Handbook* (Anthony Blond, London, 1967), p. 273.
37. J. A. C. Mackie, *Konfrontasi, The Indonesia-Malaysia Dispute 1963* (OUP, Kuala Lumpur, 1974), Harold James and Denis Sheil-Small, *The Undeclared War; The Story of the Indonesian Confrontation, 1962–6* (Leo Cooper, London, 1971), p. 8. Wing Commander L. Eley, 'Helicopters in Malaysia', *RAF Quarterly* Spring 1966.
38. James and Sheil-Small, *op. cit.* pp. 17 and 30. See also G. P. Blaker, 'Alpha and Omega, The Beginning and the End', *Regimental Chronicle* of the Royal Green Jackets, volume 65, 1963.
39. J. Paxton, *Statesman's Year Book and World Gazetteer* (Macmillan, London, 1975), p. 89.
40. James and Sheil-Small, *op. cit.* p. 81 *passim.* Mackie, *loc. cit.* See also M. C. Millman, 'Sarawak and Confrontation', *Army Quarterly* January 1966.
41. Owen Thetford, *op. cit.* pp. 304–6 and 368.
42. James and Sheil-Small, *op. cit.* p. 81 *passim*; Gardner and Longstaff, *op. cit.* p. 60 and Wragg, *op. cit.* p. 113. See also Crookenden, *loc. cit.* p. 208 and D. W. Nelms, HC Mk 1; New Chinook helicopter for the RAF', *RUSI Journal* June 1980, p. 66.
43. 'Whirlwinds over Borneo', *Officer* Number 16, Autumn 1965, pp. 17–22. See also Wragg, *op. cit.* p. 114.
44. Letter to the author, 22 August 1987 and of 22 February 1988. For the Royal Malaysian Air Force see A. Steedman, 'RMAF', *RAF Quarterly* Spring 1966.
45. Grant, *op. cit.* p. 187. James and Sheil-Small, *op. cit.* p. 148. Mackie, *op. cit.* p. 262.
46. Sheil-Small, *op. cit.* p. 86. Mackie, *op. cit.* p. 212.
47. For Aden just before the war see Charles Johnston, *The View from Steamer Point* (Collins, London, 1964). For the war years see Julian Paget, *Last Post: Aden 1964–1967* (Faber and Faber, London, 1969). For Lord Lloyd's comments see R. Bidwell, *The Two Yemens* (Longman and Westview Press, Harlow and Boulder, 1983), p. 79.
48. See the Noel-Baker papers in Churchill College, NBKR/4/3.
49. *Loc. cit.*
50. *Loc. cit.*
51. For Heath's lecture see 'Stability in the Arabian Peninsula', *RUSI Journal* May 1960. See also the review of recent events in the Arabian Peninsula in the *Army Quarterly* July 1960; the comments in Paget, *op. cit.* p. 45; in Air Chief Marshal Sir David Lee, *Flight from the Middle East* (Air Historical Branch, London, 1978), p. 208 and in Sir Kennedy Trevaskis, *Shades of Amber* (Hutchinson, London, 1968), p. 208.
52. Lee, *loc. cit.*
53. *Ibid.* p. 204.
54. *Ibid.* p. 206.
55. Paget, *op. cit.* p. 60.
56. Lee, *op. cit.* p. 211.
57. Paget, *op. cit.* p. 103.
58. Paget, *loc. cit.*, Lee, *op. cit.* p. 218.
59. Letter of 1 March 1988, Paget, *op. cit.* p. 48; Lee, *op. cit.* p. 229.
60. Lee, *op. cit.* p. 218.
61. Stephen Harper, *Last Sunset* (Collins, London, 1978), Trevaskis, *op. cit.* p. 208. For the spread of the revolt see J. Kostiner, *The Struggle for South Yemen* (Croom Helm, London, 1984), p. 72 *passim.*
62. Lee, *op. cit.* p. 226.
63. *Ibid.* p. 220.
64. 'UN Mission to Aden in open dispute', *The Times* 7 April 1967. Paget, *op. cit.* p. 149.

65. Lee, *op. cit.* p. 229, Bidwell, *op. cit.* p. 172. Ironically the Egyptians considered their aircraft a total failure in the war they were fighting against Royalist rebels in Yemen. The main effects of these aircraft may thus have been to provoke British retaliation. See Mohamed El Dahab 'Egypt in Yemen', unpublished M.Phil. thesis, Cambridge, 1988, p. 103.
66. Paget, *op. cit.* p. 251 *passim.*
67. For British help in the 1950s see Heath's lecture at the RUSI and Colonel D. de C. Smiley, 'Muscat and Oman', *RUSI Journal* February 1960. See also John Akehurst, *We Won a War, The Campaign in Oman 1965–1975* (Michael Russell, Wilton, 1982), Chapter two.
68. Akehurst, *op. cit.* p. 25. Tony Jeapes, *SAS Operation Oman* (William Kimber, London, 1980).
69. *Loc. cit.*
70. Flight Lieutenant P. A. D. Williams, 'Flying adventures with the Sultan of Oman's air force', *Air Clues* November 1966; Wing Commander P. J. Hirst, 'Sultan of Oman's Air Force', *Air Clues* August 1972; 'Supporting a Secret War', *Air Enthusiast* September 1972, p. 115 *passim*; *Air International* August 1977, p. 71 *passim*. See also Smiley, *loc. cit.*
71. *Loc. cit.*
72. Akehurst, *op. cit.* p. 52.
73. Major General K. Perkins, 'Oman 1975, the years of decision', *RUSI Journal* March 1979.
74. See note 70 *supra.*
75. Akehurst, *op. cit.* p. 141.
76. Perkins, *op. cit.*
77. *Loc. cit.* p. 183. Jeapes, *op. cit.* pp. 75 and 229.

The War in South Vietnam

1. The voluminous literature on Vietnam falls into five categories; the contemporary press accounts, the official military histories now being written in the USA, the North Vietnamese and NLF accounts particularly in David Chanoff and Doan Van Toai's *Portrait of the Enemy* (I. B. Tauris, London, 1987), the Pentagon papers detailing official US thinking and the various secondary sources. I am indebted to all of these. For a succinct summary of air operations in Vietnam see Colonel Gene Gurney, *Vietnam, the War in the Air* (Sidgwick and Jackson, London, 1985); for criticisms of the war see Ralph Littauer and Norman Uphoff, *The Air War in Indochina* (Beacon Press, Boston, 1972).
2. M. J. Armitage and R. A. Mason, *Air Power in the Nuclear Age 1945–1984* (Macmillan, Basingstoke, 1985), p. 113. A. L. Gropman, 'Air war in Vietnam, 1961–1973' in R. A. Mason (ed.), *War in the Third Dimension* (Brassey's, London, 1987), p. 34.
3. R. F. Futrell, *USAF in South East Asia, The Advisory Years to 1965* (Office of Air Force History, Washington, 1981), Chapter Five.
4. For US air assistance see Futrell, *op. cit.* Chapter ten; for convoys see Gurney, *op. cit.* p. 17.
5. General D. A. Starry, *Armoured Combat in Vietnam* Blandford Press, Dorset, 1981), p. 49.
6. Armitage and Mason, *op. cit.* p. 84.
7. J. Albright, J. A. Cash and A. W. Sandstrum, *Seven Firefights in Vietnam* (Office of the Chief of Military History, Washington, 1970), p. 40 *passim*. For US transport see R. L. Brown, *USAF in South-East Asia, Tactical Airlift* (Office of Air Force History, Washington, 1983), p. 653.
8. For US opinion see the Senator Gravell Edition, *The Pentagon Papers* (Beacon Press, Boston, undated), Vol. IV, p. 584 *passim*. For insurgent and Northern attitudes see Chanoff and Toai, *op. cit.* pp. 108–109 and 157.
9. 'Ho Chi Minh, A Leader of Lenin's Stature', *The Times* 5 September 1969.
10. M. W. Browne, *The New Face of War* (Cassell, London, 1965), p. 20 *passim.*
11. For the use of torture by the Southern government see the photographs in Browne, *loc. cit.* and Chanoff and Toai, *op. cit.* p. 95 *passim*. For press coverage see R. Day, 'Troubled reflections of a television journalist', *Encounter* May 1970; R. Elegant, 'Vietnam, how to lose a war', *Encounter* August 1981, P. Braestrup, *The Big Story* (Westview, Colorado, 1977). See also the comments in Robert Thompson, *No Exit from Vietnam* (Chatto and Windus, London, 1969), p. 164.
12. Robert Thompson, *loc. cit.*

13. R. Nixon, *No More Vietnams* (Comet, London, 1986), p. 56. Littauer, *op. cit.* p. 193.
14. Pentagon papers, p. 398.
15. J. R. McDonough, *Platoon Leader* (Bantam Books, Toronto and New York, 1986). See also *Pentagon Papers*, pp. 335 and 355. For NLF morale see Chanoff and Toai, *op. cit.* p. 185.
16. General D. A. Storry, *Armoured Combat in Vietnam* (Blandford Press, Dorset, 1981), p. 49.
17. D. Middleton (ed.), *Air War Vietnam* (Arms and Armour Press, London, 1978), p. 26. Gurney, *op. cit.* p. 155.
18. J. F. Ballard, *USAF in South-East Asia, Development and Employment of Fixed-wing Gunships, 1962–1972* Office of Air Force History, 1982, p. 49.
19. R. L. Bowers, *USAF in South-East Asia, Tactical Airlift* Office of Air Force History, Washington, 1983.
20. R. Mason, *Chickenhawk* (Penguin Books, New York, 1985), pp. 105 and 362. For helicopter operations see Gurney, *op. cit.* p. 37 *passim*.
21. Robert Thompson, *op. cit.* p. 136. For the temptation not to walk through the jungle, see R. Mason, *op. cit.* p. 408. For NLF ability to escape the helicopters see Chanoff and Toai, *op. cit.* p. 155.
22. Letter to the author. For NLF ability to hide see W. Burchett, *Grasshoppers and Elephants* (Urizen Books, New York, 1977), Chapter six. Lieutenant General W. R. Peers, *The My Lai Inquiry* (Norton, New York, 1979), p. 35.
23. Truong Nhu Tang, *Journal of a Vietcong* (Jonathan Cape, London, 1986), p. 167. Chanoff and Toai, *op. cit.* pp. 110, 154, 166, 171.
24. *Loc. cit.*
25. William A. Buckingham, *Operation Ranch Hand, The Air Force and Insecticides in South-East Asia, 1961–1971* Office of Air Force History, Washington, 1982, pp. 89 and 155.
26. *Loc. cit.* p. 74.
27. M. V. Browne, *op. cit.*
28. 'Agent Orange settlement is upheld', *New York Times* 22 April 1987. For the effects on the environment see SIPRI, *Warfare in a Fragile World, Military Impact on the Human Environment* (Taylor and Francis, London, 1980), espec. p. 79 *passim*.
29. Futrell, *op. cit.* p. 55.
30. Buckingham, *op. cit.* p. 70.
31. Peers, *op. cit.* pp. 30–33.
32. Nixon, *op. cit.* p. 17.
33. Littauer, *op. cit.* pp. 23–7.
34. R. Clarke, 'South Vietnam village wiped out in battle', *The Times* 28 February 1969. Nicholas Tomalin, 'Who really won the battle of Bien Hoa?' *Sunday Times* 2 March 1969. See also G. Wilson, 'Life in Death', *Guardian* 13 June 1973.
35. D. Bonavia, 'Years of work shattered by psychological blow', *The Times* 5 February 1968.
36. 'Villages go back to Vietcong', *The Times* 21 February 1968.
37. Fred Emery, 'Hué where marines face death', *The Times* 20 February 1968.
38. Robert Thompson, 'Vietnam on the way to victory', *Sunday Times* 21 December 1969. Compare Murray Sale 'The war that can't be won', *Sunday Times*, 2 June 1968 and George Ball, 'Lessons for US in tragic experience of Vietnam', *The Times* 22 December 1969.
39. N. Carrol, 'Vietnam how the war has changed', *Sunday Times* 15 November 1970; for NLF and North Vietnamese demoralization see Chanoff and Toai, *op. cit.* pp. 53, 65, 130 and 185.
40. Peers, *loc. cit.* 'A conventional atrocity', *Sunday Times* 23 November 1969, 'US authorities disturbed over massacre allegations', *The Times* 20 November 1969.
41. 'Wide gap in views on Vietnam', *The Times* 8 July 1969 and 'Silent majority voices its dissent', *The Times* 8 May 1970.
42. Ballard, *op. cit.* p. 221 *passim*. Martin Woolacot, 'Officers flee as Quang Tri falls', *Guardian* 2 May 1972; 'An Loc attack by North', *Guardian* 12 May 1972. Gurney, *op. cit.* p. 154.
43. Middleton, *op. cit.* p. 149.
44. A. H. Peterson, *The Role of Air Power in Providing Tactical Mobility in Past COIN Operations* (Rand P-2968, September 1964); A. H. Peterson, G. C. Reinhardt and E. E. Conger, *Symposium on the Role of Air Power in Counterinsurgency and Unconventional Warfare: The Malayan Emergency* (Rand RM-3651, July 1963).
45. John W. Taylor, 'Counter-Insurgency Air Force', *Royal Air Forces Quarterly* Summer 1963.

46. *Forces Aeriennes Françaises* July 1959.
47. For the debate on the B-26s role in the Bay of Pigs see John Ranelagh, *The Agency; The Rise and Decline of the CIA* (Sceptre, Sevenoaks, 1988), especially pp. 365, 369–71.

The Problem of Sanctuaries

1. Bernard B. Fall, *Street Without Joy* (Pall Mall Press, London and Dunmow, 1963), p. 358. Sir Robert Thompson, *No Exit From Vietnam* (Chatto and Windus, London, 1969), pp. 43–45.
2. Mark Urban, *War in Afghanistan* (Macmillan, Basingstoke, 1988), p. 207.
3. Senator Gravell Edition, *The Pentagon Papers* (Beacon Press, Boston, undated), Vol. IV, pp. 267 and 509.
4. W. Scott Thompson and Donald D. Frizzell, *The Lessons of Vietnam* (Macdonald and Jane's, London, 1977), p. 129. See also Robert W. Asprey, *War in the Shadows* (Macdonald and Jane's, London, 1976) p. 1370. Asprey launches a devastating critique of US bombing policy.
5. Thompson and Frizzel, *op. cit.* p. 153. See also Colonel A. L. Gropman, 'The Air War in Vietnam', in R. A. Mason, *War in The Third Dimension* (Brassey's, London, 1986).
6. Thompson and Frizzell, *op. cit.* p. 130.
7. M. J. Armitage and R. A. Mason, *Air Power in the Nuclear age, 1945–84* (Macmillan, London, 1985), p. 84.
8. Gropman, *op. cit.* p. 40. For statistics on bombing see Gurney, *op. cit.* p. 149.
9. Armitage and Mason, *op. cit.* p. 109.
10. Clare Hollingworth, 'Fire power is not enough', *Daily Telegraph* 30 March 1968. Sir Robert Thompson, *op. cit.* p. 139 *passim*. Asprey, *op. cit.* p. 1370 *passim*.
11. For typical Western views at the time see Mary McCarthy, 'Waiting for the all-clear', *Sunday Times* 26 May 1968 and 'The war of words', *loc. cit.*, 21 July 1968. R. Dudman, 'North Vietnam, the road to survival' and 'Down but not out', *Guardian* 26 and 27 September 1972. J. M. Van Dyke, *North Vietnam's Strategy for Survival* (Pacific Books, Palo Alto, 1972). For actual North Vietnamese views see David Chanoff and Doan Toai, *loc. cit.* pp. 44, 45, 63, 67.
12. Truong Nhu Tang, *Journal of a Vietcong* (Jonathan Cape, London, 1986), p. 243.
13. Hollingworth, *op. cit.* and *The Pentagon Papers*, pp. 335 and 355.
14. Letter to *The Times* 30 December 1972. De Gaulle is quoted in Asprey, *op. cit.* p. 1379.
15. Thompson and Frizzell, *op. cit.* p. 126.
16. Armitage and Mason, *op. cit.* p. 109.
17. M. Maclear, 'North Vietnam gears for a new type of war', *The Times* 20 January 1971; Peter Jenkins, 'Hanoi war crimes trial demanded', *Guardian* 31 March 1973 and Telford Taylor, 'The lawyers' war, the prisoners' peril', *Guardian* 11 January 1973; B. Levin, 'Salute to the brave', *The Times* 7 October 1980. See also W. Burchett, *Grasshoppers and Elephants* (Urizen Books, New York, 1977), p. 180.
18. General W. W. Momyer, *Air Power in Three Wars* (Office of Air Force History, Washington, 1976), 1978, p. 18 *passim*.
19. *Loc. cit.* See also Frank Harvey, *Air War Vietnam* (Bantam Books, New York, 1967) and Gurney, *op. cit.* Chapter VI.
20. Armitage and Mason, *op. cit.* p. 107. D. Middleton (ed.), *Air War Vietnam* (Arms and Armour Press, London, 1978), p. 26.
21. Momyer, *op. cit.* p. 123 *passim*.
22. *Loc. cit.*
23. Armitage and Mason, *op. cit.* p. 109. Gurney, *op. cit.* p. 158.
24. 'B-52s—the ageing giants that sprinkle death from 30,000 feet', *Sunday Times* 31 December 1972.
25. Gropman, *loc. cit.*
26. Thompson and Frizzell, *op. cit.* p. 169. See also Gurney, *op. cit.* p. 127.
27. IISS *Strategic Survey* 1972, p. 89.
28. Thompson and Frizzell, *op. cit.* p. 143.
29. Gropman, *op. cit.* p. 40.
30. Thompson and Frizzell, *op. cit.* p. 141.
31. Truong Nhu Tang, *op. cit.* p. 160. Chanoff and Van Toai, *op. cit.* p. 67, Asprey, *op. cit.* p. 1378.

32. Sihanouk later denied knowledge of the B-52 raids, see William Shawcross, *Sideshow, Kissinger, Nixon and the Destruction of Cambodia* (Andre Deutsch, London, 1979).
33. Shawcross, *op. cit.* p. 117 *passim*. See also Malcolm Caldwell and Lek Hor Tan, *Cambodia in the Southeast Asian War* (Monthly Review Press, New York and London, 1973), p. 210 *passim*.
34. Shawcross, *op. cit.* p. 299.
35. Truong Nhu Tang, *op. cit.* p. 180.
36. *Loc. cit.* p. 183.
37. L. Heren, 'Misinformed on Cambodia', *The Times* 30 June 1970; Murray Sayle, 'Cambodian Rainbow', *Sunday Times* 10 May 1970; J. Leslie, 'The land of the Phoenix', *Guardian* 10 October 1972 and H. H. Greenway, 'Splits widen in Cambodia', *Guardian* 28 March 1973. Shawcross, *op. cit.* p. 347. See also R. Nixon, *No More Vietnams* (Comet, London, 1985), p. 122
38. Christopher Robbins, *The Invisible Air Force; The Story of the CIA's Secret Airlines* (Macmillan, London, 1979), pp. 107–29.
39. Robbins, *op. cit.* Chapter nine on opium.
40. Armitage and Mason, *op. cit.* p. 92. See also 'US gives air support as 5,000 S. Vietnamese troops invade Laos to cut supply trails', *The Times* 9 February 1971. R. Nixon, *op. cit.* pp. 60 and 137. For a sympathetic view of the operation see Gurney, *op. cit.* p. 222 *passim*.
41. C. Mullin, 'It's a Lao road that has no turning', *Guardian* 3 January 1986. For statistics on the bombing in Cambodia see Shawcross, *op. cit.* p. 297.
42. Thompson and Frizzell, *op. cit.* p. 142.
43. IISS *Strategic Survey*, 1975, p. 95.
44. Not only did the North Vietnamese make use of the US prisoners in the negotiations but the Americans were sometimes exchanged for key cadres, see Truong Nhu Tang, *op. cit.* p. 123 *passim*.
45. Truong Nhu Tang suggests that only by widening the support of the Saigon government could it have survived, *loc. cit.* p. 127. But the South Vietnamese government never showed any willingness to bring in radicals, see 'Vietnamese politician given five years', *The Times* 27 July 1968. On the other side Turong's own account shows how naïve many Southern radicals were about Northern intentions.
46. *The Pentagon Papers* (p. 484. Even in the late 1980s the Vietnam War was still influencing US public opinion; see 'Apathy dulls senses of America's sixties rebels', *The Times* 19 March 1988. For attacks on the legality of US bombing see Littauer, *op. cit.* p. 125.
47. Dean Acheson, *Present At the Creation* (Hamish Hamilton, London, 1970), p. 524; Harry S. Truman, *Years of Trial and Hope* (Hodder and Stoughton, London, 1956), p. 452 *passim*; William Manchester, *American Ceasar, Douglas MacArthur 1880–1964* (Arrow Books, London, 1979), Chapter Ten.
48. 'Afghanistan air war', *Warplane* No. 1, 1985. For the Jason studies see Littauer, *op. cit.* pp. 45–7. The US attack on Tripoli in April 1986 which was designed either to kill the Libyan leader or to prevent him supporting attacks on US citizens might be cited as an example of a short successful operation of this type. See 'The truth behind "Reagan plan to kill Gaddafi" ', *Sunday Telegraph* 22 February 1987.
49. A. H. Peterson (ed.), *Symposium on the Role of Air Power in Counterinsurgency and Unconventional Warfare; The Algerian War* (Rand Corporation, Santa Monica, July, 1963).
50. Sir Kennedy Trevaskis, *Shades of Amber; A South Arabian Episode* (Hutchinson, London, 1968).
51. J. A. C. Mackie, Konfrontasi, *The Indonesia-Malaysia Dispute 1963–6* (OUP, Kuala Lumpur, 1974), p. 212. Tony Geraghty, *Who Dares Wins, The Story of the SAS 1950–1980* (Fontana/Collins, 1981), p. 70 *passim*.
52. R. F. Futrell and M. Blumenson, *The Advisory Years to 1965* (Office of Air Force History, Washington, 1981).

The Afghan War

There are a number of good accounts of the Afghan War both by outside commentators and by journalists who visited the war zone. See particularly Edward R. Girardet, *Afghanistan: The Soviet War* (Croom Helm, London and Sydney, 1985); Mark Urban, *War in Afghanistan* (Macmillan Press, Basingstoke, 1988); S. Gall, *Behind Russian Lines, An Afghan Journal* (Sidgwick and Jackson, London, 1983); J. Bruce Amstutz, *Afghanistan, The First Five Years of Soviet Operations* (National Defense University, Washington, 1986).

1. Yaacov I. Vertzberger, *China's Southwestern Strategy* (Praeger, New York, 1985), pp. 105 *passim* and 112. For the November 1987 poll on Soviet opinion see 'Poll reveals most Russians want Afghanistan pull-out', *The Times* 2 November 1987.

2. A. Prokhanov, 'The sense of destiny at the edge of a menacing world, *Guardian* 28 September 1986. For the state of the Afghan army see, 'Afghan Army's collapse', *The Times* 12 February 1982 and 'Afghan troops riot and mutiny', *The Times* 14 March 1984.

3. Christopher Walker, 'Can there ever be a retreat from Kabul?' *The Times* 21 January 1987.

4. Gall, *op. cit.* p. 69. See also M. Martin, *Afghanistan, Inside a Rebel Stronghold* (Blandford Press, Dorset, 1984), p. 204.

5. D. C. Isby, 'Soviet tactics in the war in Afghanistan', *Jane's Defence Review* No. 7, 1983, p. 689.

6. *Loc. cit.* According to Radek Sikorski, there may have been some Cuban troops in Afghanistan even before the invasion (personal interview).

7. For a description of Soviet enchanced blast weapons see Y. Bodansky, 'New weapons in Afghanistan', *Jane's Defence Weekly* 9 March 1985. The Soviets are also alleged to have used chemical weapons in Afghanistan at least in the early days of the war; see Isby, *op. cit.* p. 691.

8. S. Gall, 'Into battle with the holy warriors', *The Times* 25 February 1987.

9. For the guerrillas' leaders see Radek Sikorski, *Moscow's Afghan War* (Institute of European Defence and Strategic Studies, London, 1987) p. 35.

10. '500 guerrillas arrive in Kabul to talk of peace', *Daily Telegraph* 22 January 1987. 'Pakistan refuses refugee airlift', *The Times* 22 January 1987.

11. 'Moscow advocates "positive dialogue" among all Afghans', *Guardian* 23 December 1985. IISS *Strategic Survey* 1982–83, p. 87 and 1984–5, p. 73.

12. 'Germany's unwanted prisoner of war', *The Times* 5 March 1984; 'Afghanistan where they don't take prisoners', *Daily Telegraph* 11 March 1986.

13. 'Endless war in the calm of Kandahar', *Guardian* 3 February 1982. IISS, *Strategic Survey* 1980–1, p. 65.

14. 'The Afghanistan air war', *Warplane No. 1* 1985 (hereafter Warplane No. 1). 'Soviet air force in Afghanistan', *Jane's Defence Weekly* 7 July 1984.

15. Mark Urban, 'The helicopter revolution', *Aircraft Illustrated*, March 1983.

16. C. Grant, *The World's Air Forces* (Chartwell Books, New Jersey), 1979, p. 156.

17. IISS *Strategic Survey*. 1981–2, p. 94.

18. Gall, *op. cit.* p. 79.

19. Lieutenant Colonel D. R. Nelson, 'Soviet air power; tactics and weapons used in Afghanistan', *Air University Review* January–February 1985, p. 34. Isby, *op. cit.* Urban, *op. cit.* See also John Gunston, 'Special Report Afghan War', *Aviation and Space Technology*, 29 October 1984.

20. Nelson, *op. cit.* p. 35.

21. Grant, *op. cit.* pp. 71 and 142

22. 'Soviet air force in Afghanistan', *Jane's Defence Weekly* 7 July 1984.

23. *Loc. cit.* Jane's quoted a figure for 250–300 Soviet helicopters, *Warplane No. 1* had 240 Soviet Hinds and Nelson suggested 500–600 helicopters with 250 Hinds. *Defence Helicopter World* June–August 1984, had over 100 Hinds and 500 smaller helicopters.

24. 'Afghan guerrillas on the run from big Soviet offensive', *The Guardian* 9 October 1985. 'Mujahadeen say 150 Russians captured in Kabul ambush', *The Times* 8 October 1986.

25. R. Sikorski, 'Into battle with the Afghan guerrillas', *Sunday Telegraph* 7 December 1986. For Soviet attacks on crops see 'Russians try to starve out resistance', *Daily Telegraph* 3 October 1986.

26. Y. Bodansky, 'Most feared weapon in Afghanistan is Frogfoot', *Jane's Defence Weekly* 19 May 1984.

27. 'Su-24s, Tu-16 support Soviet ground forces', *Aviation Week and Space Technology* 29 October 1984. Isby suggested that close air support was left entirely to the helicopters, Isby *op. cit.* p. 685.

28. See note 7 *supra*.

29. Sikorski, *op. cit.* and *Warplane No 1*.

30. J. Akehurst, *We Won a War* (Michael Russell, Wilton, 1982), p. 141.

31. Sikorski, *op. cit.* 'Afghan rebels retreat', *Guardian* 16 July 1986, 'Afghan guerrillas take a beating', *Guardian* 22 November 1986; 'How British Blowpipe boosted Afghan rebels', *Daily Telegraph* 23 July 1987; 'Su-24s, Tu-6s support Soviet ground forces', *Aviation Week* 29 October 1984. For Abdul Haq's comment see 'Afghans deny mass delivery of Blowpipes', *The Times*, 24 June 1987.

32. 'US missile is too complex for Afghans', *Daily Telegraph* 25 August 1986; some sources give Stingers' range at three miles, see 'Moscow blames West for rebels' success', *The Times* 16 September 1987.

33. Michael Meecham, 'US credits Afghan resistance with thwarting Soviet air power', *Aviation Week and Space Technology* 13 July 1987 and John Gunston, 'Stingers used by Afghan rebels stymie Soviet Force tactics', *loc. cit.* 4 April 1988. 'Thirty die as Afghans down plane', *The Times* 10 February 1987 and 'Fear-filled flight to war-torn Kabul', *The Times* 27 November 1987. See also Sikorski, *Moscow's Afghan War*, p. 25 *passim*. For the spread of Stingers from Afghanistan to Iran see 'Iran's Stingers alarm Reagan', *The Times* 12 October 1987.

34. *Aviatsiya I Kosmonavtika* No. 11, 1984, pp. 4–5.

35. Girardet, *op. cit.* p. 43.

36. *Ibid.* p. 42.

37. *Warplane No. 1* 1985.

38. Nelson, *op. cit.* p. 41.

39. 'Moscow scorns fierce Afghan garrison battle', *The Times* 7 June 1985; 'Kabul hushes up news of siege breakthrough', *The Times* 12 June 1985; for the December 1987 battle for Khost, see 'Thousands of rebel fighters give battle with Soviet forces', *The Times* 2 January 1988.

40. *Warplane No. 1* 1985; 'Guerrillas shoot down Afghan plane', *Daily Telegraph* 2 June 1986.

41. Girardet, *op. cit.* p. 38.

42. David Isby, *op. cit.*; see also 'Afghan saboteurs blow up 20 air force planes', *The Times* 19 June 1985; 'Executions after Afghan air base sabotage', *Guardian* 26 June 1985. See also 'Rebels attack Kabul airport', *The Times* 23 October 1986. Michael Mecham, *loc. cit.*

43. J. Steele, 'Why the war must go on', *Guardian* 19 March 1986; 'Afghan villagers take brunt of indiscriminate guerrilla fire', *Guardian* 25 February 1986.

44. *Warplane No. 1* 1985.

45. *Loc. cit.*

46. 'Kabul pilots defect with helicopters', *The Times* 15 July 1985; 'Kabul frees two', *The Times* 29 July 1985; 'Afghanistan accused of bombing villages', *The Times* 20 August 1985; 'Pakistan downs Afghan jet', *The Times* 16 January 1986; 'Pakistani F-16s bag Afghan fighter', *The Times* 19 May 1986; 'Afghans rocket Pakistan', *Guardian* 30 May 1986.

47. Afghanistan where they don't take prisoners', *Daily Telegraph* 11 March 1986. For a description of Spetsnaz in general see V. Suvorov, *Aquarium* (Hamish Hamilton, London, 1985).

48. Girardet, *op. cit.* p. 41.

49. 'Afghan Generals reported arrested', *The Times* 8 January 1986. 'Polo and mischief in the mountains', *The Independent* 8 December 1986.

50. A. Hyman, 'Tribal disunity adds to Kabul disarray', *The Times* 25 November 1986.

51. 'Afghanistan arming dissident tribesmen along the Khyber', *Guardian* 1 November 1985; 'Kabul sent 300,000 rifles to Pakistan border tribes', 24 December 1985; 'Afghan guerrillas take a beating', *Guardian* 22 November 1986.

52. '100 Afghans killed in bombing error', *Daily Telegraph* 15 December 1986; 'Russian jets kill 170 civilians', *Daily Telegraph* 24 December 1986.

53. Radek Sikorski, 'The day terror came to a peasant village', *Observer* 1 November 1987.

Past and Future

1. For Northern Ireland see Desmond Hamill, *Pig in the Middle, The Army in Northern Ireland 1969–85* (Methuen, London, 1986).

2. Joseph C. Harsch, 'Queen of the battlefield; the helicopter gunship', *Christian Science Monitor* 15–21 September 1986.

3. North Korea is reported to have acquired 86 Hughes 300 and 500 helicopters against US wishes, see IISS *Military Balance 1987–8*. South Africa has French Puma and Alouette 111 helicopters.

4. See the IISS *Military Balance 1987–1988*.
5. *Aviation Week and Space Technology* 14 March 1988, p. 12.
6. See for example, 'Chemical and Bacteriological (Biological) Weapons Report of the Secretary General', A/36/613, 20 November 1981; see also *'Note Verbale* dated 22 March 1982 from the Permanent Representative of the United States of America to the UN Secretary General', 24 March 1982, A/37/157.
7. For helicopters in Northern Ireland see *Statement on Defence Estimates 1985* Vol. 1, p. 28. For Beaver operations see 'Britain apologises to Irish', *The Times* 14 January 1988.
8. Hamill, *op. cit.* p. 114.
9. 'Army acts over IRA missiles', *The Times* 7 January 1987.
10. 'Disbelief delayed response to fatal attack', *The Times* 23 March 1988.
11. Hamill, *op. cit.* p. 238.
12. *Aviation Week and Space Technology*, *op. cit.* pp. 19–20.
13. 'Ulster braced for new year missile blitz', *The Times* 1 January 1988.
14. *Loc. cit.* See also Paul Jackson, 'A near miss', *Armed Forces* January 1988.
15. B. J. Schemmer, 'Where have all the RPVs gone?', *Armed Forces Journal* February 1982. See also 'Cost key to unmanned vehicles', *Aviation Week and Space Technology* 9 August, 1982.
16. 'Israeli reconnaissance drones overfly Cairo', *Aviation Week and Space Technology* 1972.
17. An American mercenary, Eugene Hasenfus, was shot down over Nicaragua in 1986; see 'Sandinistas show a hint of cockiness', *The Times* 18 November 1987.
18. SIPRI *Anti-Personnel Weapons* (Taylor and Francis, London, 1978), p. 90 *passim*. See also G. Johannsohn, 'Fuel air explosives revolutionize conventional warfare', *International Defence Review* December 1976.
19. Reporters have continued to penetrate Afghanistan, see Radek Sikorski, 'The day terror came to a peasant village', *Observer* 1 November 1987, but few have entered East Timor or Kampuchea in recent years.
20. 'Planes bomb "hideouts" in Sri Lanka', *Daily Telegraph* 28 February 1986; 'Towns pounded from sea and air as Tamils destroy cement plant', *The Times* 22 May 1986; 'Eight die in attacks by helicopter', *The Times* 25 May 1986.
21. 'Sri Lanka raids said to kill more than 80 Tamils', *The Times* 23 April 1987; 'Tamils flee as planes attack terrorist camps', *Daily Telegraph* 24 April 1987; 'Government denies more than 100 civilians died in air raids on Tamil positions', *The Times*, 28 May 1987; 'Slow struggle on Jaffna peninsula', *The Times* 1 June 1987.

Bibliography

Adams, M., *The Middle East: A Handbook*, Anthony Blond, London, 1971.
Ainley, H., *In Order to Die*, Burke, London, 1955.
Akehurst General John, *We Won a War, The Campaign in Oman*, Michael Russell, Wilton, 1982.
Amery, L. S., *My Political Life*, Vol. 2, Hutchinson, London, 1953.
Allfree, P. S., *Hawks of the Hadhramat*, Robert Hale, London, 1967.
Armitage, M. J., and Mason, R. A., *Air Power in the Nuclear Age 1945–1984, Theory and Practice*, Macmillan, Basingstoke, 1985.
Asprey, R. B., *War in the Shadows, The Guerrilla in History*, Macdonald and Jane's, London, 1976.
Ballard, Jack S., *Development and Employment of Fixed-Wing Gunships 1962–1972*, US Air Force, Washington, 1982.
Barnett, D. L., and Njama Karari, *Mau Mau From Within*, MacGibbon and Kee, London, 1966.
Beevor, J. G., *SOE Recollections and Reflections*, Bodley Head, London, 1981.
Behr, Edward, *The Algerian Problem*, Penguin, Harmondsworth, 1961.
Bell, Lady, *The Letters of Gertrude Bell*, Vol. 2, Ernest Benn, London, 1927.
Bidwell, R., *The Two Yemens*, Longman-Westview, Harlow and Boulder, 1983.
Bond, B., *British Military Policy between the Two World Wars*, Clarendon Press, Oxford, 1980.
Bowers, Ray L., *US Air Force in South-East Asia, Tactical Airlift*, US Air Force, Washington, 1983.
Boyle, A., *Trenchard*, Collins, London, 1962.
Brown, R. C., *US Air Force in South-East Asia, Tactical Airlift*, Office of Air Force History, Washington, 1983.
Browne, Malcolm W., *The New Face of War*, Cassell, London, 1965.
Buckingham, William A., *Operation Ranchhand*, Office of Air Force History, Washington, 1982.
Burchett, Wilfred, *Grasshoppers and Elephants; Why Vietnam Fell*, Urizen Books, New York, 1977.
Caldwell, M., and Tan Lek, *Cambodia in the Southeast Asian War*, Monthly Review Press, New York and London, 1973.
Challiand, G., *Guerrilla Strategies*, University of California, Berkeley, 1982.
Chanoff, D., and Toai, Doan Van, *Portrait of the Enemy; The Other Side of the War in Vietnam*, I. B. Tauris and Co., London, 1987.
Chapman, F. Spencer, *The Jungle is Neutral*, Chatto and Windus, London, 1949.
Clayton, Anthony, *The British Empire as a Superpower 1919–1939*, Macmillan Press, Basingstoke, 1986.
Clutterbuck, R., *The Long, Long War; The Emergency in Malaya*, Cassell, London, 1966.
Cooper, M., *The Birth of Independent Air Power*, Allen and Unwin, London, 1986.
Cowton, E., *With the First in the Field*, Norwich, 1963.
Cross, John, *Red Jungle*, Robert Hall, London, 1975.
Cruickshank, C., *SOE in the Far East*, Oxford University Press, London, 1983.
Dann, Uriel, *Studies in the History of Transjordan, 1920–1940*, William Blackwood, London, 1981.
Deakin, F. W., *The Embattled Mountain*, Oxford University Press, London, 1971.
De La Ferte, Sir Philip Joubert, *The Fated Sky*, White Lion, London, 1972.
Djilas, M., *Wartime, With Tito and the Partisans*, Secker and Warburg, London, 1980.

Doglione, Colonel J. A. and others, *Airpower and the Spring 1972 Invasion*, US Air Force South-East Asia Monograph.
Dyke, J. M. Van, *North Vietnam's Strategy of Survival*, Pacific Books, Palo Alto, 1972.
Embry, Air Marshall Sir Basil, *Mission Completed*, Methuen, London, 1957.
Everett-Heath, John, *Soviet Helicopters, Design, Development and Tactics*, Jane's, London, 1983.
Fall, Bernard, *Street Without Joy, Insurgency in Indochina 1946–1963*, Pall Mall, London and Dunmow, 1963.
Foley, C., *The Memoirs of General Grivas*, Longmans, London, 1964. *Island in Revolt*, Longmans, London, 1962.
Foot, M. R. D., *Resistance; An Analysis of European Resistance to Nazism*, Eyre Methuen, London, 1976.
Fuller, J. F. C., *On Future Warfare*, Sefton Praed, London, 1928. *The Reformation of War*, Hutchinson, London, 1923.
Futrell, R. F., and Blumenson, M., *The Advisory Years to 1965*, Office of Air Force History, Washington, 1981.
Gall, Sandy, *Behind Russian Lines*, Sidgwick and Jackson, London, 1983.
Gardner, R., and Longstaff, R., *British Service Helicopters; A Pictorial History*, Robert Hale, London, 1985.
Garvin, R. J., *Aden under British Rule, 1839–1967*, C. Hurst and Co., London, 1975.
Geraghty, T., *Who Dares Wins; The Story of the SAS 1950–1980*, Fontana/Collins, London, 1981.
Gibbs, Sir Gerald, *Survivor's Story*, Hutchinson, London, 1956.
Gilbert, M., *Winston Churchill Vol. IV, 1916–1922*, Heinemann, London, 1975.
Girardet, E. R., *Afghanistan: The Soviet War*, Croom Helm, London, 1985.
Glubb, Sir John, *The Story of the Arab Legion*, Hodder and Stoughton, London, 1948. *War in the Desert: An Rif Frontier Campaign*, Hodder and Stoughton, London, 1969. *Arabian Adventures, Ten Years of Joyful Service*, Cassell, London, 1978.
Gravel, Senator, *Edition of the Pentagon Papers*, Vol. IV, Beacon Press, Boston, undated.
Greene, T. N. (ed.), *The Guerrilla and How to Fight Him*, Frederick A. Praeger, New York, 1962.
Grivas, General George, *Guerrilla Warfare and Eoka's Struggle*, Longmans, London, 1964.
Gurney, Colonel Gene, *Vietnam the War in the Air*, Sidgwick and Jackson, London, 1985.
Haldane, General Sir Aylmer, *The Insurrection in Mesopotamia, 1920*, Blackwood, Edinburgh, 1922.
Hamill, Desmond, *Pig in the Middle: The Army in Northern Ireland*, Methuen, London, 1986.
Harper, Stephen, *Last Sunset*, Collins, London, 1978.
Henricksen, Thomas H., *Revolution and Counter-Revolution: Mozambique's War of Independence*, Grosvenor Press, London, 1983.
Holmboe, K., *Desert Encounter*, Harrap, London, 1936.
Horne, A., *A Savage War of Peace, Algeria 1952–1962*, Macmillan, London, 1977.
Humbaraci, A., and Muchnik, N., *Portugal's African Wars*, Macmillan, London, 1974.
Iatrides, John O., *Greece in the 1940s: A Nation in Crisis*, University Press of New England, Hanover and London, 1981.
Ingrams, Harold, *The Yemen*, John Murray, London, 1963.
Ismay, Lord, *The Memoirs of General The Lord Ismay*, Heinemann, London, 1960.
James, Harold, and Sheil-Small, Denis, *The Undeclared War*, Leo Cooper, London, 1971.
Jeapes, Colonel Tony, *SAS Operation Oman*, William Kimber, London, 1980.
Kelidar, Abbas, *The Integration of Modern Iraq*, Croom Helm, London, 1979.
King, Peter, *Afghanistan Cockpit in High Asia*, Geoffrey Bles, London, 1966.
Kirk, G. E., *A Short History of the Middle East*, Methuen, London, 1964.
Knoebl, K., *Victor Charlie: The Face of War in Vietnam*, Pall Mall Press, London, 1967.
Koster, Joseph, *The Struggle for South Yemen*, Croom Helm, London, 1984.
Laqueur, W., *Guerrilla A Historical and Critical Study*, Weidenfeld and Nicolson, London, 1977.
Leulliette, Pierre, *St. Michael and the Dragon*, Heinemann, London.
Lias, Godfrey, *Glubb's Legion*, Evan Brothers, London, 1956.
Liddell Hart, Sir B. H., *The British Way in Warfare*, Faber and Faber, London, 1932.
Littauer, R., and Uphoff, N., *The Air War in Indochina*, Beacon Press, Boston, 1972.
Longmore, Air Chief Marshal Sir Arthur, *From Sea to Sky 1910–1945*, Geoffrey Bles, London, 1946.
Longrigg, S. H., *Iraq 1900–1950*, Oxford University Press, London, 1953.

Mackie, J. A. C., *Konfrontasi: The Indonesia–Malaysia Dispute 1963–6*, Oxford University Press, Kuala Lumpur, 1976.

Maclean, F., *Eastern Approaches*, Four Square, London, 1967.

Marlowe, J., *Rebellion in Palestine*, Cresset Press, London, 1946.

Martin, Mike, *Afghanistan, Inside a Rebel Stronghold*, Blandford Press, Dorset, 1982.

Mason, R. A., *War in the Third Dimension*, Brassey's, London, 1987.

Mason, Robert, *Chickenhaw*, Penguin, Harmondsworth, 1986.

Matthews, Kenneth, *Memories of a Mountain War, Greece 1944–1949*, Longmans, London, 1972.

McCall, Gib., *Flight Most Secret*, William Kimber, London, 1981.

McDonough, J. R., *Platoon Leader: A Front Line Personal Report of Vietnam Battle Action*, Bantam, New York, 1986.

Michel, Henri, *The Shadow War*, André Deutsch, London, 1972.

Middleton, Drew, *Air War Vietnam*, Arms and Armour Press, London, 1978.

Momyer, General William, *Air Power in Three Wars*, Office of Air Force History, Washington, 1978.

Morwood, W., *Duel for the Middle Kingdom*, Ernest House Publishers, New York, 1980.

Nixon, Richard, *No More Vietnams*, Comet, London, 1985.

O'Ballance, E., *The Indochina War 1945–1954*, Faber and Faber, London, 1964. *The Algerian Insurrection 1954–1962*, London, 1967.

Paget, Julian, *Last Post, Aden 1964–1967*, Faber and Faber, London, 1969.

Paret, P., and Shy, John, *Guerrillas in the 1960s*, Pall Mall, London and Dunmow, 1967. *French Revolutionary Warfare*, Pall Mall, London and Dunmow, 1964.

Peers, General W. R., *The My Lai Inquiry*, Norton, New York, 1979.

Peterson, A. H., Reinhardt, G. C., and Conger, E., *The Role of Airpower in Counter-Insurgency*, Rand Corporation, Santa Monica, September 1964.

Peterson, A. H., Reinhardt, G. C. and Conger, E., *The Role of Airpower in Counter-Insurgency, The Malayan Emergency*, Rand Corporation, Santa Monica, July 1963.

Peterson, A. H., Reinhardt, G. C. and Conger, E. E., *Symposium on the role of Air Power in Counter Insurgency and Unconventional Warfare, The Algerian War*, Rand Corporation, Santa Monica, July 1963.

Pirey, Phillipe de, *Operation Waste*, Arco Publishing, London, 1954.

Portway, D., *Military Science Today*, Oxford University Press, London, 1940.

Poullada, Leon B., *Reform and Rebellion in Afghanistan 1919–1929*, Cornell University Press, Ithaca and London, 1973.

Powers, B. D., *Strategy Without Slide Rule*, Croom Helm, London, 1976.

Robbins, Christopher, *The Invisible Air Forces*, Macmillan, London, 1979.

Salmon, Sir John Maitland, *Swifter than Eagles*, William Blackwood, Edinburgh and London, 1964.

Saward, D., *Bomber Harris*, Cassell/Buchan and Enright, London, 1984.

Shawcross, W., *Sideshow, Nixon, Kissinger and the Destruction of Cambodia*, André Deutsch, London, 1979.

Short, Anthony, *The Communist Insurrection in Malaya*, Frederick Muller, London, 1975.

Slugett, Peter, *Britain in Iraq, 1914–1932*, Ithaca Press, London, 1976.

Stewart, R. T., *Fire in Afghanistan 1914–1929*, Doubleday, New York, 1963.

Storry, General D. A., *Armoured Combat in Vietnam*, Blandford Press, Dorset, 1981.

Talbott, John, *The War Without a Name*, Faber and Faber, London, 1981.

Tang, Truong Nhu, *Journal of a Vietcong*, Jonathan Cape, London, 1986.

Templewood, Viscount, *Empire of the Air, The Advent of the Air Age*, Collins, London, 1957.

Thetford, Owen, *Aircraft of the Royal Air Force since 1918*, Putnam, London, 1979.

Thompson, R., *No Exit from Vietnam*, Chatto and Windus, London, 1969.

Thompson, W. Scott, and Frizzell, D., *The Lessons of Vietnam*, Macdonald and Jane's, London, 1977.

Trevaskis, Sir Kennedy, *Shades of Amber*, Hutchinson, London, 1968.

Urban, M., *War in Afghanistan*, Macmillan, Basingstoke, 1988.

Usborne, Vice Admiral C. V., *The Conquest of Morocco*, Stanley Paul, London, 1936.

Wilson, Dick, *Mao: The People's Emperor*, Futura Publications, London, 1978.

Woodhouse, C. M., *The Struggle for Greece*, Hart-Davis MacGibbon, St Albans, 1976.

Woolman, D. S., *Rebels in the Rif, Abd el Krim and the Rif Rebellion*, Oxford University Press, 1969.
Wragg, D., *Helicopters at War*, Robert Hale, London, 1983.
Wright, John, *Libya*, Ernest Benn, London, 1969.

Principal Journal Articles Consulted

Air Clues
'The struggle for South-East Asia', February 1953.
Squadron Leader E. Newitt, 'Mau Mau', October 1954.
Squadron Leader P. Barker, 'Aden and the RAF', June 1955.
Flying Officer J. A. Morgan, 'PR in Malaya', April 1956.
Squadron Leader R. C. Penning, 'Helicopter paratroop Squadron', March 1958.

Aircraft Illustrated
Mark Urban, 'The helicopter revolution', March 1983.

Air Enthusiast
J. D. Graham, 'Supporting a security war', September 1972.

Air International
'Britten Norman Defender in SOAF', August 1977.

Air University Review
Lieutenant Colonel D. R. Nelson, 'Soviet Air Power, tactics and weapons used in Afghanistan', January–February 1985.

Army Air Corps Journal
Major H. B. Dicksen, 'Independent air observation group, Eritrea 1950–1952', November 1985.

Army Quarterly
Kenneth Diacre, 'Cyprus 1956', July 1956.
'Review of events in the Arabian Peninsula', July 1960.

Air Power
Lieutenant Colonel J. F. Scott, 'Joint Experimental Helicopter Unit', April 1959.
Air Marshal Sir Robert Saundby, 'Aden revisited', Spring 1959.

Aviation Week and Space Technology
'SU 24s, TU 16s support Soviet ground forces', 29 October 1984.
Michael Meecham, 'US credits Afghan resistance with thwarting Soviet air power', 13 July 1986.
John Gunston, 'Stingers used by Afghan rebels stymie Soviet air force tactics', 13 July 1987.

Defence Helicopter World
'Soviet helicopters in Afghanistan', June–August 1984.

Flight
R. J. Blackburn, 'Aircraft versus Mau Mau', November 1954.

Forces Aeriennes Françaises
'Parachute Commandos of the air', January 1959.

'Employment of the Air Force in Algeria', June 1959.
Lieutenant Colonel Vallet, 'La grande Kabylie', July 1959.
Capitaine Menanteau', 'Bombardment in AFN', July 1959.
Capitaine Tricaud, 'Liaison aircraft in Algeria', July 1959.
'The heavy helicopter in operations to maintain order in Algeria', July 1959.
'With the Air Force in Morocco at the heroic period of pacification', December 1959.
'The Air Force in Algeria in 1959', March 1960.
Lieutenant Colonel Arpurt, 'Aspects of helicopter operations in Algeria', April 1960.

Interavia
General G. J. M. Chassin, 'Lessons of the War in Indo-China', No. 12, 1952.

Jane's Defence Weekly
Y. Bodansky, 'Most feared aircraft in Afghanistan is Frogfoot', 19 May 1984.
'Soviet air force in Afghanistan', 7 July 1984.
Y. Bodansky, 'New weapons in Afghanistan', 9 March 1985.
'Soviet maintenance in Afghanistan', part 1, 22 February 1986, part 2, 1 March 1986.

Jane's Defence Review
David C. Isby, 'Soviet tactics in the war in Afghanistan', No. 7, 1983.

Journal of The Royal United Services Institute (RUSI Journal)
'Aircraft in small wars', August 1928.
Flight Lieutenant F. M. May, 'The Arabian Survey Flight', November 1935.
Air Commodore C. F. A. Portal, 'Air Force co-operation in policing the Empire', May 1937.
Air Vice Marshal Sir Francis Mellersh, 'The campaign against the terrorists in Malaya', August 1951.
Major General N. Crookenden, 'Aviation in the British Army today', August 1952.
Colonel P. A. Tobin, 'Westland Prize Essay', August 1953.
Brigadier K. R. Brazier-Creagh 'Malaya', May 1954.
General Sir George Erskine, 'Kenya, Mau Mau', February 1956.
Group Captain K. R. C. Slater, 'Air operations in Malaya, August 1957.
Colonel D. de C. Smiley, 'Muscat and Oman', February 1960.
Major General J. L. Moulton, 'Aviation in the British Army today', August 1965.
Lieutenant Colonel T. M. P. Stevens, 'Operations in the Radfan 1964', November 1965.
Group Captain P. W. Helmore, 'Air operations in Vietnam', February 1967.
Colonel Edmund B. Edwards, 'Air operations in Vietnam', February 1967.
Anthony Verrier, 'Strategic bombing, the lessons of World War II and the American experience in Vietnam', May 1967.
Wing Commander D. Eley, 'The development and use of helicopters', May 1967.
Michael Calvert, 'Counter-insurgency in Mozambique', March 1973.
Penelope Tremayne, 'Guerrillas through the looking glass', September 1974.
Penelope Tremayne, 'End of a ten-year war', March 1977.
Major General K. Perkins, 'Oman 1975, the year of decision', March 1979.
D. W. Nelms, 'The new Chinook helicopter for the RAF', June 1980.
A. J. Young, 'RAF North-West Frontier 1915–1939', March 1982.

Officer
'Whirlwinds over Borneo', No. 16, 1965.

RAF Quarterly
Air Commodore C. M. Hodges, 'Flying secret agents to and from enemy territory', Spring 1962.
Brigadier P. W. Mead, 'Army Aviation', Autumn 1962.
J. W. R. Taylor, 'Counter-insurgency Air Force', Summer 1963.
J. E. Johnson, 'The role of Air Force Middle East', Summer 1965.
C. Eley, 'Helicopters in Malaysia', Spring 1966.
Air Commodore A. Steedman, 'Royal Malaysian Air Force', Spring 1966.

The Aeroplane
William Courtenay, 'Air power in Indo-China', 4 December 1953.
John Fricker, 'High-level helicopter operations in Malaya', 11 March 1955.
John Fricker 'Flying against the Mau Mau', 25 March 1965.
John Fricker, 'Clearing Mount Kenya', 1 April 1955.
'Airlift to Cyprus', p. 880, 1958.

Warplane
'War zone Afghanistan: The Afghanistan air war', No. 1, 1985.

Principal Aircraft Involved in Unconventional Warfare

Imperial Policing

Bristol Fighter
Fighter-bomber, biplane, wooden structure, covered in stressed fabric, carried one Vickers and one Lewis gun plus 112 lb of bombs; maximum speed 125 mph. First flew in 1916; 3,100 built during the First World War, 1,369 afterwards. Finally withdrawn from service 1932. Served in Palestine, Iraq, India and Egypt.

de Havilland 9a
Fighter-bomber, biplane, wooden structure, covered in stressed fabric, carried one Vickers and one Lewis gun and 450 lb of bombs; maximum speed 114 mph; entered service 1918 and retired 1931; 900 built during First World War and 300 afterwards. Served in Iraq, Aden, Egypt and India.

de Havilland 10 Amiens
Bomber, biplane, wooden structure, fabric covered. Entered service 1918, just too late for the First World War. Armament twin Lewis guns in nose and amidships, bomb load 900 lb. Maximum speed 112 mph, endurance six hours. Served in Egypt post-war and also helped to put down tribal disturbances in India in 1920 and 1922.

Fairey 111F
Two seat general-purpose aircraft; first flew 1926; 560 built. Armament one Vickers and one Lewis gun, 500 lb bombs; maximum speed 120 mph, range 400 miles. Served in Aden, Amman and Khartoum.

Gloster Gladiator
Fighter, biplane, metal structure, fabric covered; first flew 1934; 480 built for the RAF by 1940. Armament four Browning machine guns. Maximum speed 253 mph, endurance two hours. Served in Palestine before the Second World War and widely in the war.

Handley Page V/1500
Heavy bomber, four engined biplane. Armament twin Lewis guns in nose, dorsal, ventral and tail turrets, bomb load 7,500 lb. Maximum speed 99 mph, range 1,300 miles. Made the first flight to India in 1919, bombed Kabul in Afghan War.

Handley Page Hinaldi
Developed version of the Hyderabad heavy bomber; first flew 1927; troop carrier version appeared 1928, carried 23 troops, maximum speed 122 mph, range 850 miles. Served at Lahore in India until mid-1930s.

Hawker Hart
Biplane, metal structure, fabric covered; light bomber, one Vickers gun and one Lewis gun plus 500 lb of bombs, maximum speed 165 mph. 460 built; first flew 1928, still in service in India in 1939.

Hawker Audax
Army co-operation version of the Hart; 625 built, served in India, Egypt and Sudan.

Sopwith Snipe
Fighter, biplane, wooden structure, fabric covered. Armament twin Vickers gun. Maximum speed 121 mph. Saw action at the end of the First World War and served in Iraq until 1926. Also served in India and Egypt.

Vickers Vernon
Troop carrying transport. Twin engined, biplane, wooden structure, fabric covered. Crew of two and 12 passengers. Maximum speed 118 mph, range 320 miles. In service from 1922 to 1927, 60 built for the RAF. Converted by Bomber Harris in Iraq for bombing role.

Westland Wapiti
Day bomber and army co-operation aircraft, metal structure fabric covered. Armed with one Vickers and one Lewis gun and 500 lb of bombs; maximum speed 135 mph, range 360 miles. First flew 1927, served in India and Iraq, still in service in India in 1939.

The Second World War

Consolidated Liberator
Four-engined heavy bomber, manufactured in the USA; first flew 1939, entered service with the RAF in 1941. Armament 12,800 lb bombs. Maximum speed 270 mph, range with reduced bomb load 2,290 miles. Liberator V1s and Liberator V11c employed by British to supply Malayan guerrillas.

Fieseler Fl 156 Storch
Light reconnaissance, army co-operation and transport aircraft. Single-engined high-wing mono-plane; first flew 1936, could land in 70 feet and take off in 200. Maximum speed 109 mph, range 239 miles. C1 version used for staff transport, C2 for reconnaissance with camera. Built also in the Second World War by Morane-Saulinier which continued production after the war. Used against the partisans in Yugoslavia and by the French in Indochina.

Junkers JU 87 Stuka
Dive bomber, single engine, crew of two. Entered service 1937. More than 5,700 produced for the German armed forces in the Second World War. Armament two 7.92 mm machine guns in nose and twin 7.92 machine-guns in rear cockpit, 3,968 lb bombload. Maximum speed 255 mph, range 954 miles. Used against the partisans in Yugoslavia and elsewhere.

Lockheed Hudson
Twin-engined maritime reconnaissance aircraft; derived from the Lockheed 14 which first flew in 1937; 800 delivered to the RAF in the Second World War; all-metal stressed-skin construction. Armament, 750 lb internal bombload, seven machine guns. Maximum speed 246 mph, range 2,160 miles. Widely used to supply *Maquis* in France in the Second World War.

Martin Baltimore
Light bomber, twin engines; 1,575 produced for the RAF from 1941 to 1944. Served mainly in the Mediterranean theatre. Armament four 303 guns in wings, 2–4 guns in dorsal turret, two 0.30 in ventral position, bomb load 2,000 lb. Maximum speed 302 mph, range 950 miles. Used to supply partisans in Balkans.

Westland Lysander
Army co-operation aircraft, metal structure, fabric covered, high-winged monoplane; entered service 1938 and served in France and the Middle East before being developed for special duties (supporting guerrillas); speed 165 mph, endurance eight hours. Widely used to support the *Maquis*.

Post-1945 British Campaigns

Avro Anson
General service aircraft. Served originally with Coastal Command. Entered service in 1936; 8,138 produced in Britain, 2,882 in Canada. Retired from service 1968. Maximum speed 188 mph, range 790 miles. Widely used as a light transport after the Second World War.

Avro Lincoln
All metal, stressed-skin bomber; served with the RAF from 1945 to 1963. Armament 0.50 guns in nose, dorsal and tail turrets, bomb load of 14,000 lb. Maximum speed 295 mph. Served in Malaya and Kenya.

BAC 167 Strikemaster
Light attack aircraft developed from Jet Provost trainer. Armament two 7.62 mm machine-guns and up to 3,000 lb of underwing stores. Maximum speed 450 mph, range 724 miles. Used in the Dhofar war.

Bristol Sycamore
Light transport helicopter, carrying 4–5 passengers; 177 built from 1951 to 1959 for British and German armed forces. Maximum speed 121 mph, range 268 miles. Served in Cyrpus and Malaya.

British Taylorcraft Auster
Light observation and transport aircraft; US design but built in Britain during the Second World War. Entered service 1941. After the end of the war the more advanced Auster 6 entered service. Maximum speed 124 mph. Served in Malaya and Cyprus.

de Havilland Hornet
Twin-engined, long-range fighter; wooden fuselage, alloy wings. Armed with four 20 mm guns and 2,000 lb of bombs or rockets. Maximum speed 472 mph. Served in Malaya.

de Havilland Vampire
Jet fighter-bomber; entered service with the RAF in 1946. Carried four 20 mm guns and 2,000 lb of bombs or rockets. Maximum speed 540 mph. Served in Malaya and with the French in Algeria.

Hawker Hunter FGA 9
Ground attack version of the Hunter fighter; first flew 1959. Armament—four Aden guns, 1,000 lb bombs and 3 in rockets. Maximum speed 710 mph, tactical radius 219 miles. Employed in Aden and Dhofar.

Hawker Tempest
Single seat fighter-bomber; first flew 1942, 800 built in the Second World War. Armed with four 20 mm guns and 2,000 lb of bombs or rockets. Maximum speed 450 mph. Served in Malaya.

Hunting Perceval Pembroke
Light transport. Entered service 1953 as a replacement for the Anson. High-wing and twin engines, carrying eight passengers. Maximum speed 224 mph, range 1,150 miles. Served in Aden, Kuwait and Malaya.

North American Harvard
All-metal stressed skin trainer; first delivered to the RAF in 1938; 5,000 delivered to Commonwealth forces in the Second World War; maximum speed 205 mph, range 750 miles. Used as a bomber in Greece, Kenya, Algeria, etc.

Scottish Aviation Pioneer
Light communications aircraft. High wing, single engine; entered service 1957. Maximum speed 145 mph, range 650 miles. Served in Malaya, Aden and Cyprus.

Short Sunderland
Four-engined, maritime patrol flying-boat; served with RAF from 1938 until 1959. Armed with 0.303 guns in the tail and four in nose plus 2,000 lb of bombs; range, 2,980 miles, maximum speed 213 mph; crew of 13. Used in Malaya.

Supermarine Spitfire
Most successful British fighter of the Second World War. Armament varied according to Mark, range of machine-guns plus 1,000 lb of bombs. Maximum speed up to 460 mph. Served in Greece, Malaya and with French in Indochina.

Westland (Bristol) Belvedere
Transport helicopter. First twin-engined, twin rotor helicopter to see service with the RAF; 26 delivered, entered service 1961, crew of two and 18–19 fully-equipped troops or 12 stretcher cases; maximum speed 138 mph, operational range 75 miles. Served in Malaysia and Aden.

Westland Dragonfly
Transport helicopter, British version of Sikorsky S-51; first delivered to RAF 1950, pilot plus three passengers or two stretcher cases; maximum speed 103 mph. Served in Malaya 1950 to 1965.

Westland Scout
Light general-purpose helicopter; 150 built from 1960 for Britain, Australia, Jordan and other countries. Maximum speed 130 mph, range 317 miles. Served in Aden and during 'Confrontation'.

Westland Wessex
Transport helicopter, British version of Sikorski S-58, entered service with the Royal Navy in 1961; crew of 2–3, capable of carrying 16 troops, speed 121 mph, range 478 miles. Served in Malaya, Aden and Northern Ireland.

Westland Whirlwind
Transport helicopter, British version of Sikorski S-55, first flew 1953, entered RAF service 1955; crew of two and eight passengers, maximum speed 110 mph, range 360 miles. Served in Malaya and Cyprus.

French Post-War Operations

Alouette II
General purpose helicopter, carrying four passengers. Maximum speed 108 mph, range 373 miles. Originally built for French Navy, later for other services, 1,000 built 1955–1962. Served in Algeria with French, also during 'Confrontation'.

Bell 13/47D
Light transport helicopter with plexiglass canopy. First Bell model mass-produced for military use as well as private transport. Served in Algeria.

Bell P 63 King Cobra
Single-engined fighter; 2,000 built, serving widely with Soviet forces in the Second World War. Armament one 37 mm cannon, four 0.50 machine-guns and one 1,000 lb bomb under each wing. Maximum speed 450 mph, range 1,200 miles. Served in Indochina.

Douglas B 26 Marauder
Medium twin-engined bomber. Served widely towards the end of the Second World War. Armament 11–13 0.50 calibre machine-guns, four package guns and nose gun. Maximum speed 355 mph. Served with French in Indochina and Algeria, later re-designated A-26A (of which 1,000 were built) served with US forces in Vietnam.

Douglas C 47 Skytrain (Dakota)
Military version of the DC 3, very widely used in the Second World War, particularly to aid Yugoslav partisans and to supply troops in all parts of the world. Maximum speed 230 mph, range 1,550 miles. Served post-1945 in Indochina both with the French and later the Americans who also converted it into a gunship.

Fairchild C 119 Boxcar
Freighter and parachute carrier. Development from Fairchild C 82 Packet which served in the Second World War. Maximum speed 296 mph, range 3,480 miles. Load 30,000 lb. Served in first and second Indochina wars and in Algeria.

Grumman F8F Bearcat
Ship-borne fighter. Last fighter produced for US Navy in the Second World War. Armament: four wing-mounted 0.50 calibre machine-guns, plus bombs and rockets. Maximum speed 500 mph, range 1,500 miles. Served in Indochina.

Grumman F6F Hellcat
Single-seat fighter-bomber, built for US Navy. First flew 1942. Armament six 0.50 calibre machine-guns, rockets and two 1,000 lb bombs. Maximum speed 430 mph, range 1,500 miles. Served in Indochina.

Hiller 360
Light two-seat helicopter. Served with US army and Navy. Employed by French in Indochina.

Junkers Ju 52/3
Transport. Single-engined version first flew 1931, later three-engined version developed. Early versions carried 15–17 passengers as commercial airliners, subsequently converted to bombing and parachute transport roles. Played a leading part in the parachute attack on Crete in 1941. Some 4,845 built in the Second World War and 400 by French afterwards. Maximum speed 171 mph, range with auxiliary tanks 805 miles. Served in Indochina and Algeria.

North American B 25 Mitchell
Twin-engined medium bomber. First flew 1939, widely used by Russians and Americans in the Second World War. First aircraft to be armed with 75 mm cannon. Also carried 4,000 lb bombs. Maximum speed 315 mph, range 1,500 miles. Served with French in Algeria.

Sikorsky S 55 or H 19
General-purpose helicopter, capable of carrying up to six soldiers. First flew 1949 and served with US army and navy. 1,067 produced over ten years for 30 operators. Maximum speed 100 mph, range 400 miles. Served in Korea and with French in Algeria.

Vought F 4U Corsair
Shipborne fighter-bomber. Served in the Second World War. Armament: three machine-guns in each wing or four 20 mm cannon. Maximum speed 435 mph, range 1,500 miles. Served in Indochina.

Vietnam

Bell AH-1G Huey Cobra
Armed helicopter with two seats in tandem, prototype first flew in 1965; armed with one 7.62 mm mini-gun, one grenade launcher and rockets or missiles; range 337 miles, speed 172 mph.

Bell UH-1 Huey
General-purpose helicopter; crew of one plus up to 14 passengers; UH1-B versions carries four side-mounted 7.62 machine guns or two packs of rockets, each holding 24 projectiles; maximum speed 127 mph, range 318 miles.

Boeing Chinook
Medium transport helicopter. First flew 1961, crew of two to three plus 44 passengers or freight. Maximum speed 189 mph, combat radius 115 miles.

Boeing B 52 Stratofortress
Heavy strategic bomber, powered by eight turbofans. First flew 1952, entered service 1957. Crew of six. Maximum speed 630 mph, range 12,500 miles. D, E and F versions used in Vietnam.

Grumman OV1 Mohawk
Two-seat army observation aircraft with twin turbopropellers. Aluminium armour in the cockpit floor, maximum speed 308 mph, stalling speed 59 knots. OV1B carries side-looking radar and photographs map of territory; OV1C carries infra-red equipment.

Helio Courier
All-metal high-winged monoplane, designed for short take-off and landing. The original model first flew in 1954; other models, including one with twin engines above the wings, and the Helio Stallion were subsequently produced.

Lockheed Hercules AC 130 E
Gunship version of the Lockheed transport (which was first produced in 1952) armed with four cannons with 20 mm multi-barrels and four 7.62 mini-guns, searchlights and sensors. Entered service in Vietnam in 1970.

McDonell Douglas Phantom
Twin-engined, two seat fighter-bomber; first flew in 1958. Various versions produced from F4A to F4M. Can carry Sidewinder missiles, cannon and up to 16,000 lb of bombs, maximum speed 1,368 mph, maximum range, 1,750 miles.

McDonell Douglas A4 Skyhawk
Lightweight attack bomber with a single engine for aircraft-carriers. Production began 1953; various versions from A4A to A4N; 2,400 produced by 1970; armed with two 20 mm cannon plus bombs. Maximum speed of A4F 675 mph.

North American OV10A Bronco
Two-seat multi-purpose counter-insurgency aircraft. Twin turboprops; maximum speed 281 mph, range 228 miles. First flew 1965.

North American T 28 Trojan
Training and light ground attack aircraft, crew of two. First flew in 1949; maximum speed 352 mph, range 1,200 miles; various versions including T28D counter-insurgency aircraft and AT-28 ground attack aircraft, second with twin turbopropellers. Armed with 500 lb of bombs or rockets.

Republic Fairchild, F 105 Thunderchief
Long-range fighter-bomber with one-man crew, armed with 20 mm cannon plus 8,000 lb of weapons internally and 6,000 lb externally. First flew 1955, maximum speed 1,480, mph, combat radius 230 miles.

Sikorsky H-3 Jolly Green Giant
Transport helicopter, modified version of Sikorski S-61, first flew 1963. Crew of 2–3 plus 30 passengers, speed 162 mph, range 465 miles.

Afghanistan

Antonov An 10/12
Transport, An 10 is the passenger and AN 12 the military version for carrying paratroops etc. First flew 1957, capable of carrying 84 passengers. Maximum speed 373 mph, range 2,110 miles.

Antonov An 24/26
Transport, entered service with Aeroflot 1963. Twin turboprop, high-winged monoplane. Can carry 44–50 passengers.

Mi-2 Hoplite
Light utility helicopter to carry up to eight passengers, in service 1961. Maximum speed 130 mph, range 106 miles; some equipped with Sagger or Swatter anti-tank missiles.

Mi-4 Hound
Transport helicopter with crew of two, carrying up to 14 troops. First seen in public 1953. Armament: air-to-ground rockets and machine-guns. Maximum speed 155 mph, range 155 miles.

Mi-6 Hook
Heavy transport helicopter, announced in 1957 as the heaviest helicopter in the world. Mi-10 Harke Flying Crane version developed later. Crew of five plus 65 passengers and baggage. Maximum speed 186 mph, range 385 miles.

Mi-8 Hip
Designed as a 28-seat passenger helicopter; range 224–276 miles, maximum speed 143 mph. First flew 1962, several thousands produced for civil and military use. Served in Ethiopia–Somalia war as well as in Afghanistan.

Mi-24 Hind
Combat helicopter, in service early 1970s, crew of four plus up to eight passengers in some versions. Can carry 12.7 mm or 14.5 mm machine-guns and anti-tank and other missiles and rockets, a weapons load of 2,810 lb. Maximum speed 170 mph.

Mi 26 Halo
Heavy transport helicopter to carry 70–100 passengers. First flew 1977. Maximum speed 183 mph, range 500 miles.

MiG 21 Fishbed
Single-engined, single-seat fighter. Armament: one 23 mm cannon, four rocket pods for ground attack or two 551 lb and two 1,102 lb bomb or air-to-surface missiles. Maximum speed 1,385 mph, range at high altitude 683 miles.

MiG 27 Flogger D
Single-engined ground attack aircraft. Armed with one 23 mm cannon and external stores on five pylons for weapons load of 4,200 lb. Flogger D unlike earlier versions has laser range-finder. Maximum speed 1,520 mph.

Tu-16 Badger
Medium jet bomber and maritime reconnaissance aircraft; crew of seven, range 3,000 miles, carries 19,800 lb of bombs.

Su-25 Frogfoot
Twin-engined ground attack aircraft. Armament 30 mm cannon and various rockets, bombs and missiles weighing up to 10,000 lb.

Sources

Giorgio Apostolo, *World Encyclopaedia of Civil and Military Helicopters* (Willow Books, Collins, London, 1984).

Chris Chant, *The World's Air Forces* (Talos Publishing/Chartwell Books Inc., New Jersey, 1979).

John Everett-Heath, *Soviet Helicopters, Design, Development and Tactics* (Jane's, London, 1983).

William Green and Gerald Pollinger, *Observer's Book of Aircraft* (Frederick Warne and Co, London and New York, 1954).

Bill Gunston, *Combat Aircraft of World War II* (Salamander, London, 1978).

Jane's All the World's Aircraft 1970–71 (Jane's, London).

Reed Kinert, *Our Fighting Planes* (Macmillan, New York, 1946).

David Monday, *Axis Aircraft of World War II* (Temple Press, London, 1984).

Owen Thetford, *Aircraft of the Royal Air Force since 1918* (Putnam and Company, London, 1979).

Index